A Most Reliable Man

A Most Reliable Man

Volume II of *The Years of Deception* trilogy

Gerard Murphy

KDP Publications

First published 2020

© Gerard Murphy 2020

Gerard Murphy has asserted his moral right to be identified as author of this work.

ISBN: 9798555814784

Contents

Preface

My book *The Great Cover-Up* on the death of Michael Collins and the part played in it by Florence (Florrie) O'Donoghue fell out of a broad ranging investigation into the role of O'Donoghue in the Irish War of Independence. It was conceived initially as a single volume. However, when the quantity of material on O'Donoghue's activities reached a level that it could not comfortably fit into two volumes, let alone one, it became obvious that three books were needed to cover it all. And so, *The Years of Deception* trilogy was conceived as a forensic analysis of O'Donoghue's career during the revolutionary period.

One question people are likely to ask is if the conclusions of this investigation are so obvious and indeed self-evident then why did nobody see any of this before? I cannot answer for others except to say that people see what they want to see and overlook what they want to overlook. Indeed, I myself had to be dragged kicking and screaming to the conclusions reached in this volume, because, like everyone else with an interest in the period, I believed for many years that O'Donoghue was essentially telling the truth in his many accounts of the revolutionary period. However, there were some historians who voiced their suspicions, at least privately. It took a number of what were first accidental discoveries and then a lot of research to come to the conclusion I reached here.

It should also be pointed out that most of this work would not have been possible even as recently as ten years ago. Such has been the accumulation of new material released from archives in recent years, particularly to coincide with the decade of centenaries, much of it available online, that it allows historians – if they were in a mood to do so – to redraft much of how we understand the period. Previous writers, myself included, simply did not have enough material for dramatic new insights. Much credit for this has to go to the Irish Military Archives for the release of vast amounts of information in the form of the Bureau of Military History witness statements and, more recently, the Military Pensions applications database which allows the Irish side of the story to be written up in the same detail as the British side of the story was able to be written up to about ten years ago. Also, the vast tsunami of British military personnel records released to commemorate the centenary of the Great War has been extremely helpful in fleshing out the details of this work. Having said that, many of the sources cited, particularly in the early chapters, predate the digital era – even if digital technology allowed easier access to some of them.

It was not possible for me to include all the material I would liked to have included in this book and some very interesting stories have been left out. These will have to wait till the final volume which is now nearing completion.

Acknowledgements

A book with this level of new information will, by definition, be a child with many parents. It is not possible to acknowledge all of them here. So I will confine myself to those who had a direct input into the text.

Two people deserve special mention. Dick Kenny, as always, for his guiding hand and sceptical eye and who kept on asking questions and playing devil's advocate on many of the events described herein. A special mention must also be given to Phil Tomaselli whose book *Tracing Your Secret Service Ancestors*, a slim but invaluable tome, was the key that enabled me to unlock the vast treasure trove of British military personnel records in which secret service operatives are hidden, sometimes in plain sight, assuming you know what to look for.

Gerry White and Jim Herlihy also provided many stimulating conversations and insights into some of the dramatis personae and events described in the book – even if in the case of Gerry, it sometimes meant missing whole sections of Cork City Sports. Eve Morrison provided some documentation over the years as well as being extremely helpful in more general ways.

Denis Sexton lent me his graphological expertise, while Paul Horan allowed me access to Rathmore National School records. The following provided some useful information and help: John Arnold, Tara Breen and Johnny McCarthy, John Stephen O'Sullivan and, in IT Carlow, Ann-Marie Byrne, Orla Foley and particularly Brian O'Rourke for the many years he spent listening to me wittering on about Florrie O'Donoghue.

Also I wish to acknowledge the support of my wife Mary and my children, Áine, Grace and James for putting up with me during the years of what must have seemed to them an ever-evolving and apparently endless obsession.

Finally, I want to thank my agent, Jonathan Williams, for moving might and main in his efforts to find a publisher for this book in Ireland. That he failed to find one was not through lack of effort on his part.

Abbreviations

ADM	Admiralty
AG	Adjutant General
ASFL	Anti-Sinn Fein League
Bde	Brigade
BMH	Bureau of Military History
Btn	Battalion
CA	Capuchin Archives
CO	Colonial Office
CSO	Chief Secretary's Office
CYMS	Catholic Young Men's Society
DI	District Inspector (RIC)
DMI	Director of Military Intelligence
DMP	Dublin Metropolitan Police
DORA	Defence of the Realm Act
GHQ	General Headquarters
GPO	General Post Office
HO	Home Office
HMSO	His Majesty's Stationary Office
I/O	Intelligence Officer
IG	Inspector General (RIC)
IRA	Irish Republican Army
IRB	Irish Republican Brotherhood
IW&D	Inland Waterways and Docks
KC	King's Council
KR	Kings Regulations
MA	Military Archives (Dublin)
MI5	The Security Service
MI6	See Secret Intelligence Service (SIS)
MOD	Ministry of Defence
MSP	Military Service Pension
NA	National Archives (Ireland)
NLI	National Library of Ireland
O/C	Officer in Command

QM	Quartermaster
RE	Royal Engineers
RIC	Royal Irish Constabulary
RMF	Royal Munster Fusiliers
RNVR	Royal Navy Volunteer Reserve
SIS	Secret Intelligence Service (MI6)
SSB	Secret Service Bureau (early name for intelligence services)
TNA	The National Archives (UK)
UCC	University College Cork
UCD	University College Dublin
UCG	University College Galway
WO	War Office
WS	Witness Statement

No one can be the slave of two masters: he will either hate the first and love the second, or treat the first with respect and the second with scorn.

Matthew 6: 24-34.

I'm very wary about the role of written history. . . From my experience of dealing with historical figures, the facts are often surprising, even counterintuitive.

Jung Chang

Yeah, beware the small man, I think to myself. Always beware the small man. He'll fuck you every time. Because they never forget, do they? All that grief they got at school. Over and over, and for the rest of their miserable short-assed lives, someone's got to pay.

John Nivin

I'm not a monster. I'm just ahead of the curve.

The Joker – *Batman, The Dark Night*

Part I

Some Difficult Questions

1

A Very Reliable Informant

It was necessary that the work of MI5 should be organized in such a way as to provide means for the acquisition of information wherever mischief was likely to be brewing.[1]

After the end of the Great War, the British government convened a committee under the chairmanship of acting Foreign Secretary, Lord Curzon, to reduce the Secret Service to a fraction of its wartime size as part of the down-scaling of the war economy.[2] This it did, by one measure reducing the Secret Service Vote (the monies allocated by cabinet for information-gathering) from £1.2 million in 1918/19 to £277,000 in 1920/21.[3] The committee asked each government department engaged in information-gathering to provide an account of its stewardship over the war years. Among these was the Irish Office, the department in Whitehall that dealt with Irish affairs through the British administration in Dublin Castle. The report the Irish Office made to Curzon's Secret Service Committee, is only a few pages long. However, it contains one very interesting piece of information.[4]

After describing the activities of its intelligence-gatherers – the Crime Special Branch of the RIC and the Detective Branch of the

---

[1] MI5 D Branch Summary Report, TNA KV1/19.

[2] In the same period, almost 3.5 million officers and men were also demobbed. Denis Winter, *Death's Men: Soldiers of the Great War*, (London, 1978), p.240.

[3] Blue Notes (Intelligence) 1913-1937, TNA T 165/445. It should, of course, be pointed out that spending in Ireland greatly increased between 1919 and 1921 before dropping off almost to zero after the establishment of the Free State.

[4] Note by Irish Office. In *Report of the Secret Service Committee*, 1919, TNA KV 4/151.

Dublin Metropolitan Police, both based across the yard from each other in Dublin Castle – what might be described as the well-known intelligence services, the report contains one very intriguing detail. Along with telling us that both sets of detectives, of the RIC and the DMP, 'all have informants and are well in touch with the trend of the Sinn Féin Movement and that over the previous year clues were received from informants that led 'to the seizure of arms, explosives, documents etc., and to the arrest of the offenders', the unnamed writer goes on to say: 'The revolutionary movement has its centre in Dublin where the leaders reside and where the meetings of the directorate take place; but *Government is regularly supplied by the Inspector General with information of great value as to its plans, resources and organization, received from a reliable informant in the country* [italics added].'[5]

What this tells us is that the Inspector General, the head of the Royal Irish Constabulary, had a reliable informant at the heart of the republican movement who was passing on detailed information of its inner workings and that this individual lived down the country rather than in Dublin – though it appears he was also in a position to pass on high-grade intelligence on events in Dublin. A trawl through the monthly reports of the Inspector General confirms this: A 'reliable informant' – sometimes referred to as the 'very reliable informant' or the informant whose 'information has heretofore proved most accurate' – passed on a very substantial amount of useful intelligence to the Inspector General of the RIC on a monthly basis from the autumn of 1916 to the end of 1919.[6] What is noteworthy about this is that the information provided by the 'reliable informant' coincided exactly with the career of Joseph Byrne as Inspector General of the RIC.

Joseph Aloysius Byrne began his time as Inspector General in August 1916 and was rather rudely kicked out of the job at the start of 1920 as a result of various political manoeuvrings in Dublin Castle and in the British cabinet. These manoeuvrings were to backfire spectacularly since not only was Byrne the best man for the job, he was a force for moderation within the establishment. In 1917 he urged the

---

[5] ibid.
[6] See Inspector General's Monthly Reports August 1916 - January 1920, TNA CO 904/100-110.

government to immediately adopt Home Rule or face increased disaffection in the country.[7] In 1919 he begged it to refrain from making Sinn Féin illegal since it had received a huge mandate from the people at the end of 1918. Making Sinn Féin illegal would, in Byrne's view, be the same as making the entire country illegal. His pleadings fell on deaf ears. Draconian repression was the route taken – with negative and entirely predictable consequences.

It is also clear from RIC records that Byrne's information was not coming through normal channels – that is to say, through the RIC County or District Inspectors on the ground – since it is not reflected in the County Inspectors' monthly reports. In other words, the 'reliable informant' was not reporting to the RIC at a local level. Rather, his information was finding a more direct route to the desk of the Inspector General. Since Byrne was a military appointee to the most senior RIC post in 1916, this suggests that the 'reliable informant' was likely to be working for some branch of military intelligence which was feeding the data to Byrne, who then passed it on up the line.

In January 1917 the *Irish Times* published a special supplement to commemorate the crushing of the 1916 Rising. Under the byline 'The Darkest Week in the History of Dublin: An Orgie [*sic*] of Fire and Slaughter', the supplement was a celebration of the efficiency of the army's role in quelling the revolt.[8] And top of the list of those named in the supplement decoration by the King for his role in the events of Easter 1916 was 'Maj. and Bt. Lt-Col (Hon. Brig-Gen) Joseph Aloysius Byrne, ret. pay, late Innis. Fus.' to give him his full, gazetted title.[9]

Yet Joseph Byrne took up his posting in Ireland on 27 April when the Rising was almost over. His nomination could have had no effect on the Rising *per se*, since it was as good as defeated when Byrne, 'whose record in the Army had been excellent', was given the job of Deputy Adjutant General to General Sir John Maxwell, the newly appointed Commander of the British Forces in Ireland. His job was to deal with the legalities of prosecuting those involved in the Rising. Later that

---

[7] Inspector General's Monthly Report May 1917, TNA CO 904/103.

[8] Sinn Féin Rebellion Handbook, Easter 1916, p.92, *Weekly Irish Times*, January 1917.

[9] Sinn Féin Rebellion Handbook, Easter 1916, p.92, *Weekly Irish Times*, January 1917. *London Gazette*, 26 January 1917.

summer, after he had returned to England having completed his duties in Dublin, Byrne was appointed Inspector General of the RIC, replacing Sir Neville Chamberlain who had led the RIC up to and during the Rising. Clearly Byrne must have received his decoration for what he did *after* the Rising, when he showed 'remarkable talents for administration' and 'won the trust and liking' of the men of the RIC.[10]

His initial military posting to Dublin was for less than two months and he was back at his old job in the War Office when in June 1916 he was offered the position of Inspector General.[11] Byrne was a competent, serious man – 'in his own line, one of the best officers in the War Office' – and a devout Catholic. He went on to serve as Inspector General officially from 1 August 1916 to 11 March 1920, when he was placed on sick leave with full pay.[12] 'His own line', in the words of General Macready, who as Adjutant General had been Byrne's commanding officer at the War Office, was that, as Assistant Adjutant General, he was chair of the legal branch of that department. He was parachuted into GHQ Ireland as Deputy Adjutant General, to deal with legal matters arising out of the prosecution of the rebellion. (He was to go on to train as a barrister during his 'sick leave' of 1920/21.) As a legal expert in the Adjutant General's office in London before Easter 1916, which had responsibility for 'duties in aid of the civil power' and dealing with civilian unrest, he would, by definition, already be closely associated with the intelligence community.[13] It is a *sine qua non* that he would have been receiving intelligence, either directly or indirectly through the intelligence services such as the police, MI5 or the Special Branch. The relationship between the AG's office and the intelligence services can be gauged from the fact that, when *A Record of the Rebellion in Ireland in 1920-21* was complied by the army in 1922, of the 170 copies printed, some 34 were passed on to the AG's office, almost twice more than were passed on to any other department.[14] It is

---

[10] *The Times*, 8 January 1920.

[11] Nevil Macready, *Annals of an Active Life Vol I*, (London, 1925), p.252.

[12] Jim Herlihy, *The Royal Irish Constabulary Officers, 1816-1922* (Dublin, 2005).

[13] Keith Jeffery, 'The British Army and Internal Security 1919-1939', in *The Historical Journal*, 24, 2 (1981) pp. 377-97.

[14] Circulation list, *A Record of the Rebellion*, TNA WO 141/ 93. By contrast, the Directorate of Military Operations and Intelligence got only ten copies. I am grateful to Eve Morrison for passing on this page which is not in the published version.

also clear that Ireland was his field of expertise since it was he, along with a Colonel Hutchison, part of 'a specially selected staff', who were sent to Dublin by the War Office to support General Maxwell in the middle of the Rising.[15]

Byrne's links with the intelligence services ran very deep since, towards the end of his 'sick leave', he was seconded to the Special Branch to get to know its workings and was expected to take over its running when Sir Basil Thomson was forced to resign in 1921, which never happened since Byrne was again victim of anti-Catholic bias in the establishment.[16] In the *London Gazette* of 26 January 1916, though, Byrne's name is listed right beside that of another 'Maj. and Bt. Lt. Col., (Temp. Col.)', also on Retired Pay, Vernon Waldegrave Kell, head of MI5.[17] The almost identical description of their of respective ranks suggests that their commendation came from the same source.[18] Both were made Commander of the Bath (C.B.).

The work of the 'reliable informant' meant that during those four years Byrne came to know a lot about the inner workings of radical republicanism. While much of the information provided by the 'reliable informant' was of a routine nature – for instance, in late 1918: 'it has been agreed that four of the newly elected MPs are to go to America to carry out propaganda work and to collect money'[19] – it also sheds light on some of the more important political developments that took place between 1916 and 1920.

The 'reliable informant' made his first appearance in the Inspector General's monthly report of August 1916, three months after the Rising,

---

[15] Macready, pp.239-43, op.cit.

[16] *The Times*, 20 November 1921 and 9 December 1921.The fall of Sir Basil Thomson is worthy of a book in itself. Put bluntly, his approach of bluffing and self-promotion and the increased bureaucracy and lack of efficiency in running his Directorate of Intelligence meant that he fell foul of the government after alienating the military partly by claiming credit for the successes of MI5 and MI6 during the war. Byrne did not get the job of running the Special Branch, however. Instead, it was given to another military man, General Sir Wyndham Childs – known as 'Fido' – so named by his fellow officers because he was overly willing to do the bidding of politicians.

[17] *London Gazette*, 26 January 1917.

[18] This can be seen by simply comparing the names of Byrne and Kell with others on the same page of the *Gazette*, or any other page for that matter.

[19] Inspector General's Monthly Report December 1918, TNA CO 904/107.

when he is described as 'a reliable informant in Ireland'. At this stage Byrne was still in London and this report was written by W.A. O'Connell, his deputy.[20] It suggests that, before Byrne's move to Dublin, the 'reliable informant' was reporting directly to London, and that London was relaying that information back to Dublin. Indeed, he may have been providing information even before the Easter Rising. On 14 March 1916, the previous Inspector General, Sir Neville Chamberlain, relaying a report from London, stated that 'within the past few days, information has been received from an informant in Ireland that the Irish Volunteer leaders have been warned to be in readiness for a German landing at an early date and that in this connection general parades of Irish Volunteers on St Patrick's Day have been ordered – probably as a test of their strength.' The source of this information was MI5 since Major Frank Hall, who was MI5's man with responsibility for Ireland, stated that he had warned Sir Matthew Nathan, the Under-Secretary in Dublin Castle, by letter that 'three men would land on a boat on such and such a date' and that a rising was imminent, but that Nathan had ignored his warnings.[21]

On 23 March, a month before the Rising, Prime Minister Herbert Asquith was warned by the Director of Military Intelligence, General George Macdonogh, that a rising was planned for Easter Sunday. 'On March 23 1916, the Director of Military Intelligence informed General Headquarters, Home Forces, that he had received information from an absolutely reliable source that a rising in Ireland was contemplated at an early date, and that extremists in that country were in communication with Germany with a view to obtaining German assistance. He added that the rising was timed to take place on April 22 and that Irish extremists had asked Germany to supply arms and ammunition by that date. Acting on similar information the Admiral at Queenstown [now Cobh, County Cork] issued an urgent order for the patrolling of the Irish Coast.'[22]

---

[20] Inspector General's Monthly Report, August1916, TNA CO 904/100.

[21] Jeffrey Dudgeon, *Roger Casement: The Black Diaries*, (Belfast, 2002), p.483.

[22] Memorandum from the Asquith Papers, Box 42, Folder 5-9, Bodleian Library, Oxford. Quoted in Geoffrey Sloan. 'The British State and the Irish Rebellion of 1916: An Intelligence Failure or a Failure of Response?' *Journal of Strategic Security*, No. 5, Vol. 6, No. 3, Autumn 2013.

(It should be pointed out that most of the information on the lead-up to the Rising came from Naval Intelligence's Room 40, which had tapped the cable from the German embassy in Washington. On 10 February Room 40 intercepted a telegram containing a message from John Devoy 'on the position in Ireland'. 'We have therefore decided to begin action on Easter Monday. Unless entirely new circumstances arise we must have your arms and munitions in Limerick between Good Friday and Easter Monday. We expect German help immediately after beginning action.'[23])

Another cable from Count Bernstorff, the German Ambassador to the United States, confirmed this on 18 February. 'The Irish leader, John Devoy, informs me that rising is to begin in Ireland on Easter Saturday. Please send arms to arrive at Limerick, west coast of Ireland, between Good Friday and Easter Saturday.'[24] On 4 March the intercepted messages were even more specific, that between 20th and 23rd 20,000 rifles and 10 machine guns with ammunition and explosives would land at Fenit Pier near Tralee.[25] As one recent historian, Geoffrey Sloan, put it: 'by mid-March the British authorities had a comprehensive understanding and knowledge of the planned rebellion'. In total, some 30 messages intercepted by Room 40 indicated German support for the rebels before the Rising.[26] The fact that this information was not passed on to Dublin Castle brings us to one of the great debates about 1916: that the military may have deliberately neglected to tell the Irish authorities in order to draw the rebels out into the open and crush them, something for which there is now significant evidence.[27] However, this debate is largely outside the remit of this book.

Clearly the Admiralty and the army were working in tandem. Taken together, though, what this shows is that the War Office, presumably through one of its intelligence agencies, had a reliable informer in the

---

[23] *Documents Relative to the Sinn Fein Movement*, (HMSO London, 1921), p.9.

[24] ibid. p.13.

[25] ibid. p.13.

[26] Geoffrey Sloan, 'The British State and the Irish Rebellion of 1916: An Intelligence Failure or a Failure of Response?' *Journal of Strategic Security*, No. 5 Vol. 6 No 3, Autumn 2013.

[27] Gerry Doherty and Jim Macgregor: Hidden Histories series: Ireland 1916, 7: Who Knew What … and When? First World War Hidden History. Available online.

ranks of the IRB in Ireland with whom they could cross-check the Navy's information before Easter 1916. This information must have been coming from someone inside the IRB and the Irish Volunteers who was reporting either directly or indirectly to the War Office. The likelihood is that Byrne kept this man under his wing – either directly or indirectly through MI5 – when he moved to Dublin and became Inspector General of the RIC in late August 1916.

The 'reliable informant' disappears entirely from RIC Inspector General's reports after Joseph Byrne lost his job in early 1920. The format of the monthly reports also changed at that point. The new Inspector General, T.J. Smith, simply produced summaries of the accounts of his various County Inspectors and seems to have generated very little of his own material. Whatever the reason, the 'reliable informant' now shuffles off the stage of British intelligence records as unobtrusively as he came onto them.

2

Beyond Reproach

What the evidence in the previous chapter tells us is that Joseph Byrne had an agent at the heart of the IRB and that that individual was based somewhere outside of Dublin. He was not the only agent placed in the republican movement since the DMP had two informants, 'Chalk' and 'Granite', in the Volunteers in Dublin whose evidence, at least in predicting the Rising, was patchy at best.[28] Byrne's informant, however, produced a lot of valuable evidence, including some that is of interest to the general historian. For instance, in February 1919 he passed on information that a visiting Irish-American delegation gave the Dáil Eireann executive to believe that British Prime Minister David Lloyd George 'was very anxious to effect peace in Ireland' and was working through British envoy William Wiseman, MI6's man in New York, to find out what terms would be acceptable in Ireland.[29] To this, the informant was scathing: 'In IRB Circles this is all regarded as twaddle, and the way they view things is that the end of all talk means a fight.'[30] In other words, it did not matter what Lloyd George came up with, since nothing short of a republic would be acceptable to the Irish Republican

---

[28] Eunan O'Halpin, 'British Intelligence in Ireland, 1914-1921'. In Christopher Andrew and David Dilks (eds), *The Missing Dimension, Governments and Intelligence Communities in the Twentieth Century* (London, 1984).

[29] This is reflected in the correspondence of British diplomats at the time. See Lord Curzon to Viscount Grey, 9 September 1919, FO 800/158.

[30] Inspector General's Monthly Report February 1919, TNA CO 904/108. Actually, this may not have been the 'reliable informant' since in this instance he is merely described as the informant. However, the fact that he knew the inner workings of the IRB suggests that they are one and the same person.

Brotherhood. Presumably, if this kind of information from the heart of the IRB was being relayed to the prime minister, it might go some way to explaining why he opted for recruiting the Black and Tans and later the Auxiliaries rather than talking to Sinn Féin in 1919. Wiseman, who had a lot of influence with President Woodrow Wilson, soon left New York under a cloud, after being outed as an MI6 agent by Clan na Gael.[31]

Another example occurred a week or two earlier when the 'reliable informant' passed on information that Sinn Féin 'profess to be assured that Pres[ident] Wilson will press for a settlement and they say that if he does not, his life will be in danger in America.'[32] This refers to the hopes of Dáil Eireann for representation at the Paris Peace Conference, to give *de facto* recognition to the nascent state. In the event, Wilson ignored the Irish claims, citing that the remit of the conference was merely to set the borders of states that came into being as a result of the Great War. If threats on Wilson's life were being relayed to Washington, it was certainly not going to encourage him to support Irish demands for a seat at the table at the Paris Conference that would decide the future of Europe in 1919. (Wilson was an Anglophile anyway. His view was that the Irish rebels had stabbed Britain in the back in 1916 and that, by supporting Germany, they were guilty of treason. He would probably have ignored the Irish in any case but the notion that the IRB might be talking of threatening him was certainly not going to help the Irish cause.) However, the point here is that intelligence being passed on by the 'reliable informant' may have had important long-term political consequences.

But this does not tell us anything about the identity of the 'reliable informant', though there are indications that he might have been based in Cork. In January 1917, for instance, he reported that a large conference of the Irish Volunteers was held in Cork 'attended by 70 delegates from country districts, including many released prisoners at which reorganization was discussed'.[33] This meeting was not mentioned by the Cork County Inspector in his report for the same month – though

---

[31] Richard B. Spence, *Englishmen in New York: The SIS American Station, 1915-21*, Intelligence and National Security, 19(3), pp. 511-37, September 2002.

[32] Inspector General's Monthly Report January 1919, TNA CO 904/108.

[33] Inspector General's Monthly Report, January 1917, TNA CO 904/102.

much else that happened in Cork was. Nonetheless, it found its way directly to the Inspector General's desk. In October 1916 Frank Hall passed on a message from 'a well-informed source which has hithero [*sic*] been found reliable', to the effect that 'John O'Hurley' [Seán Ó Muirthile] is 'organizer-in-chief for the South of Ireland' and was visiting Cork and Waterford for various political ends. 'I was assured that there would be no trouble last weekend and there was not the least fear of the Sinn Fein crowd starting trouble in the near future.'[34]

Another intriguing exchange took place between Vernon Kell, the head of MI5, and Major Ivon Price, the chief of military intelligence in Ireland, in September 1916. Kell forwarded an alarmist report picked up in Berlin that another 'Sinn Fein' rising was in the offing and that a substantial batch of arms had just been smuggled into Ireland.[35] Price dismissed the suggestion, saying there was little evidence on the ground to support such claims. While General Macdonogh, the Director of Military Intelligence, claimed that the intelligence had come from the 'highest source', Kell was immediately able to check on the veracity of the suggestion that a new and substantial amount of arms might have been smuggled into Ireland. On 28 September he corrected his previous report: '"Arms smuggled into Ireland" are in fact arms which were in the hands of the Sinn Feins prior to the Rebellion and which have been concealed and not given up when the recent search for arms was made.'[36]

This is precisely the situation that prevailed in Cork during Easter week 1916 when the Volunteers agreed to hand up their arms to the Bishop of Cork, through the intervention of T.C. Butterfield, the Lord Mayor. The military then confiscated the arms when an earlier promise made by the local commandant, General Stafford and his intelligence officer Captain Dickie, was overturned on the orders of the new military governor of Ireland, General Maxwell. If this left a sour taste in Cork, it was very much sweetened by the fact that the majority of the rifles handed up were duds and most of the better munitions were smuggled out of the city before the military could get their hands on them. Dickie

---

[34] Copy Report from F. Hall to DID, 15 October 1916, TNA, ADM 223/761.

[35] Correspondence on Berlin report, September 1916, TNA, WO 35/69/8.

[36] Kell to Price, 28 September 1916, TNA, WO 35/69/8.

believed that half the serviceable rifles had been handed in. In fact, it appears to have been much less than that.

The important point here, though, is that Kell was able to find this out almost immediately. It is also clear that Hall was the conduit for this correspondence.[37] This suggests that Kell's information came from Cork – more specifically from someone who was aware of how the military in Cork had been fooled by the quick thinking of those Volunteer officers who moved their rifles out of town. Frank Hall had an agent in Cork. As late as October 1917 he was able to claim that he still had a 'reliable informant' working in Queenstown.[38]

A more clear-cut clue to the possible identity of the 'reliable informant' was to emerge in late March 1920 when Cork Lord Mayor Tomás MacCurtain was assassinated by what appears to have been undercover policemen. Joseph Byrne had been replaced as head of the RIC a week earlier, on 11 March 1920. On 19 March a conference was held in Union Quay RIC barracks in Cork between the British military authorities and the police to discuss MacCurtain's IRA activities. This was part of a scheme to arrest any 'Sinn Féin' leaders who could reliably be proven to have taken part in some atrocity or attempted atrocity. 'Only persons suspected of complicity in an outrage might be arrested.'[39] The army also had reason to believe that MacCurtain was about to go 'on the run' within days – even believing that he was about to do so the following day. Hence the urgency to have him arrested.[40] During the meeting, the military produced evidence – passed on to them by a most 'trustworthy' and 'reliable' informant who was 'beyond reproach' – that MacCurtain had been involved in the attempted assassination of Lord French, the Lord Lieutenant of Ireland, in the Phoenix Park, Dublin on 19 December 1919. At the meeting the RIC officers present – District Commissioner Clayton, County Inspector Maloney and District Inspector Swanzy – were reluctant to accept MacCurtain's involvement since they believed that he 'did not belong to the extreme military section of the IRA'.[41]

---

[37] Or at least MI5g3, run by Hall. TNA, WO 35/69/8.

[38] 'A reliable informant states.' Note from Hall re. treatment of American sailors at Queenstown (undated but almost certainly October 1917). TNA ADM 223/671.

[39] Report of the Rebellion in Ireland, 6th Division report. TNA, WO 141/93.

[40] ibid.

[41] Michael J. Feeley, BMH WS 68.

Also present at the meeting was Sergeant Michael Feeley of the RIC, who was then sent out to contact his fellow sergeants, Gilgan and Normoyle, who were in charge of the police barracks in Blackpool, the area of Cork in which MacCurtain lived. Both sergeants immediately came to the meeting and 'upheld the police view and stated that they had no evidence the Lord Mayor was absent from Cork on the date stated'.[42]

After some discussion, the military agreed to go back to 'consult with their informant' – the source of the information that MacCurtain had taken part in the attempt on Lord French's life – and presumably also that he was about to go 'on the run' – before coming to a decision. Feeley was told to expect a dispatch during the afternoon and that when it arrived he was to deal with it. Shortly before 6pm a military motor cyclist arrived with a message from the competent military authority which Feeley signed for. The dispatch stated:

Our informant has again been consulted and he adheres to his original statement that Thomas McCurtain [*sic*] was present at an attempted ambush on Lord French at [----] station in Dublin on [----]. The dispatch further stated that the information was reliable and trustworthy and that their informant was above reproach as regards his information. In view of this, Thomas McCurtain [*sic*] was to be arrested and interned. Two police were to meet a party of military at St Luke's RIC Barracks at time and place stated and they were to proceed to Blackpool to the residence of Thomas McCurtain [*sic*].

The rest of the events of that night are well known. When the police and military party who were to arrest MacCurtain arrived at his home, they found that he had been shot dead less than an hour earlier by armed gunmen with blackened faces who gained admission to the house, ran upstairs and shot him dead in his bedroom in front of his wife and children. His killers were most likely policemen in disguise. This was a seminal event of the War of Independence, for MacCurtain was the first senior republican to be assassinated by Crown forces. It led directly to an intensification in the conflict between republican forces and the British authorities and is central to the history of the War of Independence in Cork.

---

[42] ibid.

The above statement makes two important points:

That the officers in charge of the RIC in Cork were of the view that MacCurtain was a moderate and that, as a result, he was unlikely to have been at the ambush of Lord French. The military in Cork also believed MacCurtain to be a moderate – which he was. He was, however, at the ambush largely because he happened to be in Dublin and was roped in and given an automatic pistol by Michael Collins and ordered to take part. French, of course, escaped with his life and the only casualty was a Volunteer, Martin Savage, who was caught in the crossfire. As MacCurtain put it to some of his officers in Cork afterwards, 'This is all I got for it', namely the pistol. Clearly some of his own 1st Brigade officers in Cork knew he had been to Dublin and that he had some involvement in the attack. Only two Cork IRA officers left a record of knowing that MacCurtain had been present in the Phoenix Part on the day of the attempt to shoot French: Florence O'Donoghue and Michael Leahy.[43] Both will feature prominently in this book – though, as we shall see, for vastly different reasons. Certainly O'Donoghue, the Cork IRA's chief intelligence officer and MacCurtain's Brigade Adjutant, stated that MacCurtain returned from Dublin after the attempted shooting with GHQ sanction for a simultaneous attack on three police barracks by the Cork IRA.[44]

Far more important, though, is that the statement claims categorically that the military had an informant in the IRA and that this man was 'reliable and trustworthy' and 'beyond reproach as regards his information'. He must have been in the senior ranks of the IRA to even have been aware that MacCurtain was in Dublin on the day of the attack on French. What is also evident is that the military were able to contact their man between early afternoon and 6pm on 19 March in order to confirm their information on MacCurtain. Therefore, it was not difficult to get hold of him. This suggests that he was probably living in Cork. It also means that the IRA in Cork is likely to have been compromised

---

[43] Florence O'Donoghue, *Tomás MacCurtain, Soldier and Patriot.* (Tralee, 1955) Michael Leahy BMH WS 1421. It is also noted by Desmond Ryan in *Dublin's Fighting Story* (Cork, 1999), p.246.
[44] Florence O'Donoghue, *Rebel Cork's Fighting Story*, p.23.

almost before the War of Independence began. And this was no low-grade informer out to get blood money at the expense of his comrades. This man was 'reliable', 'trustworthy', 'beyond reproach'.[45] The question, of course, is who was he? And is it possible that he might also have been Joseph Byrne's very reliable informant? Given that British records between 1916 and 1919 suggest that 'highly reliable informants' did not exactly grow on trees in 1919 and that there are suggestions both in MI5 correspondence and in Byrne's reports that a man who answers this description was based in Cork, this seems to be a reasonable suggestion.

If the military decided to arrest MacCurtain because they had reason to believe he might go underground, then it follows that this must also have contributed to the decision to have him murdered that night before he would either be arrested or go 'on the run'.[46] MacCurtain had received threats to his life over the previous months from shadowy elements within the British military machine, so going 'on the run' made sense, especially since known leaders were being picked up in very substantial numbers at this time, particularly in Munster.[47] MacCurtain never got the chance to go undercover. Florrie O'Donoghue did – from the very next day – the day the army believed MacCurtain would have done so. O'Donoghue went to some lengths subsequently to claim that this was as a result MacCurtain's funeral, where senior members of the IRA made themselves publicly known for the first time. However, he was likely to have been part of the plan to go underground with MacCurtain anyway. The important point here is that the military seemed to know about it in advance – just as they knew MacCurtain had been in the Phoenix Park in December 1919. Clearly they were getting this information from someone close to MacCurtain.

---

[45] Michael J. Feeley, BMH WS 68.

[46] *Record of the Rebellion in Ireland 1920-21 – and the part played by the Army in dealing with it,* Vol. I. TNA, WO 141/93.

[47] Warning Note to Tomás MacCurtain, 18 October 1919. O'Donoghue Papers NLI Ms 31,157.

3

The Perfect Organization

In my book *The Year of Disappearances*, I attempted, among other things, to come to grips with the ambiguous contribution to the conflict of Florrie O'Donoghue, Intelligence Officer of the Cork No. 1 Brigade and Adjutant General of the 1st Southern Division of the IRA. The book ended with the unedifying spectacle of O'Donoghue's cousin and employer, Michael Nolan, a Cork draper, being exposed as an RIC informant. Indeed, Nolan's shop at 55 North Main Street – he had a second shop on Castle Street where O'Donoghue worked – was a dropping-in point for policemen on the beat. Information received from Nolan was to lead to the death of two senior IRA Brigade officers, Charlie Daly and O'Donoghue's friend and fellow employee of Nolan's, Walter Leo Murphy.[48] Unsurprisingly perhaps, in all O'Donoghue's copious writings on the period there is not even a hint of this. O'Donoghue left the employ of Nolan on the night Tomás MacCurtain was assassinated to go full-time 'on the run' and he never returned to his job as draper's assistant, though his sister Agnes ran the shop in Castle Street in his place. Here she claimed she acted as his personal secretary and was involved in all kinds of work for the IRA, including intelligence, dispatches and keeping arms right up to the Truce and beyond.[49]

Nor is there a hint in his work or in his papers of the disappearance of O'Donoghue's neighbours, James and Fred Blemens, a Protestant horticulture instructor and his son, who lived two doors away from the

---

[48] Murphy, *The Year of Disappearances, Political Killings in Cork 1921-1922,* (Dublin 2010), Chapter 58.

[49] Agnes McCarthy, MSP34REF60655.

home of his girlfriend and soon to become wife Josephine Brown on the Old Blackrock Road. The Blemenses were taken away by armed IRA men in two motor cars at the end of November 1920 just two days before O'Donoghue kidnapped Josephine's son from the home of his grandparents in Wales, with the intention of bringing the boy back to Cork and reuniting him with his mother. The Blemenses were never seen again and there does not seem to have been much effort made by the authorities to find out what had happened to them.[50]

But perhaps the biggest question mark hanging over O'Donoghue's reign as chief IRA intelligence officer – or 'spy master' as he is now sometimes called – lies in the culpability or otherwise of those who were shot as spies in the city, particularly in the spring of 1921. One of the most striking contrasts of the counter espionage campaign of the IRA in the War of Independence is between that waged by Michael Collins in Dublin and that waged by O'Donoghue in Cork. Far more 'spies' were shot in Cork, but with historical hindsight it is now possible to establish that, while most of those shot in Dublin were agents of one kind or another, most of those shot in Cork were probably not. In other words, the majority of the people Collins had shot as 'spies' *were* spies, while many of those shot in Cork city appear to have been innocent civilians – or at least there is no evidence that they were spies. A few were, of course, and we shall meet some of these in later chapters. But by and large, those shot were a mixed bag of ex-soldiers and Protestants, grouped together rather euphemistically in an alleged cabal called the Anti-Sinn Féin League (ASFL), an appellation that rather curiously – though nobody has ever thought this worth commenting on – does not seem to appear anywhere in the gigantic mountains of paper that are the archives of Richard Mulcahy and Michael Collins.

My conclusion, or at least the conclusion I was moving towards, was that the ASFL was merely a useful cover for the targeting of Protestants and ex-soldiers as scapegoats for IRA setbacks. My general view – though it went largely unstated – was that the useful information leaking to the authorities must have come from members of the IRA themselves, and that the ASFL was merely a flag of convenience to point the finger

---

[50] Murphy, op.cit. chapters 14-23.

elsewhere in order to distract attention from the real problem. At that stage I had no idea where the leaks might have been coming from. It was merely a hunch, admittedly one based on common sense. Nothing I have come across since has made me alter that view, but the story needs verification.

From the recent work of William Sheehan, it is clear that the Cork IRA, in particular the Cork No. 1 Brigade, was under severe pressure during the last months of the War of Independence and that the British forces in Cork were very much on the ascendant.[51] The 2nd and 3rd Brigades and their respective columns were still in the field and could probably have fought on, but the 1st Brigade was reduced to setting off bombs under army bands as happened in Youghal at the end of May 1921 and once-off assassinations of off-duty soldiers and civilians. The British commander in Cork, General Sir Peter Strickland's claim that if his army had a few more weeks they could have finished off the IRA is largely hyperbole. However, in the case of Cork No. 1 there is some truth in it. As he wrote in his diary when he left Cork in 1922: 'And so this is the end of two and a half years' toil, a year ago we had the perfect organization and had them beat, a short time more would have completed it thoroughly.' Another British officer, Lieutenant Colonel Lindsay-Young, was even more adamant: 'now with victory in their hands, they had been called off the kill and handed the fruits of the victory to the vanquished.'[52] The British officers, of course, blamed 'the Frocks', their politicians for, as they saw it, capitulating to the IRA, but this overlooks the fact that Ireland was a political problem rather than a military one. Military solutions to political problems rarely work – something officers more sensitive to matters on the ground, such as General Nevil Macready, the supreme commander of the British forces in Ireland, acknowledged.

So what was the 'perfect organization' Strickland claimed had been working for him in the spring of 1921? Clearly, because this was a guerrilla war, a large part of it must have been down to intelligence. The British army did not win any major battles in 1921, yet almost all the most serious IRA fighters in the city and its environs were in British captivity by the time of the Truce, picked up in ones and twos in

---

[51] William Sheehan, *A Hard Local War* (Stroud, 2011).

[52] Strickland and Lindsay-Young quoted in Sheehan, *A Hard Local War*, p.56.

increasingly effective counter-insurgency operations. Others, including Walter Leo Murphy and Charlie Daly, were dead. Sheehan suggests that this success was largely due to an increased flow of information from the population to the military. And there may be some truth in this argument: the RIC did report in January that there was an increased flow of information. However, two months later they were reporting that all such sources were drying up. The Dripsey ambush, in which a number of IRA men were shot and others captured, was down to information volunteered by civilians.[53] However, a combination of the IRA's campaign of assassination against civilians suspected – in the vaguest possible way it now appears – of giving information, and the British army's own campaign of atrocities against the population, and their property, meant that the average man in the street was even less likely to provide information against the IRA than he had been a year earlier. 'For an Irishman or Irishwoman to openly disagree with them [the IRA] is simply a novel way of committing suicide', as one correspondent memorably put it.[54] Or, as a Cork loyalist noted in a letter to General Strickland, if loyal citizens were to stand up to the IRA, 'our lives would not be worth a week's purchase'.[55]

And British forces scarcely had a better relationship with the locals in light of the reprisals and arson campaign they carried out, first by the Black and Tans and Auxilaries, and then officially by the army itself. British forces – in so-called 'khaki Cork' where only a few years earlier they had been lionized – came to be detested by the local population, especially after they had burnt down the centre of the city. They could still, of course, have got some information but with most people now too terrified to open their mouths, this would not have been enough to turn the tables so on the IRA. The 'perfect organization' came about, not because the army found a way to be nice to the population, though individual soldiers and officers were sometimes gallant to civilians.

---

[53] In this case by mutual arrangement when Mrs Lindsay, an elderly Protestant lady and Father Shinnick the local curate, agreed to tell their respective forces about the ambush. The IRA decided to ignore Father Shinnick's warning and went ahead with the ambush anyway, even though they had been told that the British had been informed. Mrs Lindsay and her chauffeur, James Clarke, were put to death by the IRA for their part in the debacle. Shinnick remained unharmed.

[54] Loyalist letter quoted in Sheehan, p. 61.

[55] Loyalist letter quoted in Murphy, *Year of Disappearances*, p.87.

(And occasionally even to IRA men themselves. One of the more fascinating aspects of some Bureau of Military History submissions of IRA witnesses is how they regularly mention courteous treatment on the part of British officers, sometimes being advised to keep their mouths shut or feign illness to avoid being murdered.)[56] The 'perfect organization' came about because the army had its agents in place in the IRA and had the wherewithal to react to information as it came in. The 'perfect organization' also came about because, after a lot of teething difficulties when the RIC was initially reluctant to cooperate fully with the army, by the spring of 1921 the two organizations were sharing information and cooperating well, particularly in the city.

In order to understand this situation, it is necessary to look, however briefly, at the development of British intelligence in Cork from the end of the Great War to the British departure in 1922.[57] Intelligence in 1918 was built, as the Record of the Rebellion put it, on 'bad foundations'. 'Prior to 1920 there was no intelligence organized along modern lines with complete and up-to-date records and capable of being developed and expanded without dislocation into an effective intelligence organization such as had been created in London and the various theatres of war, during 1914-18.' 'Till the end of 1919 there was no military intelligence operation independent of the RIC and the need for and the possibilities of such an organization was not recognized.'[58] Battalion intelligence officers rarely existed before 1919.[59] But this is clearly an example of the army praising itself at the expense of the police. Joseph Byrne had better information than the army would ever have. Indeed, when the army tried to create the intelligence organization 'along modern lines' it was the police they depended on.

The alleged early failure of intelligence is exaggerated in the two principal accounts left by the intelligence community: the military's own Record of the Rebellion in Ireland and that of the Chief of Police,[60]

---

[56] For two examples of this, see Michael Crowley, BMH WS 1603, and Dick Cotter, BMH WS 810. Also see Connie Neenan, in McEoin, *Survivors*, p.240.

[57] This is covered in much greater detail in Sheehan and in Peter Hart's publication of the Intelligence section of the army's Record of the Rebellion in Ireland, *British Intelligence in Ireland 1920-21*.

[58] Hart, *British Intelligence*, pp.43-45.

[59] Sheehan, p.71.

[60] TNA, WO 141/93 and WO 141/94.

Ormonde Winter. These tended to bad-mouth one another, each claiming credit for successes while blaming the other for failures.[61] The Record itself spends a lot of time criticizing the police, yet it was to the RIC that the army had to turn from the autumn of 1919, after Liam Lynch's group in Fermoy had shot a soldier in a raid for arms, to make up the intelligence deficit. It was the 'Special Crimes' sergeants and constables who provided on-the-job training on 'political intelligence, including the recruitment of local agents'.[62] When on 31 January 1920, the army moved to round up known IRA suspects and put them in jail, they picked up 60 leading Republicans – all already known and clearly identified. Of these, 54 were arrested in the 6th Divisional area (Munster), with eight caught in Dublin and none at all in the 5th Divisional area which covered the rest of the country outside Ulster.[63] This suggests that their information was better in Munster and specifically Cork than it was elsewhere in the country. At the very least it supports the idea that the 'very reliable informant', whom we encountered on the eve of the shooting of Tomás MacCurtain, was operating in the 6th Divisional area, that is to say Cork. It cannot be proven that he was the same man whose information found its way to the Inspector General of the RIC until the beginning of 1920, but it looks likely.

Throughout 1920 the army steadily improved its liaison with the RIC, yet the latter was to remain the main source of intelligence until the end of the year.[64] Indeed, Winter tells us that the only British agent to have penetrated the IRB had originally been recruited by a Crimes Special Sergeant of the RIC.[65] As Peter Hart commented, the RIC were also 'more successful than they are generally given credit for' and that even 'prior to mid-1920 it was not all that difficult to identify or arrest most rebels,'[66] especially when you had 'informants who were above reproach' ready to identify them and who knew their addresses and exact movements.

---

[61] Both accounts are collected in Hart's booklet.
[62] Sheehan, p.72.
[63] Peter Hart, *British Intelligence in Ireland 1920-21, the Final Reports*, p.20.
[64] Sheehan, p.73.
[65] Hart, *British Intelligence in Ireland 1920-21*, p.72.
[66] Hart, quoted in Sheehan, p.73.

By December 1920 when Martial Law was proclaimed over most of the southern half of Ireland, the army was well on its way to building on its links with the RIC to form what they considered would be an effective stand-alone intelligence organization.

The first noticeable effect of the Proclamation was that it forced the IRA to conceal their arms, when not in use, in dumps, a good many of which were discovered, for intelligence was good at this time in the 6th Divisional area and there were 45 agents, of whom 23 were believed to be reliable, working for the Divisional Intelligence Officer. These sources, however, were almost entirely dried up in February when the IRA, as a reply to martial law, to official reprisals and to the carrying of hostages on motor lorries, began a series of murders of persons whom they believed might have given information. In every case but one the person murdered had given no information – in that case the murdered man was an agent known to be untrustworthy, but the terror created was such that all those who had been giving information previously were silenced.[67]

This statement goes a long way to explain the fluctuating fortunes of the intelligence war in Cork. It also tells us that the wrong people were being murdered as supposed 'spies'.[68] Most importantly, though, it states that during the conflict, the army was running 45 agents in Cork and the surrounding area, 23 of whom were active and reliable, and that the IRA did not know who they were – the only one they got was one of the unreliables. That's a lot of reliable agents. Sheehan is surely correct to point out that 'the British Army's assessment of the effect of the IRA's shooting of informers on their intelligence network is that it had little or none . . . from the army's perspective, the widespread killing of ex-servicemen and local loyalists had no impact on their intelligence gathering'.[69] This was at the core of the 'perfect organization'. In other words, while the IRA in Cork was busily killing the wrong people – which admittedly did have the effect of reducing the amount of information coming from the general public – the British intelligence system itself remained largely untouched.

As a result, the British military's knowledge of the Cork IRA was accurate, as this summary of the IRA's structure in Cork shows.

---

[67] Hart, *British Intelligence*, p.28.

[68] And this is not just a one-off statement. It is a constant refrain running through military and police reports in both 1920 and 1921.

[69] Sheehan, p.82.

Up to the time when martial law was proclaimed there was a Brigade Headquarters and two battalions of IRA in the city. Each battalion was organized in eight companies and the total strength was about 1,000. These battalions were at one time very good and their officer class was probably the best in Ireland. [This is an interesting, if two-handed compliment.]

The position of brigade headquarters was changed frequently in consequence of the constant raids. Neither battalion apparently had any definite headquarters. By December 1920, when martial law was proclaimed, Brigade headquarters had been driven out of the city and were established near Clogheen about two miles west of Cork, all documents etc. being hidden in boxes which were buried in banks and other hiding places. It was not long, however, before these headquarters were located and the Brigade Headquarters were then moved, first to the south of the city and then to the mountains near Macroom. Meanwhile the headquarters of the two city battalions had been broken up and no effort was made to re-establish them. When the brigade headquarters was moved to Macroom a commandant was placed in charge of the two battalions in Cork City.'[70]

This is an accurate account of the travails of the city IRA from the end of 1920 onwards. Far from being 'bad, very bad', the view put forward by Florrie O'Donoghue in his many publications on the subject and seconded by Seán O'Hegarty, it suggests that British intelligence in Cork was in fact quite good. 'The two Cork battalions were resolutely tackled at the end of 1920 and constant successes were gained against them.'[71] The evidence Sheehan accumulated supports this view.

Most of the setbacks the Cork IRA suffered in the spring of 1921, such as those that occurred at Clogheen, Clonmult and Upton, have been dealt with in detail elsewhere. Many of these were the result either of the action of British agents placed in or close to IRA units or else from leakages from IRA members themselves. Often these were one and the same. The discovery of materials and the summary execution of six volunteers at Clogheen, mentioned above, was due to that group being infiltrated by Patrick 'Cruxy' O'Connor, an accountant and former army sergeant who had received the Croix de Guerre in France for bravery during World War I and who was now acting as a spy in

---

[70] Hart, *British Intelligence*, p.39. The commandant in question was Tom Crofts. Thomas Crofts, MSP34REF1887.

[71] Hart, *British Intelligence*, p.41.

Cork.[72] Another important raid, at Killeens, was also as a result of information provided by O'Connor. A raid on Rathanisky House, some five miles north of the city where fifteen members of the 1st Battalion were surrounded and arrested in February, was the work of another British agent, Bridie McKay, who was close to members of the column.[73] Walter Leo Murphy, commandant of the 3rd Battalion and Charlie Daly, who were captured and killed by members of the Hampshire Regiment at Waterfall outside the city, as we have seen, owed their deaths to information provided by Michael J. Nolan, Florrie O'Donoghue's cousin and employer.[74] In addition, the seizure of many arms dumps in the spring of 1921 and the capture of IRA leaders both in the city and outside it, was down to careful management of local agents on the ground.[75]

Some of the setbacks occurred farther afield. Over a period of little more than a month in February/March 1921, the Cork IRA suffered five very serious defeats and avoided another because of the quick thinking of Tom Barry and faulty planning on the part of the British. The first of these occurred at Upton railway station between Bandon and Cork on 15 February 1921. According to local commandant Liam Deasy: 'Cork Number One Brigade, through its Intelligence Officer Florence O'Donoghue, was sometimes able to get advance information on the movements of British troops. . . It happened that two or three days after the successful train ambush at Drishanebeg [where a Cork No. 3 Brigade column stopped a train near Millstreet and disarmed a platoon of troops, killing one and taking the remainder prisoners who were subsequently released][76] the intelligence officer informed our

---

[72] The story is not quite that simple. O'Connor had long ceased to provide information but broke down during interrogation when he was told he would face the hangman, admitting then that he had been a Secret Service agent to save his skin. O'Connor was spirited out of Cork by the military and was finally tracked down to New York where an attempt was made on his life over a year later. See cairogang.com for a very detailed and accurate analysis of O'Connor's movements and career. His full name was Patrick Joseph O'Connor and he did indeed win the Croix de Guerre.

[73] Bridie McKay may well have been on intimate terms with one of those arrested since the British suspected her of being a double agent. For a detailed description of the capture, see *The Year of Disappearances*, chapters 24 and 25.

[74] Murphy, *Year of Disappearances*, chapter 58.

[75] Sheehan, pp.86-90.

[76] O'Donoghue, *No Other Law*, pp.131-32.

headquarters that a small party of British troops, probably no more than twelve to fifteen in number would leave Cork for Bantry on the 9.30am train on 15 February.'[77] The West Cork IRA decided to attack the train as it pulled into Upton station, on the basis that the small group of soldiers would be confined to the mail car since they were in charge of the mails. However, the train made an unscheduled stop at Kinsale Junction, some two miles up the line and 50 soldiers from Kinsale climbed on board and spread themselves throughout the train. IRA scouts who spotted the troops embarking cycled furiously to Upton to warn the others but were too late.

As the train pulled into the station, the soldiers immediately opened fire on the attackers. They poured out onto the platform and quickly overwhelmed the ambush party. The result was that three IRA volunteers were killed, three others were captured, another was to die afterwards from his wounds, and Charlie Hurley, the commandant in charge of the operation was so badly wounded that he ceased to function and was to be killed a few weeks later just before the Crossbarry action. To make matters worse, six civilians were also killed and one of the IRA men captured was to turn King's evidence. What is most interesting about the case is that the British military public inquiry into the ambush failed to mention the 50-odd troops who came on at Kinsale Junction, claiming rather that the 10-man guard looking after the mails had beaten off the attackers themselves.[78] The information that led to the Upton debacle was brought out of Victoria Barracks by Josephine Brown, soon to be O'Donoghue's wife.[79]

On the same day, the flying column of the 2nd Brigade was surrounded at Mourneabbey in north Cork as they lay in wait for a British military party on its way from Mallow to Cork. This time, five IRA men were killed, four more were captured, two of whom were subsequently executed. A few weeks later the same group was surrounded again, at Nadd in the hill country some miles west of Mourneabbey. This time three IRA men were killed. Both defeats were put down to the infiltration of the column by a British army intelligence

---

[77] Deasy, *Towards Ireland Free*, pp. 219-23.
[78] Upton Inquest, TNA, WO35/159B/12.
[79] Statement attached to Military Pension Claim form, O'Donoghue NLI Ms 31,126 – Ms 31,129.

agent, Dan Shields, who had joined the Kanturk Company as an ordinary volunteer. [80]

The next day, 16 February, four IRA men digging road trenches near Kilbrittain in west Cork were surrounded by members of the Essex regiment and shot dead.[81] The most serious defeat, however, occurred at Clonmult in east Cork on Sunday, 20 February. According to Joseph Aherne, second in command of the East Cork column (of the 1st Brigade), 'we received a dispatch from the Brigade Adjutant, Mr Florrie O'Donoghue, to attack a party of eleven soldiers who were either carrying ammunition from Cobh to Cork or bringing it from Cork to Cobh. The party were to travel on the train from Cork to Cobh. The wording of the dispatch was such that it was more or less a challenge to the column to carry out the attack. It ended with the words: "If you are unable to carry out the job, please let me know immediately and I will make other arrangements." Hurley [Commandant of the 4th Battalion and column commander] read the dispatch first and then handed it to me and asked me what I thought of it. I remarked that it was an insult to the column. He said he thought the same.'[82] Aherne and Hurley, along with two others, went to reconnoitre the proposed ambush site near Cobh Junction. While they were gone, the column was wiped out after a siege at a farmhouse at Clonmult where they had been based. Twelve Volunteers were killed, many of them in cold blood after they had surrendered. The remainder were captured, two of whom were subsequently executed.[83]

The suggestion that the column had been betrayed by an ex-soldier who had been trapping rabbits in the area is probably wrong. David Walsh was captured in Glenville some two months later and confessed to the 'betrayal' when faced with an open grave. However, he appears to have been a brain-damaged ex-soldier who was barely able to speak. British military records state he had nothing to do with it and that he was not even known to them. Indeed, according to Walsh's brother, David was in hospital at the time of the siege so he could not even have

---

[80] O'Donoghue, op.cit, pp.135-36; Hart, *The IRA and its Enemies*, p.149.
[81] Deasy, op.cit. p.223.
[82] Joseph Ahearne, BMH WS1367.
[83] Tom O'Neill, *The Battle of Clonmult, the IRA's Worst Defeat* (Cork, 2006).

been at Clonmult.[84] The information that led to the massacre was picked up in Cork city on the morning of the battle by the intelligence officer of the Hampshire Regiment.[85] The column had received several warnings that they had been betrayed and planned to leave the previous day but were ordered by Brigade HQ to remain in Clonmult until the Sunday.[86]

In retrospect, it is easy to see how the column was trapped. They had been based in Clonmult for weeks, security was lax and sentries were barely being posted. The military had been waiting to pounce on Clonmult for several months, ever since a Volunteer officer was captured with a cache of photographs of a training camp that had been held there.[87] Clonmult was a disaster waiting to happen. Diarmuid Hurley, like his cousin Charlie Hurley in west Cork, was a broken man after Clonmult and was to be shot dead by the RIC outside Midleton in the same week that the unfortunate Walsh was shot in Glenville – with Walsh's 'confession' in his pocket.

These were all serious defeats suffered by the Cork IRA. In most of the cases it appears the units concerned walked into a trap or very nearly did so – as they would again a month later when Tom Barry's column was almost surrounded at Crossbarry. That they escaped was due to quick thinking on Barry' part and the fact that some of the British forces coming from Kinsale went to the wrong place – having been told to go to Kilbarry, rather than Crossbarry. Barry turned what might have been a defeat into a victory and has to be given credit for that. What most of these defeats have in common is that the information that led to them came either from British moles within the IRA or else from orders issued by O'Donoghue, based in turn on information being brought out of British barracks by Josephine Brown. You would, at the very least, have to question the *bona fides* of this information. If you get the sense of *agents provocateurs* at work here, you are probably right.

---

[84] See letters from Andrew Walsh, 19 February 1923, and General Peter Strickland, 19 July 1924, MA, A/0649. Also see Hart, *British Intelligence in Ireland,* p.91.

[85] *A Record of the Rebellion in Ireland, 6th Division Report,* TNA, WO 141/93.

[86] *The Battle of Clonmult Commomorative Journal and Calender 1921-2021.* Clonmult Ambush Centenary Committee 2020. I am grateful to John Arnold for further information on this.

[87] TNA WO35/125/6. Michael Hennessy, MSP34REF2125.

4

The Bureau and Other Stories

Florrie O'Donoghue is one of the more important figures in the Irish War of Independence. This is not so much because of what he did during the war itself – although that is also important – but because o the enormous influence he had on how it has been written about since. Not only are his well-received biographies of Liam Lynch and Tomás MacCurtain still standard reference books on the period but the vast archive he left to the National Library of Ireland is now cited and quoted from in almost every book written on the conflict. It is true to say that, probably more than anybody, Florrie O'Donoghue has framed how we write and think about the Irish revolution.

We cannot blame historians for taking O'Donoghue at face value, though there are aspects where questions should have been raised. He comes across as a clear-eyed observer and was intelligent, capable and shrewd. Those who knew him during his lifetime remember a charming, cultured man. He is spoken of in reverential, almost hagiographical, terms in the historical community on almost all sides of the many debates that characterize the writing on the period. He seems balanced and fair-minded, even if he could be scathing in his judgements when it suited him. And some of these judgements could be quite unfair, as we shall see.

He claimed, for instance, to have had a particular dislike for Richard Mulcahy, whose bad language he said he abhorred, though considering that Seán O'Hegarty, the O/C of the Cork No. 1 Brigade and O'Donoghue's closest associate in the IRA, was notorious for his vicious tongue, this appears to be a case of the kettle calling the pot black. He also spread a not-too-subtle calumny about the character of Michael Collins, implying to the writer Frank O'Connor – whom he knew well since his sister was married to the brother of Nancy McCarthy, O'Connor's first and most famous girlfriend – that Collins was a rough, boorish type and famously foul-mouthed. The latter affliction, if it could be called that, was one that Collins shared with a great many Corkmen, even to this day. In fact, the character of Collins that emerges from *The Big Fellow*, O'Connor's biography, is very different from that of previous biographies. The big, jawboned, wrestling, ear-biting Collins is oddly absent from the earlier biographies and from his own correspondence where he comes across as a more measured, astute, silent and indeed considerate man, even if he was often short-tempered with those whom he believed were not doing their jobs and was given to towering rages. And while Collins used to wrestle with Harry Boland when they were younger, one thing is sure: his closest associates would not have been as loyal to him as they were if he was the kind of boor portrayed in *The Big Fellow*.

O'Donoghue was also a religious man. This comes across particularly strongly in his accounts of the ministrations of his friend Father Dominic O'Connor, chaplain to the Cork No. 1 Brigade. After the death of P.S. O'Hegarty (Seán O'Hegarty's brother, Michael Collins's supporter and fellow non-believer), O'Donoghue made his way to Dublin, to Glasnevin Cemetery where O'Hegarty was buried, to sprinkle holy water on his grave. As one commentator put it: 'A good liaison man, for here and hereafter, one might say.'[88]

Yet there are families in Cork who to this day detest O'Donoghue because of the way he treated various Volunteer officers during the conflict and subsequently in his writings. Is he correct when he speaks of some of his colleagues in scathing terms, terms that by now have been repeated so many times, they are accepted as fact? Is he fair to Fred Murray, for instance, one of the more energetic of the early organizers of the Cork Volunteers, whom he states 'was allowed to fade out later without comment', the implication being that Murray was a coward, when in fact Murray was jailed on a trumped-up charge? Is he fair to Terence MacSwiney when he comments that 'it was part of our tragedy that he had to be a soldier. He never looked well in uniform.'

---

[88] Patrick J. Twohig, *The Dark Secret of Bealnablath*, p.133. Yet, somehow, you get the feeling that Twohig was somewhat tongue-in-cheek when it came to O'Donoghue.

O'Donoghue castigated quite a number of Volunteer leaders at various points in his writings, including Seán O'Sullivan , original O/C of the 2nd Battalion, Donal O'Callaghan, Deputy Lord Mayor and later Lord Mayor of Cork, who was also the victim of a trumped-up charge, Seán Murray and T.J. Golden. Even Liam Lynch's tendency to stammer gets a mention, as if this had any bearing on his ability as a soldier.[89]

In the case of Terence MacSwiney, we can at least check the accuracy of O'Donoghue's assessment, since MacSwiney left his own detailed papers and was written about and quoted on an almost daily basis in the newspapers of the time.[90] What comes across is a decent, fair-minded man who did his best to be Lord Mayor to all the citizens of Cork. To take one example: he felt he had to turn down, with regret, an invitation to the annual sports day of Cork Grammar School on the basis that it would have been untenable for him to attend as Sinn Féin Lord Mayor, given that a British Army band was likely to be playing there. He tried to get back the property of loyalists when it had been stolen by Volunteers and worked hard to call a halt to casual boycotting. Is it fair of O'Donoghue to dismiss him for having taken part in only one action, a failed attempt to raid for arms, when the average number of actions by most of the leadership at that time was little better?

As for how he looked in uniform, photos of MacSwiney show that he looked perfectly fine in uniform. And there is no question of his bravery. He showed that during his hunger strike. Why was O'Donoghue in his writings so grudging towards a man whose principal flaw was that he was perhaps too idealistic and maybe a little otherworldly? Why does he feel the need to pull him down a peg or two, like some recent attempts to do the same to Michael Collins?

One of the oddest things about O'Donoghue's writings is his widely flagged detestation for politics, and this may be part of his complaint against MacSwiney. But the IRA was the armed wing of an independence movement. To state that it was above politics or in some way disconnected with politics is nonsense. The supposed superiority of

---

[89] Most of these comments can be found in his memoir, published as part of John Borgonovo's *Florence and Josephine O'Donoghue's War of Independence* (Dublin, 2006).

[90] Terence MacSwiney Papers. Cork County and City Archives.

military considerations and military 'honour' over political ones sails very close to fascism. It is clear from his writings that O'Donoghue saw the IRA, or 'the Army' as he termed it, as being more important than the people of Ireland, and the will of 'the Army' as being more important than the will of the people. This is a foretaste of the kind of thinking that would sweep through Europe over the next decade, with consequences that do not require explanation here.[91]

As we shall see, O'Donoghue went to considerable lengths to massage the material that found its way into the Bureau of Military History. For instance, multiple joint submissions are used in most of the accounts he collected in Cork so that nothing could be recorded that was not agreed by all the witnesses, pages are mysteriously missing, key witnesses were apparently never interviewed, some statements never made it to the Bureau at all. In the 1940s he repeatedly tried to twist the arm of the Bureau to exclude what he believed to be inappropriate information. Disguised in a good deal of waffle about duplication of effort, waste of time and money and charges of political bias, he wrote to his fellow Bureau members that 'the investigation system in operation was dangerously faulty and needed to be refined if anything worthwhile was to emerge from all this effort'. 'In the interests of impartiality, fieldworkers had to show discrimination and acumen if they were to build a complete picture of these events; moreover, they had to be able to distinguish pertinent information from the trivial.' Civil servants who were gathering witness statements – usually either serving or former army officers – were 'deficient in these indispensable qualities and that the random and patchy methodology was not conducive to the development of this skill.' 'The fieldworkers lacked the historical sense that would enable them to detect and separate the important from the unimportant'. He did not approve of the Bureau's approach to gather a vast hoard of information that 'allowed no consideration of what future historians might need'.

In layman's language, what he was saying was that he did not want the apparently 'trivial' finding its way into Bureau records. And of course it is in such 'apparently trivial' details – often contradictory –

---

[91] For the parallels between extreme republican posturing and later Nazi and Bolshevik world views, see James Hogan's analysis in Donnachadh Ó Corráin (ed.), *James Hogan, Revolutionary, Historian, Political Scientist* (Dublin, 2001).

that evidence of skulduggery may be found, not in material which has been cleaned up and tidied in the interests of 'fairness and impartiality'. In other words, he wanted the messenger, if not shot, at least hobbled, so that inappropriate information might not find its way into the hands of future historians. Not to make too fine a point, he was calling for censorship. The director of the Bureau, Michael McDunphy, however, was having none of it: 'it was not proper for the Bureau to assume the right to determine where the truth lies' in cases where there was ostensible conflict of evidence.[92]

And of the statements that did make it, O'Donoghue sometimes wrote to the Bureau questioning their reliability. One of the more notable of these was Michael Leahy, formerly commandant of the 4th (East Cork) Battalion of the No. 1 Brigade and Vice O/C of the Brigade at the time of the Truce.[93] This is interesting because, if anything, Leahy was notable for his reliability, which was why he was selected to pilot the boat that, it was hoped, would land the huge cache of arms being sourced in Italy in the spring of 1921. Leahy was also the only other Volunteer officer to state in his Bureau of Military History submission that Tomás MacCurtain was present at the attempted assassination of Lord French – which might be another reason why O'Donoghue might have been unhappy with it.

But there are two major episodes described by Leahy which are very much at odds with O'Donoghue's version of events.[94] The first is the aforementioned failed attempt to smuggle arms from Italy – which is the only subject covered in O'Donoghue's own BMH statement, even though he was not involved directly in the operation. The second is

---

[92] The above quotations are taken from Evi Grotzaridis, 'Revisionist historians and the modern Irish state: the conflict between the Advisory Committee and the Bureau of Military History, 1947-66.' *Irish Historical Studies*, Vol. XXXV, No. 137, May 2006, pp.99-116.

[93] O'Donoghue Papers, NLI Ms 31,368. The others whose reliability O'Donoghue questions are Fred Murray, Con Collins, Roibeard Lankford, Eamonn Lynch, Denis Lordan, Liam Murphy and Flor Begley. We shall encounter some of these later on in the narrative.

[94] Michael Leahy, BMH WS 555. Leahy's account is numbered WS 555, while O'Donoghue's is WS 554. This suggests that they were written in sequence, with O'Donoghue's slightly ahead of Leahy's. However, Leahy's was dated 5 May 1951, while O'Donoghue's is dated as having been written six years later, on 9 April 1957, suggesting that he managed to get it placed beside Leahy's for 'correction'.

Leahy's account of the arrest of Terence MacSwiney in August 1920 which was to lead to his hunger strike and death. Both these events need to be looked at in detail because they identify some huge holes in O'Donoghue's story. These will be the subject of the next three chapters.

5

The Failed Genoa Arms Deal

In September 1920 Professor Liam Ó Briain, Professor of Romance Languages at University College Galway and a member of the IRB, was making a short trip to France for personal reasons. Before he left, Michael Collins approached him and asked him to cross the border into Italy to carry a message to Donal Hales, the self-appointed Irish Consul in Genoa. Ó Briain managed to get an extension to his visa which enabled him to travel on to Italy and meet with Hales. Collins had given him a sheet of paper with the letter 'M' written on it in Gaelic script. The Gaelic 'M', presumably meaning 'maith' (good), was simply a message to say 'Yes' to Hales, meaning 'go ahead with your project'.[1]

The project in question was the plan, put together by Collins and Tom Hales at an IRB meeting in April 1920, for the importation of a large quantity of arms, purchased for next to nothing from elements within the Italian military. Donal Hales, younger brother of Tom, Commandant of the West Cork Brigade, was to act as organizer for the purchase of the arms in Italy. Tom Hales was hopeful to have the arms landed in Ireland by September 1920 and was to meet his sister Madge, who was on her way to Italy, in Dublin on 27 July to carry a message to Donal to set the operation in train. However, on the very day he was to leave for Dublin, Tom Hales was arrested by members of the Essex Regiment in west Cork and was held in British jails until after the Treaty. He was also severely tortured. Madge, if she went, left without the information.[2]

---

[1] Liam O'Briain, BMH WS 565.
[2] Letter from Tom Hales to Florrie O'Donoghue, 11 June 1953, O'Donoghue NLI Ms 31,421(8).

Now it was Ó Briain's turn to bring the message to Donal Hales to go ahead with the plans for the purchase and dispatch of the guns and ammunition. It is clear from the account of another visitor sent to Italy at that point that Collins, Cathal Brugha and Richard Mulcahy were all involved in the latter half of 1920 in the planning of the importation of these arms and that all were enthusiastic about it.[3]

Donal Hales, a member of the well-known west Cork Republican family, who had been living in Genoa since 1914, was a teacher and was married to an Italian woman. An earlier attempt to get arms from Italy had fallen through. In April 1920 the Sinn Féin envoy in Rome, Seán T. O'Kelly learned that well-known poet, fascist and philanderer Gabriele D'Annunzio (1863-1938), who had in 1919 annexed the disputed Adriatic port of Fiume, was prepared to provide military assistance to the IRA. O'Kelly, along with the Dáil leadership and de Valera in particular, were wary of D'Annunzio's anti-clericalism, which de Valera felt would not go down well in Ireland. So the deal with D'Annunzio fell through, partly because of procrastination on the Irish side, and the Fiume arms went elsewhere.[4]

Hales, who had briefly negotiated with D'Annunzio was not to be deterred however. By the summer of 1920 he had made contact with another group, this time of regular Italian Army officers, one of whom, a Captain Frugione, was so incensed at British policies in Ireland that he even wanted to come to Ireland himself to fight alongside the IRA[5]. Donal Hales, accompanied by Seán Ó Seaghda, who was sent over by Collins, Brugha and Mulcahy, travelled to Rome to meet the Italian military. 'We could get as many rifles as we wished – up to 100,000. These were Italian rifles which had been used in the previous war; they were in good condition and only required cleaning. We could also get ammunition. There was some talk as to what ammunition would fit these rifles.' The rifles were to be sold off as scrap, but the Irish could have had them for a nominal sum.[6] Mussolini, who, it appears, was

[3] Seán Ó Seaghdha, BMH WS 760.
[4] Mark Phelan, 'Gabriele d'Annunzio and the Irish Republic 1919-21', *History Ireland*, September/October 2013.
[5] Michael Leahy, BMH WS 555.
[6] Donal Hales, BMH WS 292. The BMH statements of Leahy, Hales, Ó Briain and Ó Seaghda can be used to put together a largely accurate portrayal of what happened at the Italian end.

aware of the deal, later reneged on the 'nominal sum', increasing it to £10,000 which in one account gave Dublin pause for thought. Collins, however, instructed Hales to bide his time until a suitable means of transferring the money to Genoa could be found.[7]

Collins sent Leahy to pilot the ship ferrying the arms to Ireland. By the time Leahy arrived in Genoa on 28 March 1921, arrangements were well in place for the movement of the weapons to Ireland. However, even before he got there, he found the experience a highly frustrating one. Leahy had been approached by Florrie O'Donoghue before Christmas to make the trip. 'Florry [sic] O'Donoghue was adamant that I should get a proper passport photo and send it on to GHQ and Mick Collins was to have the passport ready when I got to Dublin. I hung around Cork for a while waiting and on 2nd January 1921 I left Cork.'[8] Leahy had to hang around Dublin for several more weeks, even being taken to Tom Cullen's wedding by Collins and his entourage where Leahy, a teetotaller, disapproved of the drinking that was going on. More time passed and yet 'nothing was being done about my passport'.[9] Eventually the passport issue got sorted out and Leahy arrived in Genoa on Easter Sunday.

Arrangements had already been made for the shipment of the arms since Ó Seaghda's last visit to Genoa and Rome in mid-November 1920, over four months earlier, when the 'order for the military equipment was given and instructions as to its packing, such as a false bottom ship which was to transport the equipment.' When Ó Seaghda subsequently made inquiries as to the reasons for the delay, he found that 'there was some question about insufficient lira being available for the purchase.'[10] The plan was that Leahy, a trained marine engineer, was to pilot the vessel containing the arms to a landing place on the south coast of Ireland. The ship in question was the *Stella Maria*, one of five owned by the Federacione della Mare, the Italian Seaman's Union. The ship normally sailed out of Genoa in ballast to England for cargoes of coal from Newcastle. This time, in Leahy's words, 'the *Stella Maria*, instead of travelling light, was to carry rifles, machine guns, revolvers

---

[7] Phelan, op.cit.
[8] Michael Leahy, O'Malley P17b/108.
[9] ibid.
[10] O'Seaghda, *op.cit.*

36

and proportionate ammunition to Ireland, unload at the prearranged landing place and then go on to Newcastle for coal for Italy.'[11]

Leahy found his experience in Italy a frustrating one, even if he met the colourful D'Annunzio and Madame Annie Vivanti, a well-known novelist who was married to a Sinn Féin activist and was a personal friend of D'Annunzio's. She was also prominent at carrying out propaganda work on behalf of Sinn Féin in the Italian press.[12] In late March or early April Madge Hales brought back the message to Collins that the arms were ready to go,[13] yet there was no further progress and the ship failed to sail. As Leahy put it: 'time passed and soon began to drag as I began to worry. The arms were available in plenty and were to be had, not for the asking, but for the money, and no money was coming from Ireland.' Yet when Madge Hales approached Collins on the matter of the money, she was told that the sum of £10,000 'would present no difficulty at all'.[14]

Not only was there no money coming from Ireland, there were no messages coming to Leahy from Ireland either. Leahy had been given his bare expenses by Collins and after a few weeks he was down to the last £10 note of his own money. 'My money was running out and Hales was laid up at the time. I was waiting and waiting. 3 months had gone by and finally I was flat broke so I decided that I should go to Paris to see Seán T.'[15] 'I was becoming desperate, not so much because of the state of my finances, as because of no direction of any kind coming from Ireland to further the purchase of the arms. The ship was there in port and the owners were asking when the venture was coming to a head.' Leahy made a dash to Paris to see Seán T.O'Kelly, who had no news for him either and whose advice was go on to London to Art O'Brien, Collins's man in London, who 'should be urged to get something done by General Headquarters towards securing the Italian arms'. Leahy got nothing in London either, other than instructions to return to Ireland. This he did and ended up hanging around Dublin for two further months, attached to the Purchases Branch under Liam

---

[11] Leahy, BMH WS 555.
[12] Phelan, op.cit.
[13] Tom Hales to Florrie O'Donoghue, 11 December 1953, O'Donoghue Papers NLI Ms 31,421(8).
[14] Donal Hales, BMH WS 292.
[15] Leahy, O'Malley P17b/108.

Mellows. Tired of doing nothing, he returned to Cork, arriving just two weeks before the Truce.[16]

As Leahy saw it, he had wasted six months on the project, six months in which he would have been better served with his own battalion which 'went to hell' in his absence, having had its flying column wiped out at Clonmult in February 1921. The arms had been organized, the ship was ready to sail for months, but nothing had happened: 'From that day to this I never heard just how or why the purchase of the arms in Italy was not pursued and the gun-running carried out according to plan. However, I draw my own conclusions. I used wonder too in what embarrassing position Donal Hales found himself *vis à vis* his Italian accomplices in consequence of the failure of the people at home to rise to the occasion and give him all the support and the finances necessary to carry through the project he did so much to shape.'[17]

Leahy's own conclusions, formed in retrospect, were that Collins had quietly scuppered the project because he was engaged with peace overtures with the British government, that Collins was effectively playing for time and that the lack of arms would encourage the IRA 'to settle with Britain for something less than a Republic'.[18] 'I decided then, April of 1921, that GHQ did not want arms.' This fitted with his view that '95% of the GHQ staff were fossils'.[19] However, at the time, the spring of 1921, the war was rolling on. If anything, it was becoming more intense. But this claim runs against everything Collins was thinking during those months. Reading Collins's correspondence, it is clear he would have given his eye teeth to have got his hands on the weapons from Italy. While peace feelers had been going on for months, Collins's strategy was clearly to keep ramping up the pressure as much as he could and for as long as he could. He was still very committed to the fight, indeed to intensifying it. He was still trying to import Thompson submachine guns into Ireland right up to the Truce.

A recent suggestion that it was de Valera's caution and reluctance to get embroiled in the arrangement with the sulphurous D'Annunzio that had caused the plan to stall, is also probably wide of the mark, though

---

[16] Leahy, BMH WS 555
[17] Leahy, op.cit.
[18] Appendix Note in Leahy, op.cit.
[19] Both quotations are from Leahy in O'Malley P17b/108.

de Valera did suggest to the fascist that he would be better off to try his luck in the Soviet Union![20] However, Hales's batch of arms was from the Italian military itself, not from D'Annunzio's group, which was becoming marginalized at that point anyway.

But the real cause of the failure of the project is that it had been betrayed to British Intelligence. Donal Hales noted that in Genoa 'the British Consul-General must have been told by someone that I had hidden these arms in Genoa. He was informed probably by his Intelligence Officer that these guns were in Genoa awaiting shipment.' 'How the British got the knowledge of them was extraordinary. The wife of this British Consul was Irish and she reported it to the Irish clerical students in Via Fassola, Genoa, who in turn reported it to me. It was incredible how they got this knowledge. A bargain was practically made with the Italian officials. These arms were the property of the Government but naturally the Government did not want to appear at all in the matter for reasons easily to be understood. Still the Italian Government was quite willing to give the arms. Mussolini also certainly was willing to help Ireland in every way. He always gave hospitality to my articles in his paper, *Il Popolo d'Italia*, before becoming head of the Government. The Government simply waited for the final move to be made.'[21]

There are obviously many places where the information might have been leaked: Collins or Dev might have leaked it, the Italians may have leaked it, someone close to Hales may have done so. What is clear from Hales's account is that he appears to have been genuinely astonished that the British got to hear of the plan. The idea, sometimes mooted, that he had scuppered his own brainchild simply makes no sense. He would certainly never have mentioned that the British Consul in Genoa knew about it if he did.

So where did the British Consul get his information? The information he had – that the arms were in Genoa and were ready for shipment, suggests that he did not get it locally. Because the arms – and the ship – were in Rome, not Genoa, as the Consul believed.[22] This may, of course, simply have been poor intelligence. However, other

---

[20] Phelan, op.cit.

[21] Hales, *op.cit.*

[22] Hales, *op.cit.*

evidence suggests that the information came from Britain or Ireland, not Italy, because the Royal Navy off the coast of Ireland was on the lookout for the *Stella Maria*.[23] The British knew about the plan almost from the outset. This was clear from what Collins told Leahy immediately on his arrival back from Genoa: 'I arrived back in Dublin and I awaited the bold Mick (Collins) and he claimed that they didn't send money out to me because I was being followed.'[24] 'In Dublin, Collins admitted that he had got the messages from Madge Hales and Seán T. but that the project was out of the question now – the British knew all about it.'[25] Leahy would not accept that and continued to believe that GHQ was at fault, but there is no reason for thinking that Collins made up the story. And if he subsequently instructed Donal Hales to stay quiet about the fact that the British had known all along, this was merely good housekeeping.[26]

There is no question that the British knew all about it. Their evidence speaks for itself: General Macready wrote: 'Information has been received from London and through the Admiral Commander in Chief of the Western Approaches to the effect that 250,000 rifles have been purchased by Sinn Féin agents in Italy, through the medium of D'Annunzio, and that these arms were landed at Genoa about March 9th for Ireland. No sign of the ship or ships has been seen by the Navy so far as I have heard.'[27]

While the details are slightly wrong – the number of rifles was much less than 250,000 and they were in Rome rather than Genoa – the gist of the story is correct. The fact that D'Annunzio is mentioned though, suggests that the information was sourced, not in Italy by MI6 or the Foreign Service since D'Annunzio's involvement was almost a year out of date, but closer to home, that is to say most likely by MI5 in London. (Though the Special Branch cannot be discounted.) The very mention of D'Annunzio, though, suggests that British Intelligence had been building its case for the most part of a year and that it was no

---

[23] Phelan, *op.cit.*

[24] Leahy in O'Malley P17b/108.

[25] Michael Leahy to Florrie O'Donoghue (undated) O'Donoghue, NLI Ms 31,421(8).

[26] Phelan op.cit.

[27] C.F.N. Macready, General C. in C. Ireland, Report for Week Ending 2 April 1921. TNA, CAB 24/121/101.

coincidence that Tom Hales was arrested in the summer of 1920 just as he was about to depart to Dublin in connection with the project. In other words, the British knew along and their information came from someone close enough to Hales.

The arms landing itself was to take place in west Cork, and arrangements had been made for arms dumps to be established and the guns distributed right throughout the 1st Southern Division area. 'Florry [*sic*] and the lads were to contact us off the Kerry coast and transfer the arms etc to fishing boats at sea. There was no definite venue mentioned where we were to meet the fishing boats. [But] everything was arranged.'[28] This was slightly incorrect. The landing was to take place in west Cork, not Kerry. Liam Deasy, Acting O/C of the 3rd Brigade of the IRA, had surveyed a landing place at Squince Strand near Myross after Christmas 1920 and deemed it suitable – becoming seasick in the motorboat and losing his dentures while puking overboard during his survey. Deasy reported that the captain of the Myross company 'assured us that they had made arrangements to have a hundred dumps ready to take the arms as soon as they arrived. Having satisfied myself that we had prepared for all foreseeable eventualities I departed for Rossmore to attend a Brigade Council meeting there. Two days later the meeting was held and the landing arrangements were discussed and approved. All that was necessary now was to await news telling us when the arms ship was to arrive and the machinery for landing and distributing the cargo would be put into operation.'[29]

After the meeting at Rossmore, Deasy left for an inter-brigade meeting that had been called by GHQ to complete the plans for the distribution of the arms. This was held at Donoghmore in early January 1921. Those present were Deasy and Charlie Hurley representing the 3rd Brigade, Liam Lynch and George Power representing the 2nd Brigade, and Florrie O'Donoghue and Seán O'Hegarty representing the 1st. The plan was to hand over most of the arms to the 1st Brigade at

---

[28] Leahy in O'Malley P17b/108.
[29] Liam Deasy, *Towards Ireland Free*, pp.205-06.

Inchigeela, with the Kerry brigades to receive their portion at Ballyvourney. Arms dumps and transport were worked out in detail.[30]

So it is clear that many people knew about the plan, including at least two senior officers from each of the Cork brigades, several staff members at GHQ, and obviously members of the Myross IRA who were to run the actual operation itself. There had been at least a half-a-dozen meetings of the Cork brigades at which the plan had been discussed. Deasy and O'Donoghue had been summoned to Dublin in 18 December 1920 to put together the plan. On their way to the meeting, O'Donoghue was pulled aside by security forces at Kingsbridge Station in Dublin and searched, while Deasy was waved through. It was also out of this meeting that Mick Leahy was nominated to pilot the ship because of his expert knowledge of the coastline.[31]

The failure of the operation led to a lot of finger-pointing that lasted for decades afterwards. Obviously the more people who knew about the landing, the greater the likelihood of becoming known to the British. In *Towards Ireland Free*, Deasy's book on the War of Independence and probably the best book written on the conflict by a combatant from an Irish military point of view, Deasy gives no hint as to how he thought the information had got out. The sheer amount of detail he includes on the matter, however, and the naming of the individuals and companies involved, suggests that he was pretty sure the leak did not come from the 3rd Brigade. In his Civil War memoir, *Brother Against Brother*, he suggests in passing that 'the whole scheme had been sabotaged by British Intelligence in Italy. This was very disappointing but it had to be accepted as a fortune of war.'[32]

It is clear though that the British knew about the arms plans from the outset and the only way they could have known it is that if it had been leaked from inner circles of the IRB where the plan had been hatched as early as April 1920. It is certainly no coincidence that Tom Hales was arrested on the very day he was to go to meet his sister to send the

---

[30] Deasy, *op.cit.* p.194.
[31] Deasy, *op.cit.* pp.179-80.
[32] Liam Deasy, *Brother against Brother*, p19.

message to Donal Hales that the arms importation was to go ahead. Or that he was brutally tortured to get more information out of him afterwards – which, despite claims to the contrary, he did not appear to give. Collins was very concerned about the arrest of Tom Hales and about the fact that 'the thumbscrews were applied to Hales to get information out of him'. He urged Art O'Brien to organize a visit to Hales, 'one of our best men', in prison as soon as possible.[33] He also put in place a plan to have Hales sprung from prison the following spring. As early as 29 July 1920 Collins was aware of the potential for leakage. He telegrammed Art O'Brien: 'You will remember recent correspondence. Do you still think it would not be advisable to send Donal a line?'[34] On 21 September Joe Vize, one of Collins's most trusted arms smugglers, was sent to London to liaise with Art O'Brien on the matter of the 'Italian Furniture'.[35] This was around the time that Collins first consulted with the Cork Brigades on the matter. Two days later, O'Brien replied to Collins that Joe Vize had become aware that postal communication concerning the matter had been interfered with and cautioned Collins in future to send everything important by hand.[36] Joe Vize himself was arrested on 14 October and held in various prisons until he escaped a year later.[37] In March 1921, when Madge Hales passed through London on her way to Genoa, the IRA man given the job of meeting her, 'a good lieutenant' was arrested by the police in suspicious circumstances.[38] This was precisely when British Intelligence in London were able to confirm the shipment.

Indeed, the unfortunate Leahy may have been inadvertently responsible for adding to the problem because of the orders he was following: 'I sent a photo of the ship to Collins through Seán T. O'Kelly in Paris.'[39] If Leahy was being followed, as Collins said he was, then his correspondence would almost certainly have been monitored. If Leahy sent a photograph of the ship to O'Kelly and the letter was intercepted,

---

[33] Collins to Art O'Brien 4 September 1920, O'Brien Papers, NLI Ms 8426/3.

[34] Collins to Art O'Brien, 29 July 1920. O'Brien Papers, NLI Ms 8426/3.

[35] Collins, Memo to 'L', 21 September 1920. O'Brien Papers NLI Ms 8430/9.

[36] O'Brien note to Collins, 23 September 1920, O'Brien Papers NLI Ms 8430/9.

[37] Joseph Vize, Military Pension Application W24SP9904.

[38] Memo from 'L' to Donal Hales, 11 March 1921, O'Brien Papers NLI Ms 8428/V.

[39] Leahy in O'Malley Papers, UCDA, p17b/108.

which it would have been if Leahy was being watched, then this would have confirmed what British intelligence and the Royal Navy probably already knew. But the most suspicious detail in the entire saga is the unaccountably long delay between the time Leahy provided O'Donoghue with passport photos for his false passport and him actually receiving the passport – a delay it seems of at least a month, and maybe even two months. Why did it take so long for a fairly straightforward forgery job that should have been done in two days?

O'Donoghue, of course, had a different view and was marginally involved in the project since its inception, going to Dublin with Deasy to meet with GHQ on the matter, being involved in a range of meetings in Cork to deal with the prospective landing, suggesting to Leahy to make sure to get passport photos and arranging for Leahy's false passport. His Bureau of Military History account, clearly meant to trump that of Leahy since it is one number above Leahy's though written six years later, states: 'My recollection is that we did not have any definite information about the complete failure of the project at the Italian end until after the Truce … . It was after the Truce that we learned that Commandant Leahy actually came back to Dublin on the day we met at Shanachrane [7 May 1921]. I do not know why the project failed in Italy.' The implication here is clear enough: O'Donoghue is claiming he had no idea why the project failed but seems to be pointing the finger at Leahy.[40] When he expressed the same view in an article before *No Other Law* was published he was reprimanded by Monsignor M.J. Curran, who was Vice Rector of the Irish College in Rome at the time. 'I was particularly interested in your remark that the failure to import the Italian arms was due to the Italian end. That is not what I have been told or led to believe. Are you quite sure it was not the Irish end?' Monsignor. Curran went on to write that Donal Hales had reluctantly told him a year later that 'Mick Collins' and 'the people at home had stopped it'. According to Curran, 'the Italian War Office was completely helpful in the matter but that for some reason or other Headquarters at home called it off. If so, it would be unfair to the Italians to pass the blame on to them.'[41] At around the

---

[40] Florence O'Donoghue, BMH WS 554.
[41] Monsignor M.J. Curran to Florrie O'Donoghue 7.4.1953, O'Donoghue NLI Ms 31,421(8).

same time O'Donoghue got another letter from Tom Hales stating that 'the Italian end was not responsible for [the] failure'.[42]

O'Donoghue wheedled his way out of it and wrote to Curran: 'Perhaps I was rash in saying that the failure was at the Italian end and I am indebted to you for the additional information which you gave me which will be the basis for further inquiries. The only first hand-account I had came from Mick Leahy, the man we sent out on instructions from GHQ. He admits that he does not know, and never knew, the full story.'[43] Yet in the statement O'Donoghue submitted to the BMH, dated 9 September 1957, he stuck to his story that 'he did not know why the project failed *in Italy*' [italics added].

The likelihood, however, is that the information that led to the plan being abandoned originated in Cork. In May 1921 GHQ decided to take responsibility for landing the weapons away from the Cork brigades entirely when a decision was made to change the venue from west Cork to Helvick Head on the Waterford coast. Considering that all the arrangements were in place for the storage and transport of the arms in Cork, with distribution out of Cork, the decision to change the venue to Waterford must have been taken for a good reason. Pax Whelan, the Commandant of the West Waterford Brigade, was summoned to Dublin in early May and given instructions by Collins and Mulcahy to organize for the landing of the weapons in his area. A week or two later, Paddy Paul, O/C of the East Waterford Brigade, who was then given direct responsibility for the transport of the arms, was in Dublin and spoke to Richard Mulcahy. Mulcahy urged the need for the utmost secrecy on the matter. Paul wrote to O'Donoghue after the initial serialization of *No Other Law* in the *Irish Press* to complain that he was not mentioned by O'Donoghue as having attended the meeting at Tubbareenmire, near Glenville, in early May where the matter was discussed and, presumably, Paul's role was outlined. O'Donoghue corrected himself and included Paul in the final published edition.[44]

This tells us at the very least that Collins and Mulcahy were still very committed to landing the guns as late as May 1921, as well as being

[42] Tom Hales to Florrie O'Donoghue, O'Donoghue NLI Ms 31,421(8).

[43] O'Donoghue to Monsignor Curran, 10 June 1953, O'Donoghue NLI Ms 31,421(8).

[44] P.J. Paul, BMH WS 877.

aware of the danger of the leakage of information. As we shall see in Volume III, the month of May 1921 saw a deep rift develop between Collins and Mulcahy in Dublin and O'Donoghue in Cork. Mulcahy never fully trusted O'Donoghue, or indeed Seán O'Hegarty, subsequently and there was significant animosity between them for the rest of their lives. But Mulcahy was right in this instance, for Waterford was to prove more secure and the Helvick area was used successfully for the landing of arms in the post-Truce period.

In summary, it is not possible at this juncture to establish exactly how information of the Genoa project was leaked, but the evidence is the British were aware of it right from the start. It appears that the British were also aware of Leahy's involvement and had him followed. The delay in the issuing of his passport is highly suspicious, as is the fact that he was ordered to send photos of the *Stella Maria* to Art O'Brien and that the Royal Navy were on the look-out for that very vessel. Leahy is simply wrong in his own assessment of the reasons for failure. If GHQ were '95% fossils' and 'did not want' the arms in April 1921, then why were they still trying to land them at Helvick Head in May? Collins was still writing to Art O'Brien, hoping for progress in the matter as late as 10 June 1921.[45] Collins had his own agents in various parts of British Intelligence, including Dublin Castle, the Dublin Metropolitan Police and the Special Branch in London. He even had David Neligan enrolled as a secret service agent by the spring of 1921. It is far more likely that Collins was correct, that Leahy was being followed and that Collins became aware of it and, as a result, did not send on the money. Collins was no fool and certainly would not send good money after bad. If Leahy put a letter in the post with a picture of the *Stella Maria* in it, then this is as good as proof that the game was up. Certainly by the end of 1921 Collins was at the very least suspicious that the Cork Number 1 Brigade, and O'Hegarty in particular, was interfering in the business of arms purchasing.[46]

There are a myriad of questions arising from this episode and they go right back to its inception: the arrest of Tom Hales when he was about to organize the smuggling effort, the raid on the mails when Joe Vize went to London, the arrest of the man sent to meet Madge Hales in

---

[45] Memo 'M' to 'L' 10 June 1921. Art O'Brien Papers NLI, 8430/17.
[46] 'MoC' to 'AoB', 1 December 1921, Art O'Brien Ppaers NLI 8430/23.

London while on her way to Genoa, the delay in Leahy getting his passport when it should have been possible to have it done in days. The very fact that O'Donoghue was searched in Kingsbridge Station on his way to the December 1920 meeting, while Deasy was waved on through, is in itself suspicious. In fact, Leahy's entire trip looks very much like a set-up: his getting his passport photo to O'Donoghue, the passport taking weeks to be prepared, Leahy's orders to send a picture of the arms ship to Collins, when it was very likely to be intercepted, the fact that the Royal Navy knew about it and the likely landing point was also known. Clearly Leahy's identity and his role in the affair were known to British intelligence even before he left Ireland, though Leahy himself was almost certainly an innocent party in all this since he would hardly have mentioned all these details had he been in any way guilty. And why did O'Donoghue make a BMH submission on it when he had nothing to say on the subject, other than to make a further smokescreen?

All this could be a lethal game. When Leahy returned to Cork at the end of June, he states that he immediately contacted Florrie O'Donoghue and went with him directly to west Cork.[47] He was lucky. Because the same week a barman at a city centre hotel, also called Michael Leahy, was visited by a stranger in plain clothes who asked him his name. When he replied, Leahy was taken upstairs to a room in the hotel and shot through the head. The would-be assassin then calmly came downstairs, strolled out into the street and told passers-by to call an ambulance since a man had been shot in the hotel.[48]

---

[47] Michael Leahy, BMH WS 1421.
[48] *Cork Weekly News*, 25 June 1921. Apparently, Leahy miraculously survived the attack.

6

A Sorry Tale

One of the more bizarre events of the War of Independence in Cork took place during August 1920. That this has not been seriously questioned by historians of the period seems rather odd since it does not depend on newly released sources. It was commented on by Mick Leahy though, and it will become clear from what follows why O'Donoghue might not have been happy with what Leahy had to say.

The event was the capture by the British Army of Terence MacSwiney, Lord Mayor of Cork and O/C of the Cork No. 1 Brigade of the IRA at Cork City Hall, on the evening of 12 August 1920. The story is well-known. The army threw a cordon around the City Hall, where a number of meetings – a Brigade meeting, a Sinn Féin court, even an IRB meeting – were in progress. After several hours of sifting through their various captives, the army led away a dozen men consisting of most of the Cork No. 1 Brigade staff, including the Lord Mayor. The dozen captives immediately went on hunger strike. A few days later, these were released with the exception of MacSwiney, who remained on hunger strike until his death some 73 days later, an event that attracted unprecedented attention to Ireland from around the world.

Since the eleven or so men released comprised most of the leadership of the Cork No. 1 Brigade, it is clear that had the British held on to their captives they would have dealt the Brigade a serious blow. The accepted view of historians is that the release of the men was down to 'monumental incompetence' on the part of the British forces in that they did not know the identity of those they had captured, even though most of them gave their correct names on the basis that they assumed the British already knew who they were. As O'Donoghue's biographer John

Borgonovo put it: 'Remarkably, the British military snatched defeat from the jaws of victory.'[49]

However, this judgment is based on an acceptance of the first published account of the capture, written by O'Donoghue himself in *No Other Law*, published in 1954. O'Donoghue's account is full of authentic detail and appears on the face of it to point to a serious level of incompetence on the part of the British. O'Donoghue says that the raid came about as a result of information received by the army when they captured some 'local mails' on 9 August indicating that that a Brigade meeting would be held in the City Hall on the night in question: 'There was not in the manner in which this information fell into British hands any question of treachery, or even of culpable negligence on the part of anybody concerned; it was an accident of war which gave the astute Intelligence officer of the British 6th Division in Cork a slight edge which he fully utilized. He had a stroke of luck and he made the most of it.'[50]

One of the charges made against MacSwiney at his subsequent trial was that he had in his desk the key to the police cipher code that was being used that week by the RIC. The RIC routinely sent its confidential telegrams in cipher; these would have to be deciphered by recipients who would have needed a key to do so. The cipher and key were regularly changed for security reasons. Encrypted messages were worthless without the correct key to the cipher. The army claimed they had found the cipher key during a second raid which they carried out on the Lord Mayor's office specifically to search for it – a claim dismissed by O'Donoghue who said that MacSwiney was a victim of a set-up and that the British had planted the code in his desk in order to charge him with an indictable offence – even though there was more than enough material found in the first raid to indict MacSwiney anyway. At the trial, the British case was that an RIC encrypted message was found hidden behind a sheet of iron in a carpenter's shed to the rear of the City Hall where the twelve men were caught – one of them was seen putting it there – and that the cipher key to this message was later found in a drawer in MacSwiney's office.

---

[49] Borgonovo, *Spies, Informers and the 'Anti-Sinn Fein Society', The Intelligence War in Cork City 1920-1921*, pp.5-6.

[50] O'Donoghue, *No Other Law*, pp.89-93.

O'Donoghue claimed that the police cipher key was normally in his custody but that in the early afternoon MacSwiney had him to attend a meeting of the 8th Battalion Council to be held that evening at Kilnamartyra and he had departed for mid-Cork immediately. This means, of course, that O'Donoghue could not have been present when the raid took place. The key, according to O'Donoghue, was then in the possession either of Joe O'Connor or of Nora Wallace, one of the Wallace sisters who ran the shop that served as the IRA's headquarters in Cork city during this period. According to O'Donoghue, 'it was Joe O'Connor who brought the cipher key to the City Hall on the night of 12th August.' And it was O'Connor who, on the basis of this, hid the cipher key in the shed behind the City Hall where the men were being held before being led away. 'Joe O'Connor found it impossible to destroy the sheet of paper containing the cipher key, but he managed to dispose of it in a crevice of the woodwork of the shed in which the men were first held. The document could not therefore be found anywhere except where Joe O'Connor disposed of it' – the implication being that it could not have been found in the Lord Mayor's desk. But O'Donoghue is already lying even at this point, because what was found in the carpenter's shed was not the key but the encrypted message.

According to O'Donoghue on a memo to Michael Collins at GHQ, MacSwiney was framed by the British. 'It was sworn that this document was found in his desk in the City Hall. This is untrue.' But now O'Donoghue changed his story again, this time stating that both the message and the key were found together in the shed:

The only point not made clear is in connection with the Code. This was not in Terry's possession at any time. When I was leaving town I gave it to one of the Brigade Officers and he had it on him at the City Hall that night. Not wishing to destroy it if possible, he hid it outside at the back behind a partition. One of the soldiers saw him hide it and drew the attention of the officer to the matter. Terry was one of a number of men who was in the vicinity of this place at the time. It was perjury of Lieut. Kells to swear that he found the code in Terry's desk. The code and the message were together in the back yard and were not found in anybody's possession.[51]

---

[51] Quoted in Collins to Art O'Brien 'Memo to L.' 10 September 1920, Art O'Brien Papers NLI, MS 8430/9.

O'Donoghue's accounts agree on one point: either the code, or the message and the code, were found together as one document and were hidden by Joe O'Connor behind the partition of the carpenter's shed at the back of the City Hall. This is the version of events put out by O'Donoghue, which is now generally accepted.

Yet even contemporary newspaper accounts of the raid and the subsequent trial of Terence MacSwiney suggest that this version is incorrect. O'Donoghue's main argument is that the document could not have been found in MacSwiney's desk since it had been hidden in the shed. He claimed that the 'cipher code' was the document found there. But, according to the British, what was found in the shed was the actual encrypted RIC message and the key to the message was later found by the military in the drawer of the desk in MacSwiney's office.[52]

According to the newspapers, there were three raids on the City Hall that week. The first was the one in which the men were captured. This took place at around 7.30pm on the Thursday night, 12 August, and the men were taken away to Victoria Barracks at around 9.30. Two hours later, however, the British came back and carried out a second, very thorough, search of the premises which went on for several hours. This time they turned out every scrap of paper in the place, with the result that the building was strewn with documents the following morning. Four days later they returned and searched the building again. There were also raids on the home of Seán O'Hegarty and also one at Belgrave Place, where Terence MacSwiney's sisters ran their school, Scoil Ita, and where Terence often stayed – in fact he had been there that very afternoon. What this suggests is that the British were searching for something specific.[53]

According to evidence presented by the army at the court martial, it is clear that there were at least two pieces of paper involved, not one. It is also clear that, at first, the raiding party did not recognize the significance of the RIC message. It was only later that night that they realized that in order to read the RIC coded message, they would need its key and that there was a likelihood that the key might be found somewhere in the building. So they went back to search for it. 'None of

---

[52] In *No Other Law* he claims that there was just one document involved. In his report to Collins, he said that the message and the code were together.
[53] *Cork Examiner,* 13, 14 and 17 August 1920.

the search party recognized the importance of this code [the original RIC coded message] at the time because there were no police present. The key to the code was found in the Lord Mayor's room. The officer who found this key was not present at the first search and did not know what it was.' The original message was found by a Private Norris in the carpenter's shed, the key was found during one of the later searches by a Lieutenant Kells, who gave evidence to that effect and whom O'Donoghue claimed perjured himself. 'Kells' was in fact Lieutenant A.R. Koe of the Hampshire Regiment, one of the most important British intelligence officers in Cork at the time.[54] Koe stated at the court martial that he had found the cipher key in MacSwiney's desk along with over thirty other papers, several of which would on their own be of a sufficiently 'seditious' nature to convict MacSwiney. In other words, the British had no need for the key since they had enough evidence without it.

Koe stated that he found the key between 11.00 and 11.30pm in MacSwiney's office during the second search of the Hall. If they were trying to frame MacSwiney, the army could simply have said they found the cipher key in his drawer in the first place. Why would they stage a series of elaborate searches in which nothing was left unturned when they could have simply said they had it already? They were in full control of the inquest anyway. If the intention was to frame MacSwiney, this was a very roundabout way of doing it There was no need to frame him. All the evidence suggests that there were two separate documents involved and O'Donoghue was being disingenuous when he claims there was only one – or if there were two that they were both together. And it appears that everyone, including Collins, was taken in by this.

According to the British military report to Dublin Castle, the raid, which was carried out in the first place because a 'captured letter' stated that:

A battalion of the Irish Republican Army had been officially summoned to attend [a meeting] at City Hall, Cork at 7pm on 12th instant. Accordingly, it was decided to send a party of troops to investigate the matter.

---

[54] *Cork Examiner,* 17 August 1920. Proceedings of the Court Martial, Cork 16 August 1920. TNA HO 144/10306.

When the troops entered the Hall the persons therein were engaged in escaping. A small party, of which the Lord Mayor was found to be one, were arrested in the back yard of the Hall in a hut.

The Lord Mayor and two others were observed tearing up papers and were separated from the others. Close to where they were standing was a piece of corrugated iron leaning against the wall. Behind this was found an envelope addressed 'very urgent' to 'The Commandant, 1st Cork Brigade, IRA, Cork'.

In this envelope was found a copy of a cipher telegram sent the previous day by the County Inspector RIC to the Inspector General RIC relative to the removal of hunger strikers.

The decipher of this telegram was correctly written on it. The key to this cipher was found in the Lord Mayor's desk. At the Court Martial he admitted the responsibility for the control of this key.[55]

The military went on to state that several other letters were found in MacSwiney's desk which prove that he was commander of the 1st Brigade of the Cork IRA and a few of them were read out in the court.[56] Also found behind the sheet of corrugated iron were two further letters, including one from IRA GHQ concerning the setting up of a bomb factory in the area. That alone would have been enough to convict MacSwiney had the military decided to use it.[57]

However, MacSwiney was still probably the victim of a set-up, even if it was not quite in the way O'Donoghue claimed. Because in his own evidence, while he claimed full responsibility for the possession of the cipher, MacSwiney also stated that 'the code was not in my desk, though I know where it was and am sure that it was put in my desk.' MacSwiney too claimed that the code and the message had been separate. Had it been found with the message, there would have been no need for the rigmarole of the searches; they could simply have produced it, stating that they saw MacSwiney and two others trying to hide it in the shed. The obvious scenario is that they found the telegram, belatedly realized that there must be a cipher key to it somewhere, went looking for it until they either found it in his desk or located it elsewhere and put it in his desk to make a more cast-iron case.

---

[55] GOC Ireland to Under Secretary, 21 August 1920, TNA HO 144/10306.

[56] These include a receipt book for monies received from various battalions and a document containing a speech by a Captain of A. Company 1st Battalion in which MacSwiney was named as Brigade Commandant.

[57] Lieutenant Colonel H. Toppin to Sir John Anderson, 23.8.1920. TNA HO 144/10306.

O'Donoghue also claimed that there was a secret passageway from the City Hall behind a hidden door through which MacSwiney and the others could have escaped, but that for some inexplicable reason on that evening, MacSwiney had 'inadvertently' left the key to the passageway at his sister's house in Belgrave Place – 'Though it is doubtful if he could have made any effective use of it, so quickly was the whole area surrounded.' However, since O'Donoghue was the man detailed to look after MacSwiney's security and had been sharing a room with him for the previous few months while both were 'on the run', it would have been up to *him* to ensure that the key to the secret door was in the City Hall where it was needed.[58] Clearly O'Donoghue was at least partly culpable for MacSwiney's arrest, if only out of negligence.

In fact, it may have been more than negligence. Dan O'Donovan, in a letter to Moirin Chavasse, MacSwiney's biographer, stated that 'during the course of the meeting we got word that there was a raid – immediately there was a scatter. In expectation of such an occurrence, Terence MacSwiney had arranged with several officers that we could go on the roof . . . we tried to get on the roof but the door to the exit was locked and his sergeant at arms was so excited he could not find the key. So then we went through the Concert Hall and out the back and into the carpenter's shed.'[59]

O'Donoghue's reaction to this is interesting. In a letter to Mrs Chavasse, he rubbishes O'Donovan's claims: 'There are nine errors of fact in a short statement and even with the most generous stretching I could not find nine things that are true in it.' O'Donoghue then goes into full faux-pedantry mode – the dismissal of a piece of evidence based on hair-splitting tangential errors – while ignoring the main points: 'Charlie Hurley was not at the meeting. Charlie Hurley was not killed at Crossbarry. The meeting was not called as a result of a dispatch from the Chief of Staff,' and so on. 'I do not see how you can continue to place any reliance on anything in it. I am not suggesting that the fault is Dan Donovan's. He was probably giving the very best of his recollection many years after the event. He was in a very different position to one who can weigh and compare a number of documents.'

---

[58] O'Donoghue, *No Other Law*, p90.

[59] Dan Donovan to Moirin Chavasse, (n.d.) O'Donoghue Papers NLI Ms 31,282(2).

O'Donoghue then goes on to make the claim sometimes used by historians when they want to paint a coat of whitewash over something: 'Although the general picture may be broadly true, the witnesses were not always conscious of the need for that degree of accuracy a historian looks for.' Naturally, there is nothing in his letter about the 'sergeant at arms' failure to find the key or the fact that the door onto the roof could not be opened.[60] The question of course is who exactly was MacSwiney's 'sergeant at arms' on the day? Was he the man who had been his security coordinator over the previous few months, since the death of Tomás MacCurtain, that is the say, the man who claimed that role, O'Donoghue himself?

It is also worth noting that the IRB meeting called for 7.00pm that evening was to appoint a replacement for Tom Hales who was County Centre, who had been arrested in July. All divisional Centres were to attend. Since O'Donoghue was in all likelihood the man who sent out the instruction and was a divisional Centre and would almost certainly have known of the meeting, it is hard to believe he was not there himself – or that he would have scampered off to Kilnamartyra with such an important appointment in the offing.

Another significant detail in the court martial documents is a reply to a query made by Dublin Castle on the 'captured letter' that led to the sweep in the first place. It will be recalled that this was 'some local mails' of which O'Donoghue claimed: 'there was not in the manner in which this information fell into British hands any question of treachery, or even of culpable negligence on the part of anybody concerned; it was an accident of war'. If this were 'an accident of war', the British in their internal correspondence were very coy about it. 'The captured letter showed the information contained in paragraph 1 of page 1 above but it is considered that it should be treated as confidential how this letter was captured *or even if it was captured* [my italics]'.[61] This implies that the 'captured letter' that led to the raid was not captured at all but was acquired by some other means. Clearly O'Donoghue's statement above should also be called into question.[62]

---

[60] O'Donoghue to Chavasse, 17 April 1954, O'Donoghue Papers, Ms 31,282(2).
[61] GOC Ireland to Under Secretary, 21 August 1920. TNA HO 144/10306.
[62] O'Donoghue, *No Other Law*, p.90.

7

'They could not have nominated a better man'

Mick Leahy had something else to say on the capture of MacSwiney. He states that O'Donoghue himself was one of those captured and then released. In O'Donoghue's account, as published in *No Other Law*, the IRA officers captured were:

Terence MacSwiney, O/C Cork No. 1 Brigade
Seán O'Hegarty, Vice O/C Cork No. 1 Brigade
Joseph O'Connor, Quartermaster, Cork No. 1 Brigade
Daniel Donovan, O/C 1st Battalion, Cork No.1 Brigade
Michael Leahy, O/C 4th Battalion, Cork No. 1 Brigade
Liam Lynch, O/C Cork No 2. Brigade.

O'Donoghue names six others as also having been captured: Patrick McCarthy of Mourneabbey, Michael Carey, Laurence Cotter, Thomas Mulcahy, Patrick Harris and Thomas McCarthy, the last five with Cork city addresses. Everyone, with the exception of Lynch and Leahy, gave their correct names and addresses and all, bar MacSwiney, were released four days later after having been moved from the military detention barracks to Cork Jail. According to O'Donoghue: 'it would be fruitless now to speculate upon the reasons for this action. It has been suggested that it was an error and that a cancellation of the release order came to the jail after the prisoners had left. It seems incredible that if men like Liam Lynch and Seán O'Hegarty had been identified they would be released … What is certain is that if all the officers captured had been recognized and detained it would have been a staggering blow to two of the Cork brigades.'[1] 'No explanation of Liam's release seems feasible except that his captors did not recognize him or take the normal precaution of having a police check on the identity of the prisoners.'[2]

So far, so good. The cock-up was simply a failure of British intelligence. But is this believable? All the men, bar Lynch and Leahy, gave their correct addresses. O'Hegarty was named in the newspapers as being one of the captives. His home and that of Mary MacSwiney was searched while the men were still being detained. If the newspapers knew that O'Hegarty was one of the captives, then the British knew it – and they raiding his house at the same time! Considering that the British army had been very successful in rounding up known IRA men the previous spring – only to release them again when the British government backed down in the face of hunger strikes – they almost certainly knew the identity of most of those they had captured. Lynch and Leahy might have been let go, since they gave false names, but the others? This seems so improbable as to beggar belief.

Most of the accounts of that night follow that of O'Donoghue, and it is clear they were written after *No Other Law* was published since they all repeat O'Donoghue's list of those captured. Mick Leahy's account, however, completely contradicts O'Donoghue's version of events:

In the month of August 1920, I received a dispatch from Florrie O'Donoghue, Brigade Intelligence Officer, instructing me to shoot an RIC sergeant in Cobh whose name I cannot now remember. I do recollect that he was from Cooraclare, Co. Clare. I came to Cobh, made the necessary inquiries, but found there was no RIC sergeant of the name given me in the town. I therefore decided to go in to Cork, see Florrie and get a description of the wanted man who might be in Cobh but under another name. The following morning I went by boat across the harbour to Passage West and thence by rail to Cork. I inquired the whereabouts of Florrie O'Donoghue and found he was in the City Hall with Terry MacSwiney, then Lord Mayor of Cork. I went to the City Hall, saw Florrie and got the description of the RIC man. It was then my intention to return to Cobh to carry out the shooting when Terence MacSwiney told me that there was a meeting of senior officers of the Cork brigades that night in the City Hall, about 8.00pm. Although I was only a battalion commandant at the time, Terry ordered me to stay and attend the meeting.'[3]

---

[1] O'Donoghue, *No Other Law*, p.92.
[2] ibid.
[3] Michael Leahy, BMH WS1421.

A rather obvious, if minor question is: if the meeting of senior officers was so important, why did MacSwiney order O'Donoghue to decamp to a less important meeting in Kilnamartyra? Leahy's account goes on to follow the general trajectory of that of O'Donoghue, with the men hiding in a carpenter's shed at the rear of the hall when they were captured, even to the extent of their tearing up papers and hiding the scraps in the wood shavings in the shed. But he then goes on to make a statement that is quite at variance with O'Donoghue's version of events in that he names O'Donoghue himself among those who were captured – and he does not mention Joe O'Connor. In a shorter list given to Ernie O'Malley, he again includes O'Donoghue and omits O'Connor.[4] He is quite adamant on this. 'All the Brigade officers were there.' What is very pointed about Leahy's BMH account is that it was written two years after *No Other Law* was published. It is unlikely that Leahy would not have read O'Donoghue's book at that point. If so, why did he not go along with everyone else and repeat O'Donoghue's list? This suggests that Leahy was contradicting O'Donoghue and knew that he was doing so.[5]

So what does the British account tell us about the identity of those captured? The court martial file,[6] which is a large one, has a disclaimer on the cover stating 'the remnants of this file have been destroyed', which indicates that some kind of cover-up was certainly going on. However, it does contain a list of those captured. Like O'Donoghue's list, this contains twelve names. Ten are the same, allowing for the fact that Liam Lynch gave his name as James Casey and Michael Leahy called himself Thomas Power. But there are two major differences: Joseph O'Connor and Laurence Cotter are not included and are replaced by Patrick Connors and one Laurence McCarthy.[7]

---

[4] Leahy in O'Malley P17b/108; Mick Murphy BMH WS112; Seán O'Hegarty to 'The Organization', 23/7/1921, O'Donoghue, MS 31,237(1).

[5] Paddy McCarthy, who was one of Liam Lynch's drivers stated in his account that the meeting was called to carry out some operation that involved the officers being armed, presumably for some 'job'. He includes Joe O'Connor among those captured. Patrick McCarthy BMH WS1163.

[6] TNA, HO 144/10308. The file was originally scheduled to be released in 2030 but it seems the process was speeded up.

[7] Lieutenant. Colonel. H. Toppin to Sir John Anderson, 23.8.1920. TNA, HO 144/10308.

Patrick Connors is the easy one to identify. This refers to Patrick 'Cruxy' O'Connor, the British Secret Service agent who had penetrated the Cork IRA. Described as a 'Company Officer IRA' in the report, he was O'Hegarty's 'golden boy' at the time and never likely to be too far away from O'Hegarty's circle. The fact that no IRA account mentions O'Connor as being one of those taken may be understandable since they would hardly want to admit that a well-known spy was in their midst when they were captured – particularly at a high-powered meeting with the Lord Mayor. However, it is clear from British records of his arrest some six months later that O'Connor had long since ceased to provide information and that the military in Cork were not aware even at that stage that he had been a Secret Service agent.[8]

O'Donoghue went to considerable lengths in *No Other Law* to suggest that Joe O'Connor was one of those captured and claims that he was the one who hid the cipher message before his capture. 'The Brigade Quartermaster [O'Connor] wished at the Courtmartial to make a public statement as to these facts and take responsibility for the document. This was not sanctioned as it was believed it would have no influence on the Lord Mayor's sentence.'[9] O'Connor in his IRA pension application also claimed that he was among those captured but that the British did not recognize him.[10]

On the other hand, can we dismiss the possibility that this may have been eyewash and that O'Connor, a brother of Father Dominic and O'Donoghue's best friend – and best man at his wedding to Josephine, was covering for O'Donoghue? Because, in her IRA pension application, O'Donoghue's sister Agnes stated that it was *she* who kept the RIC cipher codes for Florrie at the draper's shop in Castle Street where O'Donoghue used to work and which was a clearing house for IRA documentation.[11] And another odd thing was that Father Dominic himself was stopping Volunteers on their way to the City Hall while the raid was in progress and asking them to pass on to him any

---

[8] *Record of the Rebellion in Ireland, 6th Division Report*, TNA, WO 141/93.
[9] O'Donoghue, *No Other Law*, p.91.
[10] Joseph O'Connor MSP34REF1878.
[11] Agnes McCarthy, sworn statement in MSP34REF60655. At the time O'Donoghue made his claim Nora Wallace was safely dead, so nobody could contradict him on that point.

documentation they might have been carrying – for safe-keeping. It is almost as he had prior knowledge of the raid.[12]

If 'Joseph O'Connor' was in fact Patrick 'Cruxy' O'Connor, then who was Laurence McCarthy? There was no Laurence McCarthy prominent in the IRA in Cork at that time.[13] However, the building that housed the draper's shop on Castle Street that O'Donoghue ran was owned by one Laurence McCarthy, who was a cousin of Michael Nolan, O'Donoghue's employer and cousin. Indeed, the shop itself was taken over by Laurence McCarthy when Nolan had to get rid of it after being exposed as an RIC informant after the War of Independence.[14] Was 'Laurence McCarthy' actually Florrie O'Donoghue? It is interesting to note that Josephine Brown too claimed that she was on her way to the City Hall the same night in order, she states, to encourage MacSwiney – who was not supposed to know anything about it anyway – to hurry up with the plan to rescue her son Reggie from Wales.[15] Had she and Father Dominic some as-yet undocumented role in the affair?

In the British army report, four of the captured men are stated categorically to be members of the IRA, including Seán O'Hegarty, yet they were all let go. The reason the military authorities gave for the release in their report to Dublin Castle was that there was insufficient evidence to convict the men. Yet the documents found in the carpenter's shed and the fact that they were seen hiding them and destroying them would have been more than enough to put the whole lot in jail, not just MacSwiney.

The astonishing thing is that, despite knowing they had captured 'John O'Hegarty, Brigade Quartermaster, IRA', as they called him, they let him go. Clearly, someone wanted O'Hegarty released. The British Army's Record of the Rebellion, in its account of the arrest of Terence

---

[12] 'G' Company, 2nd Battalion, Cork No. 1 Brigade activities, MA/MSPC/A/1/(G) 2.

[13] And no Laurence McCarthy arrested and interned by the British either. The arrest records are now searchable online at Findmypast.ie. Apart from a man in Dublin of that name, the only 'Laurence McCarthy' arrested was the man taken with MacSwiney and then released.

[14] Michael Nolan TNA CO 762/147.

[15] Borgonovo, *Florence and Josephine O'Donoghue's War of Independence*, p.121.

MacSwiney, strays into territory that seems very alien from an Irish perspective:

After McSwiney's arrest there was a good deal of discussion amongst Cork rebels as to who should take his place as Brigade Commandant. Amongst those involved in the dispute were Sean Hegarty (a storekeeper in the Cork Workhouse, who was dismissed from the Post Office service after the 1916 rebellion and whose name was mentioned in the House of Commons in connection with the murder of Mrs Lindsay), Fred Murray (an alderman of Cork city who had previously come under notice on several occasions, particularly in connection with the murder of a policeman in Cork and with the hunger strike at the beginning of 1920) and Donal O'Callaghan, Deputy Lord Mayor (who was strongly suspected of being involved in the attempted murder of Maj-General Strickland). All these rebels were anxious to be Brigade Commander but there was only one vacancy. To add to their trouble, it was arranged that a letter be sent through the ordinary post and that that letter would contain a request for money to reward one of these people for information he had supplied. The letter was captured as it was intended that it should be and the ruse worked very well. O'Callaghan had to clear out of the country at short notice and Hegarty was elected Commandant. As he was not a brave man and was chiefly concerned with his own safety, the appointment suited the Crown forces exceedingly well – they could not have nominated a better man for the position from their own point of view.[16]

Leaving aside the inaccuracies in the account – O'Callaghan played no part in the attack on General Strickland (it was led by O'Hegarty, though the fact that the British had the belief that it was O'Callaghan is itself suspicious) – what the account states, quite unambiguously, is that the British wanted O'Hegarty to become Brigade Commandant. O'Callaghan was stitched up by the leaked letter suggesting that he was an informer so that O'Hegarty got the job. Fred Murray was already in jail after a similar stitch-up for a crime he did not commit. Was this to prevent him becoming O/C?

But the real question is why did the British want O'Hegarty in charge of the Cork IRA? Did they believe, as they stated, that he was not brave and was primarily concerned with his own safety? Is this further

---

[16] *A Record of the Rebellion in Ireland, 6th Division Report*, WO 141/93. O'Callaghan fled to America accompanied by Peter MacSwiney, brother of Terence. *Cork Holly Bough*, Christmas 2019, *Cork Examiner*, 5 January 1921.The reason the British suspected O'Callaghan had been involved in the attack on Strickland was that they had information that the Acting Brigade Commandant had led the attack. They believed at the time that this was O'Callaghan – or at least they may have been led to believe it by their mole in the IRA.

evidence of their incompetence? Were they, as is sometimes claimed, victims of an IRB sting, in which O'Hegarty's IRB staged a coup and used the British to help remove Murray and O'Callaghan in order that O'Hegarty should get the job, with O'Donoghue as second-in-command? Because it is clear from his own British army intelligence file that the British knew exactly who he was when they released him in the wake of MacSwiney's arrest, [17] something that the MacSwiney court martial file confirms.

The obvious explanation is that, since they wanted O'Hegarty to become Brigade Commandant, it would have aroused suspicion if they had let him go and held on to everyone else. The plan, it seems, was to put MacSwiney in jail, just like they had earlier jailed Fred Murray, both on dubious charges, so that O'Hegarty could get the top job. In the process they also blackened O'Callaghan's name. There is only one conclusion: that the raid was part of a bigger plan to ensure that O'Hegarty became Brigade Commandant and that it would have fallen apart if O'Hegarty had not been released.

IRB correspondence at the time, and O'Donoghue's subsequent denigration of Fred Murray and O'Callaghan, suggest that O'Hegarty and O'Donoghue were determined to get complete control of the IRA in Cork. And it is clear that they got this with British help. Murray and O'Callaghan were badly treated, with O'Callaghan not just being the victim of the false allegation that he was taking money for information but also being blamed for not alerting the men at the City Hall that night that the raid would take place. To make matters worse, he was also blamed for the lack of IRB activity in Cork between the summer of 1920 and the spring of 1921. As O'Hegarty put it in a letter to O'Donoghue: 'Then of course Domhnall Óg [O'Callaghan] who was responsible for Cork City and County left without letting us know he was going and as a result our men have not been meeting in Cork since. The SC [Supreme Council] on a suggestion from the special meeting I refer to have appointed you to the position Domhnall occupied, namely

---

[17] The file, which is scant enough and was compiled only in 1922, does contain some very interesting details nonetheless. John (Sean) Hegarty intelligence file, TNA WO 35/207.

Centre for Cork City and County.'[18] Considering that O'Callaghan was manipulated into leaving the country in the first place, this is disingenuous, to say the least. So not only was O'Hegarty appointed O/C of the Brigade but O'Donoghue replaced O'Callaghan as IRB Centre for Cork. It is clear that the entire episode was staged to suit the British and the reason was that they wanted O'Hegarty to be promoted to Brigade Commandant.

According to himself, O'Donoghue was MacSwiney's personal bodyguard, even sharing the same bed as him in the months between the death of Tomás MacCurtain and MacSwiney's arrest. If Leahy is correct, O'Donoghue's claim that he had left for Kilnamartyra in the afternoon is a lie. The British army's own record suggests that he was one of those captured and that he gave the name Laurence McCarthy. Who was the 'sergeant-at-arms' who failed to open the door to the roof of the City Hall but O'Donoghue himself? The reason the men were subsequently released was that the British wanted both O'Donoghue and O'Hegarty to be on the streets where they were needed.

That leaves one question: how did the cipher key get from O'Donoghue's care – or at least that of his sister in the shop in Castle Street – into MacSwiney's desk? The likelihood is that British military intelligence located it there with O'Donoghue's help and had it transferred to MacSwiney's desk. This is indeed a tangled web.

To summarize: the British staged the entire operation in order to put O'Hegarty in a position of control of the republican forces in Cork. Unfortunately, O'Hegarty and probably O'Donoghue himself were caught up in the swoop. All the men were then released in order to avoid suspicion. In this analysis, O'Donoghue's account of the events of that evening, with its evasions and dissimulations, is a carefully constructed combination of fact and fabulation. The net effect was that coup was now complete; the old order of MacCurtain, MacSwiney, Fred Murray and O'Callaghan was overthrown, replaced by that of O'Hegarty and O'Donoghue. This was a nasty business – O'Donoghue was to continue sowing allegations about O'Callaghan and Murray for many years afterwards, but O'Hegarty was now Commandant of the Cork No. 1 Brigade of the IRA and O'Donoghue became Head Centre

---

[18] Seán O'Hegarty to Florence O'Donoghue, 14 March 1921, O'Donoghue, MS 31,237(1).

of the IRB in Cork. All the control was in the hands of these two men; all the eggs were in one basket, the basket where the British wanted them. MacSwiney was dying on hunger strike; Murray and O'Callaghan were hung out to dry. For the next twelve months, the Cork No. 1 Brigade stumbled from one disaster to the next. No matter how you look at it, this was a situation 'which suited the Crown forces exceedingly well'. This was very far from 'monumental incompetence'. The obvious implication of this is that the British wanted O'Hegarty to be in command in Cork because either he himself, or someone very close to him, was extremely useful to them and 'they could not have recommended a better man for the position'.

8

A Minor Interlude

We have seen how Michael J. Nolan, Florrie O'Donoghue's cousin and employer at his drapery shop at 55 North Main Street, Cork, acted as a British informant and took credit for the information that led to the death of Walter Leo Murphy, commandant of the 5th Battalion of the Cork No. Brigade.[19] According to O'Donoghue, Walter Leo was his best friend.

Florence O'Donoghue was born on a small farm under the twin shadows of the Paps Mountains near Rathmore, Co. Kerry on 22 July 1894. He was the only son of Patrick and Margaret Donoghue (neé Cronin) and had four sisters.[20] He arrived in Cork from Kerry as a sixteen-year-old in the spring of 1911 to work with Nolan, his mother's first cousin, as a shop assistant in his drapery store.[21] The shop was at the front of a large three-storey house and – presumably in lieu of a portion of their wages – the shop assistants lodged on the premises. Initially, the staff consisted entirely of girls and, perhaps because he had been raised in a family of sisters, O'Donoghue got on well with women and was well liked by them in return.[22]

However, O'Donoghue soon had male company when he was joined by a number of other lads who also came to work in the shop.

---

[19] Murphy, *The Year of Disappearances*, Chapter 58.
[20] O'Donoghue refers to four sisters in his memoir: Agnes, Nell, Margaret and Lizzie.
[21] Although he stated in his military pension application that he did not arrive in Cork until the winter of 1916, the 1911 Census finds him already there in April 1911.
[22] Borgonovo, *Florence and Josephine O'Donoghue's War of Independence*, p.12 and p.25.

According to his own account, he joined the Cork Catholic Young Men's Association (CYMS) where he eventually rose to the rank of Honorary Secretary, showing, like his future boss Michael Collins, a yen for detailed secretarial work. It appears he also had plenty of physical energy, regularly cycling the 90 miles round trip home to Rathmore in the summer months and setting up a football club and reviving a cycling club that had been in abeyance for years. 'There is a medal somewhere which I won for the first 50-mile road race that we held.' He became secretary of the cycling club and, as if that was not enough, he also took a course at the Cork School of Commerce.[23]

A popular young lad with plenty of friends, he quickly got over his initial homesickness at finding himself in a strange city and lived an active and congenial life as he moved into his early twenties. He was twenty when the First World War broke out. O'Donoghue at this point portrays himself as entirely apolitical. 'The whole weight of such opinion as I had any contact with, newspapers, periodicals, public speeches and private discussions, was unquestionably pro-British. I never at any time heard a bit of doubt or protest, or anything but admiration for England and a hatred for Germany.' A few of his friends 'with whom I was intimate, Michael Lehane, Jack Stack and Tommy O'Meara, joined up [the British army]. We talked about it but to the suggestions that I should go with them I did not respond. My refusal had nothing whatever to do with the national question or the issues involved, because my ignorance of both was profound. My decision was, I think, dictated by about equal parts of an instinctive dislike of what I had seen of British soldiers in uniform with their swaggering ways and flashy uniforms in the streets of Cork, lack of initiative, and a sense of responsibility to my parents and sisters.'[24]

This refusal 'to respond', of course, can be interpreted to mean he was refusing to join up. Or it can be interpreted to mean he was refusing to respond to the fact that his friends had joined up, which is not quite the same thing. However, it is clear that his passions at the time were his work with the CYMS and his cycling and football clubs. 'War was then a novelty' – a novelty he did not, at least on the face of it, appear to take seriously. His abilities, however, had already been recognized by his

<hr>

[23] ibid p.14.
[24] ibid, p.16 and p.25.

employer when, in 1913, Michael Nolan acquired the lease on a second shop around the corner on Castle Street (from his cousin Laurence McCarthy, as we have seen) and set it up as a men's outfitters and put the nineteen-year-old Florrie in charge of it. [25] There he was joined by two new assistants, the brothers Denis and Michael Lehane, with whom he seems to have been very friendly.

However, his account of the Lehanes does not quite add up either. He states – twice – that Michael Lehane joined the British Army at the outbreak of the war and that he was replaced in the shop by Leo Murphy, who according to O'Donoghue, introduced him to republicanism, something he claimed he had known nothing about up to that point. Denis Lehane, he states 'did not stay very long. One Sunday night he left a note for Michael and, without a word to anybody, walked out. It was years later that we heard that he had arrived in the United States.'[26] Except that it appears that it was Michael Lehane who left for America and Denis Lehane who joined, or rather tried to join, the British army. For Michael Lehane departed for America on the *Lusitania* on 20 March 1915.[27] It seems it was he who left the note for his brother rather than the other way around. Denis Lehane disappeared all right, but he did not end up in America. Rather, the evidence suggests, he ended up as one of the first people to be executed by the Volunteers and buried in Knockraha.

O'Donoghue is probably correct to say Denis Lehane walked out though. It appears he made his way to Tralee where he joined up for six years' service in the Army Special Reserve infantry, more specifically as a reservist in the Royal Munster Fusiliers. He was posted to Aghada on Cork Harbour on 2 June 1915. However, he was then discharged from the army 'as a consequence of having made a misstatement on enlistment'. (He claimed he was nineteen when in fact he was only sixteen. He was discharged from the army for being underage.)[28]

---

[25] Guy's Postal Directories for Cork, 1913, 1914, 1915.

[26] Borgonovo, op.cit, p.15.

[27] Passenger Lists, Ancestry.co.uk. The Lehanes' older brother, Daniel (Reg. No 7035), a 'sober, reliable and well-behaved man', did serve in the British army from 1913. He contacted tuberculosis in the trenches and was invalided out in August 1916, as 'no longer fit for service'. He died of TB on 16 February 1919. Ancestry.co.uk.

[28] Denis Lehane, RMF, Regimental No. 5558, British Army Pension Records, Ancestry.co.uk.

Lehane now disappears completely from official records and there seems to be no death certificate for him and no subsequent record of his existence.

Michael Leahy, the East Cork IRA commandant, however, remembered picking up an agent called Dinny Lehane in the harbour area whom he believed was an undercover RIC man. There was nobody of that name in the RIC at that time – the last Denis Lehane in the RIC having died of influenza in Tipperary in 1919.[29] But it is easy to see how Leahy might have thought he was dealing with an undercover policeman since most 'spotters' in civilian clothing at that time were RIC men. It seems this was early on in the campaign, probably as early as 1917 or 1918 and possibly even earlier, since Leahy states that Lehane was the first person he 'personally executed'.

The first I personally executed was an RIC man named Dinny Lehane. There was a barge which went up from Haulbowline to Cork for stuff. Curfew was on and D. L. was in the barge on duty when he saw a fellow in Cork in civvies apparently drunk. He knew this lad might be shot if the British came upon him during curfew and this lad made towards the barge. The fellow said he was going somewhere and he stayed on the barge all night and he was given a mug of tea. Then the man on duty charges off and he saw the RIC man making a bee line to get away. He collared him [and] sent for some of the boys. They found papers. He was an RIC man and had a list of men who were on the run whom he was spotting.'[30]

Lehane was moved to Knockraha to await his fate.

Ned Mulcahy,[31] a blacksmith who was a real [indecipherable word] was the Governor of Sing Sing. The RIC man was sentenced and we got a firing party and Mulcahy was sent to get the grave ready.

'We're letting out that prisoner of yours,' I said, to take a rise out of Mulcahy. But later I said we will kill him, but not with guns.

'Have you a hammer? Send him down to the store and get your sledge and let him have it.'

'You can't ask me to do that,' he said.

'I am,' I said. 'I'm giving the order.'

'[I can't] damn it,' he said, 'do this.'

'Get your sledge,' I said.

---

[29] RIC Membership Rolls. HO 184 series.

[30] This account was given to Ernie O'Malley by Leahy. Michael Leahy, O'Malley Papers, P17b/108.

[31] His correct name was Ned Moloney, not Mulcahy.

He got his sledge. He picked it up and he taking [ages?]. I said: 'I've known you for many a long year and many the piece of iron you softened for me when you were working but unless this deed is done I'll put you where no man will ever find you again.'

I thought it had gone on long enough so I told him we would shoot the man. We fired and the RIC man dropped.

'Turn his face to the East,' Mulcahy said. Before that, the man had said he was not a Catholic. Now when he was brought to be shot he wanted a priest.

'Sorry, we can't,' I said. So I had to say the Act of Contrition for him and he had to repeat it after me. Then we knelt down and said the Rosary before we shot him. I was a bit worried about it then but I felt no more since.'[32]

Was this the Denis Lehane who had worked in Nolan's shop with Florrie O'Donoghue? The lack of a death certificate for him and the fact that these events took place in the harbour area where the reservist Lehane had been posted suggests that this may have been the case. If so, then it appears that O'Donoghue was covering up for him by stating that it was he rather than his brother who went to the United States, which in turn suggests that he may well have been aware that Denis Lehane was a British agent. With Michael Nolan supplying information to the RIC and Denis Lehane disappearing while in all likelihood working as a spy and RIC men regularly calling to the shop, it appears that the draperies on North Main Street and Castle Street were quite a little hive of espionage activity, though not on the IRA side.

---

[32] Leahy in O'Malley Papers, UCDA P17b/108.

9

A Man of Exceptional Charm and Charisma

According to Jamie Moynihan, his fellow IRA officer, Florence O'Donoghue 'was a man of exceptional ability and charisma, with a personal charm which attracted and influenced many other people.'[1] He organized the Volunteers along regular army lines: 'The structures Florrie put in place throughout Mid-Cork were accepted nationally in later years. The smallest group was the section (composed of eight to ten men), four sections made a platoon, four platoons formed a company, a number of companies made a battalion (the number of companies in a battalion was dependent on local volunteer numbers), several battalions formed a brigade, a number of brigades formed a division, several divisions formed a corps, and three or four corps formed an army.'[2]

There can be no question that O'Donoghue was one of the more professional and competent officers serving with the IRA. His orders and instructions to Volunteers as evidenced by the material in his papers are an example of what would now be called 'best practice' in the business of organization and the gathering of information, and are a rich source for historians, and justifiably so. He was careful, diligent and showed an enormous capacity for work. For a farmer's son and a draper's assistant, his professional approach to his work – in contrast to the more haphazard methods employed by many in the Volunteers – is suggestive of a military competence rare in the chaotic history of the IRA.

---

[1] Jamie Moynihan, *Memoirs of an Old Warrior*, ed Donal O'hEalaithe, (Cork, 2014) p.320.

[2] ibid., p.24.

He also set up IRA intelligence in the South, something that was almost non-existent up to that point. 'History will recognize Florrie O'Donoghue as the architect, planner and deviser of the IRA's code of intelligence, a near-perfect system which proved invaluable to the Volunteer organization, not only in the 7th and 8th Battalion areas but also throughout Co. Cork during the period 1919-21.'[3] 'Florrie's ingenuity knew no bounds at that time.'[4]

Moreover, if the accounts of his stewardship of IRA intelligence are to be believed, his rise to prominence within the Volunteer movement was extraordinarily rapid. According to himself, he had no interest whatsoever in the 'National Question' until well after the 1916 Rising. In his IRA pension application, he states that he came to Cork in the winter of 1916 – though the 1911 Census finds him there in April 1911. It was when Walter Leo Murphy joined the staff of Nolan's drapery in late 1916 that O'Donoghue said he became interested in the movement. Murphy was interested in separatism and was later to set up the 3rd Battalion of the Cork No. 1 Brigade in the Ballincollig area, west of the city. In his memoir O'Donoghue states: 'Neither of us knew anybody who was a Volunteer, nor did we know if we would be accepted as recruits. But sometime in the winter of 1916-17 we decided to go to the Volunteer Hall and offer our services. Here the initiative lay more in Leo's character than in mine, though I feel sure that in one way or another, once I had reached conviction in my own mind, I would have been driven into service in some form. We were accepted without question or formality.' He claims that his motivation was that he had become aware of the 1916 Rising and was impressed by the writings of Pearse and MacDonagh but is vague in his notions of what 'national freedom' meant. He claims that in the summer after the Rising 'a fresh and exhilarating wind was blowing in Ireland'; but felt that, in Leo's case, 'there was also a call to serve'.[5]

In his IRA pension application, O'Donoghue claimed his first 'action', if it could be called that, was that he 'assisted in procuring 3 rifles from Connaught Rangers'. He dates this as occurring at some time

---

[3] ibid., p.39.
[4] ibid., p.320.
[5] Borgonovo, *Florence and Josephine O'Donoghue's War of Independence*, Chapter 2.

between '30 April 1916 and 31 March1917' – though in his memoir he implies that it happened in 1919.

I remember one of our lads coming to me one day in the shop to say that there were three Connaught Rangers in a pub nearby who wanted to desert. They had their rifles with them but no ammunition. They wanted £2.0.0 each and three complete sets of civilian clothes. The cash was not too difficult to procure; three sets of clothing and shoes were a tougher problem. Eventually we got the stuff together and the three lads began to change. Everything was going well until one of them discovered that the pants we had provided were too big. The deal was held up until we procured a better fitting one. I remember thinking at the time that if the average British soldier was of the same standard as these Connaught Rangers they were not such formidable opponents as we thought. I often wondered what became of them. We never saw them subsequently.[6]

This is a persuasive piece of recollection. It is detailed and so convincingly banal that it would not occur to one to even question it. Yet it is full of inconsistencies. For a start, by including it in the chapter on events in 1919 in his memoir O'Donoghue implies that this happened during 1919 rather than 1916/17 as he claims in the pension application. In fact, as we shall see, it can be dated precisely – to 5 February 1917 – around the time he said he joined the Volunteers. In other words, he could hardly have known who 'our lads' were since, by his own account, he knew nobody in the Volunteer Hall at that stage. The three soldiers wanted £2 each for the rifles and they were looking for civilian clothes. But if this is true, would the provision of three sets of male clothing prove 'a tougher problem' to someone who worked in a men's outfitters – and who ran the shop himself? Would someone who was used to measuring men for clothes every day of the week not be able to provide a pair of trousers that would fit – with racks of them on hand? This suggests that O'Donoghue is being economical with the truth in the above account.

British records tell us precisely where the three Connaught Rangers rifles came from. On 5 February 1917, three miniature rifles were taken from the munitions store at the fort at Crosshaven where the Connaught Rangers were based. The army's intelligence report of the week stated: 'Three miniature rifles were taken from the store of the 4th Connaught Rangers, Crosshaven on 5 inst, but it is believed they were taken by the

---

[6] ibid, p.80.

men for their own use.'[7] Surely if soldiers had taken the rifles and deserted with them, this would have been reported as a case of desertion. On the other hand, if they wanted rifles for their own use, say to go shooting game, they would hardly have taken miniature rifles with no ammunition but would more likely have taken decent service rifles.

This all happened around the time when O'Donoghue claimed he first went to the Volunteer Hall to offer his services. Is it possible that he acquired these rifles to improve his credentials with the Volunteers? If so, the British army did not even let him have decent ordnance but sent him in with three miserable guns which were worthless since they had no ammunition – something that would have been exactly in character for the army to do. This has all the appearance of a set-up. It was not the only time dud munitions found their way to the IRA from the security forces. Seán A. Murphy argues convincingly that a cache of Canadian-made Ross rifles were allowed to be taken by the IRA, probably with the help of naval intelligence in 1919 and that these were later used in the Kilmichael Ambush. The Ross rifles had the habit of blowing up in the hands of the person firing them, with the result that it was not uncommon for the bolt to be driven back through the head of the shooter, something apparently that may have occurred at Kilmichael.[8] And the Cork No. 1 Brigade column may have had as many as half-a-dozen of these flawed Ross rifles at Coolavookig. [9] Murphy quotes General Boyd of the British Army's Dublin District: 'I understand that a certain amount of ammunition of a highly dangerous explosive nature had been issued to the intelligence staff of Divisions by GHQ for the purpose of being gradually distributed to Sinn Feiners of extreme views with an object which is obvious.'[10] When David Neligan joined the British Secret Service as one of Collins's agents in Dublin, he was surprised to find a Captain boasting of how they were planting ammunition to be found by the IRA that would go off prematurely: 'If they use it, they will get a shock.'[11] O'Donoghue's Connaught Rangers have all the appearance of Greeks bearing gifts.

---

[7] B.J.C. Doran intelligence report 7February 1917. TNA, CO 904/157.
[8] Seán A. Murphy, *Kilmichael: A Battlefield Study*, pp.102-12.
[9] Jamie Moynihan in O'Malley UCDA P17b/112.
[10] Major General G.F. Boyd to GHQ 24 April 1920, quoted in Murphy, op.cit., p.102.
[11] David Neligan, BMH WS 380.

73

O'Donoghue's opinion of the Volunteers he had just joined was not exactly high. 'At first I was not impressed by what I saw – rather the reverse.' The 'stark reality' was 'groups of shabby youngsters gossiping in the Volunteer Hall or muddling through some clumsy drill. These lads were different to any I had made contact with through the Catholic Young Men's Society, the School of Commerce, the Gaelic football or cycling clubs and at first I felt that I did not quite understand them. . . . If a few of its officers and some of its members had scant respect for any laws, foreign or native, if occasionally they were not above preying on the wealthy commercial life around them, nevertheless they were wholly reliable, intrepid men whose loyalty to the organization was absolute.' Not absolute enough that that he was entirely happy to be involved in some of their early 'stunts', such as the seizure of arms from private homes. 'For some unaccountable reason we were picked by some of the tough men as two of a party of twelve for an arms raid on the house of a Captain Clarke at Farran, about twelve miles from the city.' The raid was unauthorized and outside the Company area but, as O'Donoghue put it, 'neither impediment troubled these pirates'. 'It was my first experience of a Volunteer operation – if it can be called that – and I did not feel too happy about it. The contrast between this and "Our camp fires are burning low; out yonder lies the Saxon foe" seemed fantastic and absurd. The foe in this case probably wasn't a Saxon anyway, I thought, and I felt an uneasy guilt at the idea of invading with arms the privacy of a man's home, whether he was a foe or not.'[12] This is evidence of O'Donoghue's essential, or at least apparent, decency – something which was to stand him in good stead all his life. In the event, the Clarke family – of tobacco fame – were disturbed during dinner. A shot was fired by the Volunteers when the Clarkes were slow at handing over their arms and Captain Clarke was hit in the hand and the Volunteers got away with some fowling pieces and ammunition. But O'Donoghue still felt unhappy about it. Looking back at it afterwards, he saw it as the antithesis of idealism; 'whatever the poets said, this was the reality'.

What comes across at this point in O'Donoghue's account of his own early development is of an idealistic young man full of energy and

---

[12] All these quotations are taken from O'Donghue's own account in Borgonovo, *Florence and Josephine O'Donoghue's War of Independence*, pp.24-34.

drive. It is equally clear that he imbibed at least some of this idealism from the Catholic Young Men's Society and his football and cycling clubs and that the Volunteers rather failed to live up to these ideals. 'Two voices called then, one the cautious, practical voice of the workaday life that regarded this playacting as soldiers as not quite respectable and suited only to the lower orders. I got much good and well-meant advice to the general effect that I would ruin my business prospects if I continued to associate with the rabble' – some of this advice came from Michael Nolan. 'The other advice came out of something deeper. It was quiet, assured, spoke only to the heart, and knew no doubts. There is an obligation to do what you believe to be right; be not afraid, go forward, this is your destiny. And so a decision was made.'

At that stage of his life, O'Donoghue was what would traditionally in Ireland have been regarded as a good, reliable lad. He stands out from the vast majority of his peers within the Volunteers as having no background in the republican movement and no interest in politics. He rarely if ever makes a political statement, being concerned only with military matters which he placed on a higher plane than mere political considerations. He seems to have been only dimly aware of the 1916 Rising, at least initially and of the subsequent executions. He states he gained his republican idealism from reading the writings of Pearse and MacDonagh, yet the fantastical writings of Pearse, with his talk of blood sacrifice could not be farther from the pragmatic approach taken by O'Donoghue during all his years as an IRA man and afterwards. If he was swayed into action by the thought of a glorious death as envisaged by Pearse – echoing much imperialist thinking in the years before the Great War – why did he not continue to fight for the republican ideal during the Civil War, rather than sitting on the fence? O'Donoghue's espousal of republicanism is not convincing and there is no concrete evidence in his writings that Pearse and MacDonagh ever had the slightest influence on him.

Yet his rise to prominence within the Volunteers was meteoric. No sooner had he joined the Volunteers than he claimed he saw a notice in the Volunteer Hall to the effect that a Cyclist Company was being formed. O'Donoghue put his name forward. The Cyclist Company was to be under the command of Donnacha MacNeilus, a Donegal engineer who was based in Cork. 'To my astonishment he [MacNeilus] proposed me for the position of 1st Lieutenant and to my greater astonishment I was elected unanimously. I do not know whether there was any pre-arrangement, I never enquired, but this was a complete surprise to me. There it was again, the unforeseen turn of events creating a decision in which I had no part.'[13] This is a refrain which is repeated again and again in O'Donoghue's memoir: the role of chance in promoting him quickly up through the ranks.

He was particularly suited to the Cycle Company. As a prodigious cyclist, distances of 100 miles in a weekend over the rutted roads of the time were no problem to O'Donoghue. And when MacNeilus, who worked nights in his job at the Shell factory on North Main Street, was unable to take time off work, it was often left to O'Donoghue to organize the company himself. When MacNeilus had to go on the run after being sprung from jail for having shot a policeman during an arms raid in November 1918, O'Donoghue was now in sole control of the Cyclist Company. He had around 25 members in his cycle troop; each member had to use his own bicycle which he himself had to maintain. Using British army cycle company manuals, O'Donoghue set about training his company.

Around April or May 1917 O'Donoghue claimed that he had met Tomás MacCurtain for the first time who, amazingly again, immediately seemed to entrust him with all Brigade despatches. By the end of 1917 MacCurtain gave him the additional job of organizing lines of communication between the various battalions throughout the county, using members of the Cycle Company as dispatch riders. The Volunteers had no effective dispatch and communications system up to that point. 'I was to take charge of this work and use the Cycle Company for the first stages of these lines of communication. I would be appointed Brigade O/C Communications and would attend Brigade Council meetings in future.'[14] While O'Donoghue mulled over his new appointment 'Tomás, Terry and some others who wore uniforms were arrested the next day. I must have been unrecognized or regarded as of no consequence because no attempt was made to arrest me.' This is

---

[13] John Borgonovo suggests the IRB may have arranged for O'Donoghue to be placed within the Cycle Company since MacNeilus was an IRB man. Borgonovo, op.cit., p.43.

[14] O'Donoghue in Borgonovo, op.cit., p.34.

another oft-repeated refrain in O'Donoghue's memoir, the fact that Providence always seemed to spare him being arrested. 'I believe that the hand of Providence saved me, for the first of many times, from death or arrest that night' he states of a night some months later, when guiding the outlawed MacNeilus, he nearly stumbled into Crosspound RIC barracks while a raid was on nearby, in which local Volunteers were arrested.

Indeed, O'Donoghue's chronologies of 'activities' in the city, especially in the years of 1916-19 read, for the most part, like chronologies of Volunteer setbacks, consisting mostly lists of dates when various Volunteer officers and men were arrested. It is possible that this is what he was really interested in and that these were in effect his 'achievements'? It is tempting to read it like that, especially when people like Seán O'Hegarty are referred to as 'J Hegarty' in these chronologies.[15]

Once he accepted his role as O/C Communications, however, O'Donoghue threw himself into it with gusto, expanding his sphere of influence by organizing his Cyclist Company to run the network based on the principle, as he put it, of: a. safety and secrecy, b. speed and reliability and c. economy of manpower. He imposed a system of communications whereby no names were to be written on dispatches so that if they were captured by the police, they would have no idea who the O/C mentioned was or where a particular battalion was located. This commonsensical approach to security does not appear to have been thought of up to then. It is the kind of system that would be put in place by anyone who knew something about military communications. From mid-1920 he also put in place an around-the-clock tap on the military telegraph system that operated from Victoria Barracks, something that also required significant technical skills.[16]

But O'Donoghue's real gain while running the Cycle Company was that, as he put it: 'I began to acquire for myself an intimate knowledge of the County Cork bye-roads on my Sunday organizing journeys'. It is clear from O'Donoghue's account that over a two-and-a-half-year period he got to know County Cork extremely well. For areas within a

---

[15] These can be found in O'Donoghue, NLI Ms 31, 339(2) and Ms 31,401.

[16] The tap was in place on the telephone lines around Grenagh and may have been run by Frank Busteed. See Frank Busteed MSP34REF4903.

25-mile radius of the city, he would make round trips and return on the same day – on his Sundays off. But for longer trips – and the far reaches of the county in west Cork were much further than could be covered in a day – he would leave at around midnight on the Saturday night – after having worked up to 11.30pm in the shop – cycle through the small hours to his destination, catch some sleep in a hay barn before going to Mass, do whatever work he had to do and return that evening to the city. And, according to himself, he made such trips almost every weekend. Occasionally he was accompanied by MacNeilus or by his next-in-command, Denis Kennedy, but mostly he says he was on his own.[17]

It is probably true to say that as a result of this punishing regime there was nobody in Cork who had the level of knowledge of the county that O'Donoghue had. As a result, he got to know all the officers of the various companies and battalions in the areas he visited. This meant that nobody, except perhaps Tomás MacCurtain, had anything like the level of intimate local knowledge that O'Donoghue had, which put him in an extraordinarily central and important position.

Then in February 1918, just a year after he claimed to have first joined the Volunteers, MacCurtain promoted him to the role of Brigade Adjutant, a post he held up until April 1921 when he was moved out to the country as Adjutant of the 1st Division. He was not yet twenty-four years of age. Again, 'Tomás must have prepared the ground because the appointment was unanimous.' As Adjutant, he was now effectively secretary to the Brigade, and all paperwork passed through his hands. Much of this work was carried out at the shop of the Wallace sisters, effectively Brigade HQ, just around the corner from his workplace. His *modus operandi* was to do as much of the Volunteer work as he could during his lunch break. He would bolt his lunch as quickly as he could and spend the rest of the hour on his Volunteer tasks. After the assassination of Tomás MacCurtain when he went on the run, O'Donoghue still continued to use Wallace's for this work. This was to continue until he left the city at the end of April 1921, after which the military shut down the shop.

But well before that, if he can be believed, and within months of joining the Volunteers, in May or June 1917, O'Donoghue was sworn into the IRB. This is truly astonishing since the IRB was a secret oath-

---

[17] O'Donoghue in Borgonovo, op.cit., p.36.

78

bound society devoted to armed revolution where, in O'Donoghue's own words, 'recruitment was a very slow and careful process' and in the years after 1916 continued 'with the same painstaking caution'.[18] O'Donoghue's elevation was extraordinary for someone – according to himself – so recently (only a matter of months) committed to 'the struggle'. For someone like O'Donoghue with no experience of republican politics – indeed with something of a disdain for such politics – this induction seems nothing short of amazing. At the time O'Donoghue was sworn in, there were less than 50 IRB men in County Cork, even though there were over 1,000 Volunteers in the city alone. The IRB which had organized the 1916 Rising, was dedicated to physical force methods and despised democratic politics.

O'Donoghue is almost amusing in his suggestion that some hidden providential hand was pulling the strings to raise him up through the ranks of the republican movement and put him into key positions so quickly. As we have seen, by the summer of 1921 he was IRB Centre for the county after nudging Donal O'Callaghan aside, in addition to being Adjutant of the 1st Southern Division, and this with the help of British dirty tricks.

His next step, and this is one it seems he carried out entirely on his own initiative, was to set up an intelligence-gathering system in the city itself. This started in 1919 when he structured the battalion and company system to put in place men whose prime function was the gathering of information. This was then extended to placing agents in hotels and railway stations and in the police and, ultimately, in the British army itself. As John Borgonovo put it: 'He targeted the three components of British communication – mail, telephones and telegraph . . . he built special intelligence teams, which opened letters, tapped phone lines, and intercepted and decoded telegrams. These compartmentalized sections then forwarded the information to O'Donoghue's full-time six-man intelligence staff for compilation and analysis.'[19]

---

[18] O'Donoghue, *No Other Law*, p.188.
[19] Borgonovo op.cit, p.69-71. See also O'Donoghue's own lecture on the development of an intelligence service, delivered during the Second World War, O'Donoghue, NLI, MS 31,443.

While the last part of this may not be entirely accurate – his six-man intelligence staff was more involved in gathering information themselves and passing it on to O'Donoghue for analysis – but the overall picture is largely correct. O'Donoghue built a centralized web of communications with himself at the middle of it like a spider. There is no question that this operated efficiently and was cleverly run. There were scores of people involved, from hotel porters to night watchmen to shopkeepers to clerks in offices. There were also several policemen apparently supplying O'Donoghue with information, the best-known one being a Special Crimes sergeant called Costelloe, whom it appears he visited several nights a week – and was once almost shot for doing so: the IRA men watching Costelloe believed that his nocturnal visitor was a British agent of some kind. (They were right.)

And while many of these contacts were useful – it was hotel porters who noticed Timothy Quinlisk, a British spy (who was outed in early 1920), and allowed an IRA hit-squad to assassinate District Commissioner Smyth; it was a railway porter who spotted District Inspector Swanzy's hat in transit to Lisburn that alerted the IRA to the fact that he had been moved to Ulster – it still begs the bigger question: if the IRA's intelligence in Cork city was so good, then why did it lead to IRA losses rather than to IRA gains? Why was it that, despite this vast plethora of intelligence-gathering, the IRA in the city was on its knees by the time of the Truce, with arms dumps being located on an almost daily basis and most of its senior officers either dead or in jail? By July 1921, the British were able to report that the two city battalions had ceased to function – not completely true, of course, but not an empty boast either. One statistic says it all: of the 18 Volunteers killed by British forces in the city during the War of Independence, not a single one was killed in actual combat. All were killed either during raids on their homes, often by undercover operatives, or as a result of being captured either with or without arms. This was of course a 'shoot to kill' policy, but it was based on accurate intelligence. By 1921 the initiative, especially in the city, was now certainly with the British.

There are dozens of serious questions that should have been posed about the intelligence operation run by O'Donoghue during the last year of the conflict. Why were the homes of British intelligence officers not targeted? Why were the wrong people – for the most part – shot as spies? Why were actual spies often allowed to escape after being caught

– some of them even ending up with plum jobs in the new Free State? Why did the British want Seán O'Hegarty, and by extension O'Donoghue, running IRA affairs in Cork? Why was O'Donoghue never arrested, even though the British certainly knew who he was? Why is there no intelligence file on him, even though there is one on nearly every other senior officer in the country? Why does he, like the Scarlet Pimpernel, keep turning up everywhere? – whether it is appearing out of a hotel in Dublin to inform an IRA hit squad on its way to Lisburn to shoot DI Swanzy that the job is off, or in the east end of London claiming he was there to shoot an intelligence officer who was based in Cork, just before the plan fell flat on its face?[20] From the death of Tomás MacCurtain to the abortive gun-running from Genoa, from the arrest of Terence MacSwiney and the succession stakes of the Cork No. 1 Brigade to the death of Michael Collins, there are very serious questions to be asked of O'Donoghue's stewardship of IRA intelligence in Cork. It is very difficult to accept that his own accounts can be taken at anything like face value.

To give another example: for the first four months of 1921 O'Donoghue states that he and Joe O'Connor, the Brigade Quartermaster – a quartermaster it has to be said, of a dwindling supply of ordinance – were the only senior IRA officers left in the city. 'Conditions in the city were extremely difficult from the burning of Cork onwards, making it nearly impossible for known men to remain in the city, and this fact influenced the formation of the Brigade Column, and the attachment thereto of men who could no longer remain in the city. Nevertheless, the Brigade Staff work was carried on without serious hitch, and I was almost in daily communication with GHQ and the Brigade O/C.' Considering that O'Donoghue was known to the authorities and moved with impunity between his office on Cook Street and the Wallace's and Josephine's home on Blackrock Road, his immunity to arrest is uncanny.

When in May 1922 the IRA in Macroom apprehended and executed three British intelligence officers and their driver who were on their way to Berehaven, the military in the city, who were trying to find their missing men, called to the Cork Workhouse where Sean O'Hegarty worked and took away 'a well-dressed young man' to help them with

---

[20] Connie Neenan.in O'Malley, UCD P17b/112.

their inquiries. There is no proof that O'Donoghue was the 'well-dressed young man', but as the well-dressed young man closest to O'Hegarty and who was never far from O'Hegarty's side when O'Hegarty himself was over forty it is reasonable to suggest it was him.[21]

O'Donoghue is also interesting, even amusing, on the subject of British spies in the No.1 Brigade. The only spy he admitted to have penetrated the city IRA was 'Cruxy' O'Connor. On the subject of O'Connor and spies in general, O'Donoghue wrote:

I was sceptical of popular ideas about spies . . . . Looking at the facts I could not see spies being successful against the tight organization we then had. By this time everybody of any consequence knew everybody in the Brigade, in the adjoining Brigades and at GHQ. We were not accepting anybody at his own valuation. The man who could horn in successfully would need to be a genius. Traitors and informers were a more dangerous possibility. I dare say we were all subconsciously sensitive to the havoc worked by these wretches in former national movements. Ours was remarkably free of this stain. In a Brigade of eight thousand men we had during the whole course of the struggle only one solitary case of a Volunteer turning informer and in this case it was the result of pressure put upon him while a prisoner. The lives of seven [actually six] of his comrades were lost because of his crime. He gave information that enabled the British to raid the place where they were sleeping at Ballycannon, just outside the city. They were surrounded while asleep and murdered before they had a chance to resist. The British smuggled the informer to America subsequently, but we traced him. At a time when every man and every shilling was needed, we went to the trouble and expense of sending three men after him to America. He was shot in New York.[22]

When Kim Philby was outed as a Soviet spy in the 1960s, most of his friends and colleagues refused to believe it. He was so charming and debonair they found it impossible to accept that he was anything other than what he said he was. To be a good Secret Service agent, or even a good Intelligence Officer, you have to be a convincing liar. O'Donoghue likewise appears to have been very charming and witty, though he makes a few statements that hint of a certain vulnerability: 'I hated firearms', he states at one point, and while he accepted the fact

---

[21] *Evening Echo*, 6 May 1921.
[22] O'Donoghue in Borgonovo, op.cit., p.83. This is a well-known story. O'Connor was not killed in the assault in New York, however, but survived his wounds. See Murphy, *Year of Disappearances*, pp. 66-67.

that he might be injured or die in combat, he then goes on to say: 'I was terrified of torture'. But, then, who isn't?

He was also quick on his feet to deflect attention away from what he wanted it deflected from – a case in point being a British agent close to the centre of national affairs. In the summer of 1920 the secretary of the Cork County Board of the GAA was found to be working as a spy for the RIC. Cornered in the South Chapel by members of the 2nd Battalion, he was allowed to escape thanks to the intercession of the local priest. He immediately fled to South Africa and was never seen in Cork again. When his friends, who were IRA men themselves but who did not know why he had absconded, protested to O'Hegarty and O'Donoghue, they were told that he had to flee because of threats from a criminal gang whom he had, supposedly, witnessed robbing the payroll of the staff of the asylum. So convincing were O'Donoghue and O'Hegarty's dissimulations that articles are still being published today, almost a hundred years later, giving this version of events.[23] O'Donoghue was, of course, highly dismissive of the possibility of spies penetrating 'the tight organization we then had', but he might say that, mightn't he? 'The man who could horn in successfully would need to be a genius.' This sounds very much like a case of self-praise.

---

[23] See Murphy, *Year of Disappearances*, p.64 for a slightly more detailed account of this case. For O'Hegarty and O'Donoghue's cover-up, see Jim Cronin, *Making Connections: A Cork GAA Miscellany*, pp.166-69 and *Cork Holly Bough*, Christmas 2013.

10

Cool-Headed and Intelligent Men

O'Donoghue continued to work at the drapery store until 19 March 1920, the day before Tomás MacCurtain was assassinated. He never worked at Nolan's again, not even returning when the conflict was over – unlike Seán O'Hegarty who went back to his job as storeman at Cork Workhouse with the return of peace. According to his own account, he went on the run and, as we have seen, spent the next few months as a personal bodyguard to Terence MacSwiney, often sleeping in the same bed, at the home of the Hurley family on Sundays Well Road, a solid middle-class area of the city. 'Our enemies having the curious idea that the "respectable element" in the population could be ruled out of participation in our villainies.'[24] MacSwiney in this period divided his time between his sister's house in Belgrave Place, the Cork Asylum where he was given refuge by the matron, and Hurleys. To kill time between leaving Hurleys and taking up his duties as Lord Mayor, MacSwiney and O'Donoghue would go either to Belgrave Place or to O'Donoghue's own base at North Main Street. Clearly, he had not cut off all contact with Nolan at this stage.[25] This protection was on foot of instructions from Richard Mulcahy, who was close to MacSwiney and had been best man at his wedding. Mulcahy was worried about MacSwiney's security in the wake of the murder of Tomás MacCurtain and wanted 'cool-headed' and 'intelligent' men in MacSwiney's guard.

> I was alarmed to hear that you had been going around Cork during the day and even staying at home at night without any protection. . . . We have adopted here a

---

[24] O'Donoghue did the night shift, with another Volunteer, Charlie McSweeney, doing guard duty during the day. Borgonovo, pp.94-95.
[25] ibid.

system of protection to all Volunteers who have received notices and to any prominent people so circumstanced, who will accept our protection. Usually in the case of Volunteers, they are required to stay away from their own homes, they have a man or two with them in whatever place they are sleeping. . . . The matter of discriminating between military raiding and murder parties might be a difficult one for persons who are not cool-headed but with cool-headed and intelligent people that difficulty should not be very great.[26]

In other words, it was now standard practice for senior Volunteer leaders to go 'on the run' and that MacCurtain was probably about to do so when he was assassinated a fortnight earlier. MacSwiney obviously got his 'cool-headed' and 'intelligent' guard, though it is equally obvious from Chapter 6 that that guard was not much use to him when push seemed to refuse to come to shove.

After MacSwiney's arrest in August 1920, it becomes more difficult to keep track of O'Donoghue. It seems he assumed the role of a commercial traveller and called himself George Egan, a representative of Glenavon Woollen Mills, with an office in a commercial block at 15/16 Cook Street in the city centre. 'I had the firm's official cards with my fictitious name printed on them, and if inquiry was made the firm would have acknowledged me as genuine.'[27] Few knew about the existence of the office and the only IRA man who ever visited, according to O'Donoghnue, was Joe O'Connor. At least one other person did know of his disguise, however, and this was Josephine Brown with whom he was romantically linked by this time. Mail addressed to 'George Egan' was by now being delivered to Josephine's address on Blackrock Road. It is probably fair to say he was by now living with her, at least some of the time.[28] When he was promoted to Adjutant of the newly formed 1st Southern Division in April 1921, he protested vigorously that he wanted to remain in the city, but he was over ruled.[29] He then had to take to the hills, literally, much to his annoyance.

[26] Richard Mulcahy to Terence MacSwiney, 8 April 1920. Father Dominic Papers, Capuchin Archives, CA/IR/1/5/2/1-11.

[27] Borgonovo, p.99.

[28] Both the business card and a postcard delivered to George Egan with address at Rockboro Terrace, Blackrock Road can be found in O'Donoghue NLI Ms 31,498.

[29] 'Adjutant Cork appointed Adjutant: Would prefer to work as Intelligence officer re Cork No 1, though it would be very difficult to get a new Adjutant as the Bde is

But how did he manage to avoid arrest, first while running the drapery store on Castle Street and then when 'on the run' and operating between Wallace's sweet shop and the office in Cook Street? It is inconceivable that he would not have been recognized by British forces during this time, particularly by the RIC. He had carried Tomás MacCurtain's coffin in full Volunteer uniform and was photographed and named in the press as one of the pallbearers. By his own admission, he was known by sight to the RIC men who regularly visited Nolan's shop. He was getting mail at the home of a forewoman typist in Victoria Barracks. He is named in the 6th Division Record of the Rebellion as adjutant of the brigade.[30] He was even seen by D.I. Swanzy[31] with Terence MacSwiney one night on York Hill.[32] He puts all this down to the legendary 'incompetence' of British security forces and his immunity to arrest down to 'Providence'. Nearly every senior IRA officer and Sinn Fein politician in the city was arrested at some point or other between 1916 and the Truce of July 1921. Mick Murphy, for instance, the commandant of the 2nd Battalion, who had gone to the Brigade Flying Column in the spring of 1921, was back in the city less than 24 hours when he was arrested by undercover RIC men in June 1921.

Yet O'Donoghue was never captured – unless, of course, he was accidentally picked up with Terence MacSwiney and then released – while men like Connie Neenan and Mick Murphy were going from pillar to post trying to avoid being captured and in many instances recaptured after having being released. While hundreds were being locked up, O'Donoghue was able to ply his trade with impunity in the heart of the city of Cork, right under the noses of the British. He wrote little or nothing about his activities during these eight months between the arrest of Terence MacSwiney and his departure to west Cork and Kerry at the end of April 1921. During that period up to twenty alleged 'spies', most of them either ex-servicemen or Protestants, were shot dead by the IRA in the city, only one of whom, according to British

---

hard hit owing to lack of good staff officers.' Agenda of Kippagh meeting. Mulcahy Papers UCD, P7/A/18.

[30] *A Record of the Rebellion in Ireland, 6th Division,* WO 141/93.

[31] District Inspector Oswald Swanzy of the RIC, soon to be assassinated in Lisburn for his alleged role in the shooting of Tomás MacCurtain.

[32] Borgonovo, pp. 95-96.

records, was an actual spy. The contrast with Collins's killing of British agents in Dublin could not be greater.[33]

Even after he had been promoted to adjutant of the 1st Southern Division and was moved to the Cork/Kerry border from late April 1921, both he and Joe O'Connor were able to slip into and out of the city every other weekend. At a time when known IRA men were liable to be shot dead in the street by British hit squads, Florrie O'Donoghue was even able to get married in a public space – the South Chapel right in the heart of the republican and RIC-monitored south inner city in April 1921.[34] This apparent immunity to capture is unparalleled among middle-ranking and senior IRA officers in Cork city. (The other two exceptions were Seán O'Hegarty and Joe O'Connor, but they can be grouped with O'Donoghue in this context.)

The most striking evidence of his apparent invisibility to the British are the events surrounding the kidnapping of Reggie Brown, Josephine's seven-year-old son, from his grandparents' home in Barry in south Wales at the end of 1920. The story of the snatching of Reggie Brown is well known and is part of the mythology surrounding 'the spy in the barracks', as Josephine became known. The accepted version of events is that after the death on the Western Front of Josephine's first husband at the end of 1917, she lost the custody battle for her sons, Reggie, who was ordered by a court in London to be brought up by her husband's parents in Wales. At the time of the hearing, Josephine already had her second son, Gerald, who was a mere baby at the time with her at her home on the Blackrock Road. But Reggie was in Wales and the Browns were not going to give him back.[35]

---

[33] Obviously, Collins's Squad sometimes killed the wrong people but the majority of Collins's targets were spies of one kind or another, while the majority of O'Donoghue's were not.

[34] His marriage certificate states that on 27 April 1921 at the Catholic Church of St Finbarr, Florence O'Donoghue described as a Clerk, of 65 North Main Street and son of Patrick O'Donoghue, Farmer, married Josephine Marchmont Brown, typist, of 2, Rockboro Terrace, daughter of Henry James Brown, Head Constable RIC. The celebrant was Father Timothy O'Leary CC and the witnesses were Joseph O'Connor and Teresa O'Reilly. Even the marriage cert contains errors: O'Donoghue's address was 55 North Main Street, not 65 and Josephine's father was Henry James McCoy, not Brown.

[35] Josephine's version of events, which is largely adhered to here, has to be treated with caution. It is broadly true but contains many significant evasions.

By her own account, Josephine was heartbroken. By this time, she was working in the headquarters of the British army's 6th Division in Victoria Barracks in Cork as forewoman over a staff of twenty-five female clerks and typists, which meant she would have had access to much of the documentation being handled by the clerical staff at the barracks. Sometime in the autumn of 1919 she claimed that she had made contact with Florrie O'Donoghue through Father Dominic, who was by then chaplain to the 1st Brigade. O'Donoghue, after apparently first clearing the matter with Michael Collins, did a deal with her.[36] If she would provide him with information from the British army's offices, he would endeavour to get her son back for her. This romantic and timeless story has done much to enshrine both O'Donoghue and Josephine in the pantheon of republican heroes – indeed it is a wonder that it has not been turned into a movie at this stage. Historians of the conflict almost uniformly agree that Josephine was 'as good as her word': she started passing information out to Florrie, and Florrie, for his part, after some delays, travelled to Wales and, on 1 December 1920, removed Reggie from his grandparents' home and over the next few weeks had him smuggled to Ireland. This is the story of the snatching of Reggie Brown from Wales and the bones of it are true.[37]

Questions begin to arise only when we look at British reactions to this. It is clear from the newspapers accounts of the kidnapping published in south Wales, that O'Donoghue – accompanied by two other IRA men, Seán Phelan and Jack Cody – did not simply stroll into the Brown household and that Reggie, as he put it, was 'quite unperturbed' and 'showed no reluctance to come with us'. In O'Donoghue's version of events, 'I may have told Mr Brown we were armed – I do not remember definitely – if I did that was the full extent of any threat to them.'[38] The *South Wales Echo* and the *Western Mail* gave more dramatic versions of events. According to the *South Wales*

---

[36] Collins does appear to have provided some help to O'Donoghue to establish contacts in Cardiff. GHQ to Adj, Cork No.1 Brigade, 19 October 1920. O'Donoghue Papers Ms 31,192(1).

[37] A detailed account of it, from both Florrie and Josephine's point of view, is available in John Borgonovo's edition of their joint papers. *Florence and Josephine O'Donoghue's War of Independence, A Destiny Which Shapes Our Ends* (Dublin, 2006).

[38] Borgonovo, op.cit, p.131.

Echo, men with distinct Irish accents entered the home and pushed a revolver in Mr Brown's face. 'Mr Brown remonstrated with the men but was told if he did not let them alone they would blow his brains out.' According to the *Western Mail* 'The revolver was pushed into his face and he was threatened that if he were not quiet "he would be blown to kingdom come".' The *Echo* went on to add: '. . . when the lad was being taken away he fell on his knees and prayed and asked to be allowed to remain with his "mam and dad".'

In a sense these details do not matter – although common sense suggests it could not have been as calm as O'Donoghue states – except that they illustrate how the kidnapping was viewed in Cardiff at the time. The *Western Mail* led with the story for a week. Indeed the *South Wales Echo* was to pursue the case for many years afterwards with interesting results. On 4 December the *South Wales Echo* reported that Scotland Yard were interviewing friends of Mrs Brown in London and for a time believed Reggie was being held in London, which he was not.[39] When the *Western Mail* sent a reporter to Cork to interview Josephine, she, not unsurprisingly, made a good job of pretending to be as appalled as everyone else. 'Oh it cannot be true that he is kidnapped, my favourite child. It will break my heart if he is not returned.'[40] In Cork, enquiries were made to the police and the local newspapers. According to O'Donoghue Scotland Yard sent two detectives to Cork and, even though they interviewed Josephine, and General Strickland (at least according to O'Donoghue), and the Cork newspapers printed the fact that Reggie was in Ireland, they left Cork empty-handed and the case seems to have been dropped.

This seems incredible in the cold light of day. Here we have an unsolved kidnapping case that is the talk of Wales and is carried by most British newspapers for well over two months, in which newspapers are even stating that the boy is with his mother in Cork (he was not at that point – but he was not too far away. He was in fact with her sister in Youghal, whose address the Brown family already knew) and Scotland Yard appear to walk away from it. According to John Borgonovo, who has written extensively on the subject: 'despite intense

---

[39] See notes 10 to 15 in Borgonovo, p.137, which discuss the newspaper coverage in Wales.

[40] Borgonovo, pp.134-35.

newspaper coverage, British officials never suspected IRA involvement in the kidnapping', and indeed, based on newspaper evidence, this does appear to be the case.[41]

However, the Home Office file on the kidnapping, or rather part thereof, has survived and, while it does not shed much more light on the events, it gives a very strong hint of how the case was viewed from within the British security establishment. As late as 1924 the Brown family were still looking for information on Reggie's fate. The file consists of inquiries made on behalf of the Brown family by the London news representative of the *South Wales Echo*. The result of the inquiry was a legal debate as to the various avenues to which the family might have recourse to get the boy back and concludes with a letter from the Secretary of State stating that 'he regrets to say that he is not in a position to take any action or offer any advice in the matter'.[42]

The ins and outs of the legal debate need not concern us here; suffice it to say that they revolve around the likelihood that Josephine was party to the kidnapping but that, because there was no direct evidence of this, there was no legal avenue to pursue. But the file does contain some useful pieces of information. The superintendent of the Barry Dock police wrote about the inquiries he had made in the years after the kidnapping:

Persistent appeals have been made to me by A.A. Brown and his two daughters for the recovery of Reggie Brown.

I told them I was quite helpless in the matter. Ireland being in such a lawless state that I could not rely upon the co-operation of the Irish Police, consequently nothing was done with the exception of writing to different addresses in Ireland and finally locating the wife and child of the deceased Private Brown or Marchment at 2 Rockboro Terrace, Old Black Rock Road, Cork.

From later information, it has been ascertained that the mother of Reggie Brown is now married to a man named O'Donoghue . . . . There is another element in the case. The mother is a Catholic and the Browns are Protestants and this fact will be exploited by the mother to prevent the Browns recovering the child.[43]

---

[41] Borgonovo, p.134.

[42] Sec. of State to Mr H. Woodward (n.d.), TNA, HO 45/11571.

[43] Glamorgan Constabulary to Head Constable Cardiff, 24 November 1923, TNA HO45/11571.

This tells us that by 1923 the Welsh police knew that the boy was living with his mother at Blackrock Road and that they also knew Josephine was now married to Florrie O'Donoghue. So they knew where Reggie lived. The file also supports the view offered by the Welsh newspapers that the kidnapping was not as smooth as O'Donoghue's suggested.

If the account given of the 'kidnapping' can be relied on, the men who carried it out may have committed an assault or an offence against 5.56 of the Offences against the Person Act of 1861 but as their names are not known no warrant could be obtained against them and I do not see how any police action would be possible, even if the Irish authorities were anxious to enforce the order of our High Court which is improbable – an order which gives custody of a child to English Protestants instead of its mother – a RC – is not likely to be viewed favourably by Irish courts, unless grave misconduct can be proven against the mother.[44]

And so the matter stood. There was no legally easy way to get the child back. The only immediate result of the inquiry was that in 1925 the rumour was put out in south Wales – presumably by the O'Donoghues themselves in order to throw the Browns off the scent – that Reggie had died in Ireland.[45] To a neutral looking in upon the debate, this looks pretty hard-hearted, but the most important thing relates to what is not in the file.

Because the file – or rather the folio – consisted originally of a series of eight separate files. Files 1-5 are stated to have been destroyed, as has file No 7. Only two remain: files 6 and 8, and these were still being picked over as late as October 1961. Almost everything official relating to the investigation itself and the circumstances surrounding the kidnapping has been removed. Considering that this was an unsolved kidnapping case, there seems to be no good reason for shredding the investigation papers and retaining just the innocuous material. This destruction of the essential files on the case – highly selective as it must have been – strongly suggests the involvement of the security agencies. While this is a Home Office record, we'll never know if military or

---

[44] H.B.S. to 'D' Division, 14 December 1923. TNA HO45/11571.
[45] See newspaper clippings and note from Joe O'Connor in O'Donoghue NLI Ms 31,126-129.

civilian intelligence had a hand in the destruction of the files but it is fair to say there is a high possibility that they did.

Another fascinating story that is likely to be connected to O'Donoghue is that given to Ernie O'Malley by Pat Margetts, a Galway-born British soldier serving in Victoria Barracks, Cork. A line or two from this are frequently quoted by historians when they wish to make the point that there was leakage of information to the authorities from within the IRA. But what Margetts has to say in detail is rarely scrutinized and it is worth doing so here because it points the finger very strongly in one direction.

Margetts was serving with the Argyll and Southern Highlanders. While working as a guard at the Detention Barracks in Galway he was so angered by the way drunken Auxiliaries were treating civilians that he decided to help the IRA in any way he could.[46] For a relatively brief period – January to May 1921 – he was posted on guard duty to the Detention Barracks at Victoria Barracks, Cork, now the location of Cork Prison. The most notable prisoner he guarded was Paddy 'Cruxy' O'Connor who, as we have seen, had betrayed the IRA at Ballycannon outside Cork city, an affray in which six Volunteers lost their lives. Margetts watched the interrogation of O'Connor, a 'process of kindness', according to Margetts, in which a stream of intelligence officers went into and out of his cell, including 'a Captain of the Hampshires, an Intelligence Officer whose name I now forget'. 'It was close to 11 o'clock when I felt that Connors was giving information but I could not get out to pass on the word for I was on duty and also there was a curfew and it would have been difficult to knock up anyone.'

When asked by O'Malley if it were military or RIC who were responsible for the Ballycannon debacle, Margetts claimed – rightly – that it was police, but that there was little difference between them by this stage. 'There was a very close co-operation between the RIC and military in Cork, closer than any area . . . . I talked to Connors myself. He looked scared; anyhow he had a furtive look in his eyes and he

---

[46] He even met his future wife after a row in which he disarmed a drunken Auxiliary. Pat Margetts in O'Malley UCD, P17b/111.

looked at you from under his eyelashes but he had not been ill-treated nor were there any marks on his face.'

What is significant about Margetts's account is that his time in Cork was limited, a few months, and he knew very little about the IRA organization in the city to which he wanted to pass on what information he had. In his account he mentions only the Detention Barracks where he worked and Wallace's shop in the city centre where he dropped off his information – which was effectively the IRA headquarters in Cork city.

We really had great freedom in the Detention and that explains how I was able to get around so easily. The first time I went to the Wallaces in Brunswick St I had some information and I was in uniform. Sean Hegarty was upstairs and he was very angry at my coming in and endangering the women. (Wallaces was Bde Hd Qts. It was continuously used by Sean Hegarty but nothing I think was ever found there.) Eventually I think my coming in there in uniform was a safeguard. I never saw Hegarty as often as I went in there, but I believe he never trusted me. *It would have been better for him and for his command if he had looked more carefully at his own men. For they needed looking and some of them were giving information as well as Connors* [my italics]. But I was trusted by the Volunteers, so go in and see Sheila, for Nora is dead now. Sullivan and I were very friendly indeed. He was from Clonmult and he was executed.[47]

This reflects how limited Margetts' perspective was in Cork. He mentions only the Detention Barracks and Wallace's as places of contact with IRA men. And he left Cork in May. So whoever he was talking about when he stated that it would be better for Hegarty and his command 'if he had looked more carefully at his own men, for they needed looking and some of them were giving information as well as Connors', he is likely to be referring to someone he saw at the Detention Barracks and again at Wallace's. Seeing as he mentions O'Hegarty's 'own men' and 'his command', this would suggest that it was someone he noticed at IRA HQ at Wallace's. And as Florrie O'Donoghue, O'Hegarty's right hand man, was the IRA officer most likely to be at Wallaces at any one time, there is a strong liklihood that it is he whom Margetts is talking about. In fact, for most of Margetts's time in Cork, including the time when O'Connor was in custody, O'Hegarty was away in mid-Cork with his column and the HQ at Wallace's was

---

[47] ibid.

93

effectively being run by O'Donoghue himself – which would explain why Margetts never met O'Hegarty there. Margetts may also have picked up something from Pat O'Sullivan, one of the survivors of the Clonmult massacre who was subsequently executed.

What is also implied by Margetts's account is that it was something of a mystery to him why the British did not raid Wallace's or at least close it down. After all, if he, a British soldier in uniform, was able to find it within weeks of arriving in Cork and walk in in uniform with his information why were the British military not able to do so? What is hugely significant is that, within two weeks of O'Donoghue leaving Cork city to take up his position as adjutant of the 1st Southern Division, they did in fact raid Wallace's and ordered it to be shut down, something they had curiously never managed to get around to doing in the two years O'Donoghue had been working there.[48] What all this suggests is that the British knew who O'Donoghue was, that he was around town all this time and that they turned a blind eye to his movements. Then as soon as he left for west Cork and it was no longer useful to them to allow Wallace's to remain functioning, they raided it immediately and shut it down. Indeed, a week after he left for west Cork, the British army's 6th Division was able to report that 'a close touch is now [being] kept with the doings of rebel Flying Columns'.[49] From a British point of view, clearly the city's loss was the country's gain.

O'Donoghue, according to himself, had another, 'narrow shave' at the Cook Street address. 'I was never raided. One morning when I had been there for some time, I thought the bluff would be put to the test. Joe O'Connor had just dropped in when the block was surrounded and a

---

[48] It was closed down on 14 May 1921 by order of General Higginson, O'Donoghue NLI, Ms 31,148.

[49] This is part of General Macready's weekly report on the state of Ireland on 30 April 1921. However, the reference to keeping track of flying columns comes from the 6th Division in Cork and the reports from the various Cork IRA brigades are attached (dated 3 May). The report on the 1st Cork Brigade is short and accurate – 'the Brigade is in a bad way' – suggesting intimate knowledge of the day to day position in which the Brigade found itself. The reports on the 2nd and 3rd brigades are more diffuse and consist largely of a list of engagements and the occasional intercepted communication and are more speculative, suggesting poorer intelligence. Report of the C. in C. on the Situation in Ireland, 30 April 1921, TNA CAB 24/123/13.

house-to-house search started. We bundled up our arms and documents, put them in the prepared hiding place and waited. Nothing happened. After a couple of hours, whistles were blown, and to our astonishment we saw the party gathering to their lorries and moving off. We found out later that some soldiers had looked in on the floor below us, walked round in a casual way, asked a few harmless questions and left. Probably they reported having searched our building, though they did not come up to our floor. Police or Auxiliaries would have been more thorough.'[50] Or perhaps not.

---

[50] Borgonovo, pp. 99-100.

11

'Volunteers for Intelligence Work'

As we have seen, after the assassination of Tomás MacCurtain at the end of March 1920, O'Donoghue, who was intimately involved in organizing the IRA's response to the killing and was one of the pallbearers at MacCurtain's funeral, decided to go 'on the run'. As a result of the funeral, prominent IRA men were now publicly known figures – this was a decision they had made themselves. 'The Brigade Staff in uniform marched immediately behind the hearse in the funeral; we shouldered the coffin in and out of the City Hall, in and out of the Cathedral, and at the graveside. We did that deliberately after consultation, believing that the time for further concealment was ended. And no matter what the cost, the event called for an open avowal by us of our positions of responsibility.'[1]

The result of this decision was that all prominent Volunteers who took part in the funeral procession, if they were not known to the police already, were now well known both to the authorities and to the people at large. Anonymity – if it had ever even existed – was firmly in the past. O'Donoghue left his employment at Michael Nolan's. 'On commencing whole-time duties I had to decide whether or not I would follow the example of other city men who had gone on the run and take to the country, or whether I would remain in the city. The city was the natural centre and focal point for the Brigade, and from no other point could the routine work of my two departments be handled so conveniently. The country was safer or course, but I had seen good men go into safe areas only to stagnate. We had that problem earlier. I

---

[1] O'Donoghue, quoted in Boronovo, op.cit., p.91.

decided to stay in the city.'[2] And so O'Donoghue became 'George Egan'. The central conundrum all of this is that neither 'George Egan' or Florence O'Donoghue, nor even Florence Donoghue, for that was what he was known as in 1911, was ever arrested or molested by the army or by the RIC.

And there are other issues – for instance with the intelligence materials in his own papers. The contrast between the materials taken by Josephine from the barracks and forwarded to Michael Collins and those 'retained' by O'Donoghue could not be greater. It is clear that O'Donoghue sent mostly worthless files to Collins during the War of Independence, while those in his own papers were far from worthless.[3] Many of them were intimately connected with matters on the ground during the conflict. And then there are what are euphemistically called O'Donoghue's 'working notebooks', which in reality consist mostly of loose pages from notebooks written in O'Donoghue's hand. Some of these derive from the summer of 1922 after he resigned from the IRA and are concerned with the peace negotiations that were taking place between pro- and anti-Treaty factions over the summer of 1922. But they read very strangely, especially when you bear in mind that these were meetings that O'Donoghue had attended himself. Why would he need to keep minor details of meetings he attended, especially since he was technically no longer a member of the IRA? Why did he feel the need to write down these details? Presumably he was not thinking about writing a history book while that history was still being made – and would not get around to doing so for thirty years. There is no evidence that his memory was faulty or that he needed to cobble together *aides-mémoire*. The following are some examples of these 'loose notes', from July 1922. But who were they written for?

Daly went to see Lynch but did not succeed; met Deasy in Mallow. Deasy would not commit to this or any other subject. I would have been surprised if he did.

---

[2] O'Donoghue, quoted in Borgonovo, op.cit., pp.93-94.
[3] This is not strictly true. The files smuggled out during the War of Independence are largely worthless. In the autumn of 1921 though, the quality of both the material being smuggled out of barracks and passed on to Dublin seems to have improved considerably, though there are still notable evasions on O'Donoghue's part. This is a subject we shall return to in the last volume of this series.

There was a meeting today of O'Rahilly, Daly, Dowdall, Egan, O'Cuill and myself. Rahilly's proposals were discussed – Dowdall, O'Rahilly and Egan left for Dublin to contact Govt people.

Another attempt to contact Lynch, this time by Fr Duggan. I had a talk with LL[?] before he left today and suggested that he should not discuss these matters with Deasy but go to Lynch and see him alone.

Duggan's back . . . Lynch said he had had six months of negotiations and was fed up with them . . . war or peace for him, he was tired of the situation.[4]

As noted in my book on the death of Michael Collins, O'Donoghue was far from 'neutral' at that point.[5] He was ostensibly trying to get both sides together to try to end the Civil War. But, still, why keep scraps of paper about meetings that he had just attended? Why even bother to write them? He had just been there. No other veteran of the conflict kept detailed accounts of meetings the way O'Donoghue did. They read as if he was either talking to himself or providing detail for some third party. The suggestion that he was putting together material for his future career as a historian makes no sense. Nobody worries about the history when he is in the middle of making it. Besides, his career as a historian did not get going until the 1940s.[6]

Similarly, he was gathering in his tiny gnomic handwriting in pocket notebooks the details of the Army Conventions and meetings of the IRB Supreme Council from February to April 1922 – taken almost certainly every day while the meetings were going on. His notes of Brigade and Divisional meetings even contain the names and addresses of many of the participants, something you would imagine he could not possibly have any need to write down since he would have known them all already. There seems to be no logical reason why he would feel the need to record such details. He was not a newspaper reporter or a detective gathering material for a case. It makes no sense that anyone would make

---

[4] These notes are of 5-8 July 1922 and are of significant historical value. But why should O'Donoghue record the minor details of what he already knew? O'Donoghue NLI MS 31,187.

[5] Gerard Murphy, *The Great Cover-Up: The Truth about the Death of Michael Collins* (Cork, 2018).

[6] These can be found in O'Donoghue NLI MS 31,179 – MS 31,189.

detailed notes in tiny writing of meetings while at the meetings and list the names and addresses of his friends and colleagues. But it would make perfect sense if he was making these notes for someone else's benefit.

And his understanding of the operations of British intelligence officers sent into the field, compared to accounts from other former Volunteers, is uncannily accurate. In *No Other Law*, his biography of Liam Lynch, O'Donoghue quotes General Macready's own biography: 'As soon as the rebels began to attack and molest the troops, there was a dearth of volunteers for Intelligence work and when during the summer of 1920 authority was obtained from the War Office to enlarge and improve the whole organization, little difficulty was found in obtaining keen volunteers who were already well acquainted with the localities in which they were stationed.' What is interesting about this is that it states that these 'volunteers for intelligence work' were either locals who were in the army or men with local contacts.

O'Donoghue goes on to dismiss such operatives. 'These "volunteers for intelligence work" were courageous men. Those of them we encountered in the Cork Brigades were officers, some of senior rank. They left their posts in civilian attire, sometimes very poorly dressed, and penetrated the countryside in an effort to obtain information or establish contacts for the purpose. Creditable as it was to their sense of duty, this type of activity disclosed a boy scout mentality, and a complete absence of any sense of reality of the situation that then existed. Moreover, their contacts were of necessity limited to a narrow circle of persons antipathetic to the Army and the national struggle, whose information could rarely be more than general and belated.'[7] Yet he had a high opinion of his more professional British opponents.

Perhaps this is as good a place as any to say what my personal feelings were to the soldiers and police opposed to us. Except occasionally, in the case of some particular reprehensible outrage by the Auxiliaries or Black and Tans, I never felt any burning hatred of them individually or collectively. I often wondered what that violent hatred in some of our men sprang from, and questioned if there was not some cold, analytical streak in myself. I hated passionately the conquest which the forces of occupation represented; I hated, passionately and painfully, the terrible thing that conquest had done to the minds of our people, but against the men who were the instruments of

---

[7] O'Donoghue, *No Other Law*, p.118.

conquest I could not feel any bitter hatred. For a few of them I felt genuine admiration because they were soldiers activated by a sense of duty, doing that duty as they saw it without viciousness or excess. The more my Intelligence work enabled me to read their minds, the more familiar I became with their responsibilities, problems and difficulties, the more the possibility of any violent hatred of them as persons vanished. That frame of mind made it sad to see men die in so unworthy a cause.'[8]

In his account of the operation of the intelligence section of the police, its chief, Ormonde Winter, makes an intriguing comment. Writing about the successes and limitations of the work of members of the Special Crimes section of the RIC, detailed with gathering information on subversive activities, Winter writes that:

The secret society known as the Irish Republican Brotherhood had been an organization concerning which it has been exceedingly difficult to obtain information, and informers, members of the IRB, have been impossible to obtain. The only member of the IRB who turned informer and whose information has been of the utmost value was obtained through the agency of a Special Crimes Sergeant.'[9]

He does not name either the IRB man in question or the Special Crimes Sergeant. But there are some grounds for believing that the latter may have been Sergeant Jack Maliff, the leading Special Crimes RIC detective in Cork. Maliff was one of those who supported the application of O'Donoghue's cousin Michael Nolan for compensation for losses he incurred as a result of IRA intimidation he received after passing on information on Walter Leo Murphy. Indeed, Maliff may also have been the man who recruited Nolan as an informer.[10] Mick Murphy gives a detailed account of an effort to shoot Maliff – who overlapped between his duties in the RIC and interrogation at the military detention barracks – in Cork in January 1921.

Jack Maliff, a prominent rugby player and a 'G' man who was very powerful and was picked out to act in Cork Military Barracks where he was interviewing prisoners and terrifying them. He knew our men. Word came out to us about him but he could not be found. But one day at the Mardyke when Munster were playing Leinster in rugby I was told we could find Maliff there. So I went there when I had got 2 Volunteers,

---

[8] O'Donoghue in Borgonovo, op.cit., p.69.
[9] Hart, *British Intelligence in Ireland*, pp.71-72.
[10] Murphy, *Year of Disappearances*, Chapter 58.

100

Denis Hegarty and Frank Mahony, our I/O. Both of them are now dead in the USA. We went to the 'Dyke and I had never been up to this time at a foreign game in my life. The lad on the turnstile was a Volunteer and he told us that Maliff was in there and where he would be. And there he was on the touchline, so we decided we would kill him when he was coming out from the match and do it at the Courthouse. When the crowd had thinned out he had another 'G' man with him called Ryan. The guns were put up behind them but they weren't killed. We put 14 bullets into Maliff and we gave Ryan a few. I'll tell you what happened when we were shooting. We were on the left step when he was on the right foot and at that point you would wobble. After that, there were lorries flying all over the city and there was hell to pay generally.[11]

Maliff's importance as an intelligence organizer in Cork can be deduced from the cover of a long-since shredded file in Irish military intelligence. It reads:

British Intelligence   SCI/445
Re:- Mailiff – Ex. Det. RIC
Connection with British Intelligence
Services at Rushbrook[12]

This comes from the post-Treaty era, probably 1922-23, since Maliff is here referred to as an ex-detective. But its implications are clear: that British Intelligence was still running some sort of operation from Rushbrook on Cork Harbour well into the Free State period, and that Maliff was believed to be connected with it. This is all the more interesting since this is the first of many links we shall see between the Queenstown area and intelligence-gathering. There is, or rather was, also an undated, though probably early document relating to meetings at sea in O'Donoghue's papers, which has disappeared since his archive

---

[11] Mick Murphy, O'Malley Notebooks, UCD, P17b/112. Neither Maliff or Ryan was killed, though both were badly injured. Murphy and his men were poor shots even at that proximity. Several others were injured in the affray. One of them, a customs official from Youghal called John Pring, died of his wounds.

[12] The reference to Maliff is on the inside of the reused cover of a file on attempts to track down Sandow Donovan and the Gray brothers, who opened fire on a Navy launch between Haulbowline and Cobh in March 1924 in which one person was killed and 25 wounded. MA, A/0917.

was catalogued.[13] Josephine appears to have had connections with the Queenstown area herself and Dinny Lehane was picked up there while working on the barges between Haulbowline and Cork. All this suggests that Maliff may well have been the Special Crimes Sergeant to whom Winter was referring.

More generally, Winter's account of the IRB is largely a potted history going back to James Stephens and the 1840s. 'It is the most secret and has always been the most dangerous of Irish secret societies and information as to its current activities is always difficult to obtain. Its branches cover all parts of the world where Irishmen live.' However, by late 1917 the RIC seems to have known quite a bit about the 'Organization', as they knew its members called it, its constitution and its intricate system of electing officers. The structure, divided into divisions and subdivided into county, district and circle centres, each with a 'Centre' was understood, as was the structure and membership of the Supreme Council. Even the oath of allegiance is quoted. This would reflect what the Inspector General Joseph Byrne was able to gather from his 'reliable informant'.[14]

In early 1915 a copy of the IRB Constitution fell into the hands of the police. 'As a consequence an effort was made throughout Ireland to try to find out what progress the organization was making but 'owing to the secrecy involved, little could be learned'. Only in Cork did any information appear to be forthcoming, where it was established that a new 'circle' had been set up in Cork city and that Tadhg Barry was the Centre. 'At the end of 1915 an informant declared that the IRB and Sinn Féin were in close union and that organizers were visiting the country advising their followers to stand loyally together and be ready at an hour's notice to strike a blow for Ireland.' This is remarkably like what the 'reliable informant' was saying and what was being passed on to the Director of Military Intelligence in London around that time.

---

[13] 'Notes re meeting at sea' O'Donoghue, NLI Ms 31,148. These notes have been removed since the archive became publicly available. The IRA was not exactly known for holding meetings at sea.

[14] Chapter 6 'The Irish Republican Brotherhood' in *A Record of the Rebellion in Ireland* (Intelligence) Vol. II pp. 47-53. TNA, WO 141/93. This chapter was excluded from *British Intelligence in Ireland*, Peter Hart's edition of the Record, for reasons of space (Hart, p.16). Though it is now part of the Army's Record, it first appeared as an appendix to Winter's account.

By the end of 1917 seven of the eleven members of the Supreme Council were known to British Intelligence and it was also known that four of them held leading positions in the Sinn Féin Executive while the other three were 'well-known Sinn Féin extremists'. Information on the workings of the IRB seemed to have reached a peak between 1917 and 1919, with nine different new centres from various parts of the country being reported, even including one from Blackrock, County Cork. In 1920/21 very little new information was forthcoming, reflecting the fact that no activity was taking place. In other words, the material in Winter's possession broadly reflects what was happening on the ground in the IRB, with the implication that Maliff may well have been the Crimes Special Sergeant who had originally found this particular source.

Despite their mutual distrust, there was still significant cooperation between the military and the police. According to the Army's own Record of the Rebellion, 'some [intelligence] officers successfully passed themselves off as officers of the IRA and obtained information of great value. This, it need hardly be said, not only demanded at times courage of rare quality but always required exceptional local knowledge.' 'Irish persons who were prepared to act as genuine secret service agents, i.e. as Sinn Féiners or as IRA were difficult to find . . . a few however were used with success . . . where adequate precautions were taken, numerous agents were never suspected.'[15] The Record also refers to the usefulness of female agents: 'Specially selected women, as usual, proved excellent intelligence clerks, but the difficulty of their accommodation limited their employment.'[16]

Two other things need to be said in connection with this. Jack Maliff was one of the very few RIC Special Crimes detectives who was allowed to live in Ireland after Independence, despite the fact that he was known to the Irish authorities to be working for British Intelligence. It appears that, despite his fearsome reputation – or perhaps because of

---

[15] There were at least two of these in the Cork IRA, Dan Shields and Cruxy O'Connor, the latter being a Secret Service agent. But these were not officers. There was nobody with the level of 'exceptional local knowledge' that O'Donoghue had.

[16] Hart, *British Intelligence in Ireland*, pp.48-49, pp.54-55, p.59.

it, he was not intimidated after Independence.[17] He even went on to become chairman of Cork Constitution Rugby Football club in later years.

In 1918 the army general commanding British forces in Cork, General Beauchamp J.C. Doran, set up an army cycle corps to augment an intelligence-gathering operation that he had been running since the end of 1916. Reading between the lines, it may even have been set up in response to the Volunteers' own cyclist companies, though, rather curiously, he did not seem to feel the need to operate within a forty-mile radius of Cork city, focusing instead on more outlying counties such as Clare, Limerick, Kerry, Tipperary and the far reaches of west Cork. 'The newly arrived cyclist troops [are] having a good effect and a number of interesting reports have been coming to me from these Brigades.'[18] Clearly, if there was no need to have cycle companies operating in areas within a forty-mile radius of the city, you would have to ask why. Was O'Donoghue using his own work as a cycle company organizer to gather information from these areas for the British authorities?

There is also a link between O'Donoghue's cycle company and British Intelligence. Jack Healy, one of the principal cycle merchants in Cork – who presumably sold bicycles to both the British Army Cycle Corps and to members of the IRA Cycle Company – worked for several years as a courier for the Special Intelligence Branch at Parkgate Street under Major Ivon Price, the head of military intelligence in Ireland.[19] Healy, along with Price himself, was demobbed in 1919 with the end of the Great War, so he could not be regarded as a 'spy' during the War of Independence. But he had been a military intelligence motorcycle

---

[17] Although he did flee to America for a time in 1922 and appears to have spent much of the early 1920s living in England. RIC Pensions records and Passenger Lists, accessed at Findmypast.com. Ellis Island Records accessed online.

[18] B.J.C. Doran Report 31.5.1918. TNA CO 904/157.

[19] Jack Healy, TNA CO 762/81. Healy claimed in his Irish Grants Committee submission that he was an agent for Dublin Castle's intelligence department from 1916 until 1919. Healy was a native of County Clare and his claim is for the loss of motor cycles. However, he was also a well-known bicycle merchant. It appear that he was not supplying information during the War of Independence – he claims he ceased working for Dublin Castle in 1919 when Price's unit was stood down – but many ex-RIC men vouchsafed for his loyalty.

courier from 1916 to 1919. He was also a member of O'Donoghue's IRA Cycle Company.[20] As we have seen, Price was removed from his role as intelligence chief and returned to the RIC as County Inspector for Cavan/Fermanagh on 1 February 1919.)[21] He was to return to Dublin Castle as Assistant Inspector General in October 1920, but this was closing the stable door after the revolutionary horse had well and truly bolted. But there is a chain of connections for the 1917-19 period and cyclists, couriers and cycle companies are at the centre of them. This suggests that the reason why General Doran did not bother to employ a cycle corps in the vicinity of the city was that he did not need to. Why organize cycle companies when you have the IRA Cycle Company working for you? It was a perfect fit. After all, why bark if you've got a dog?

Perhaps this is a good time to summarize what has been established up to this point on the many anomalies surrounding O'Donoghue's IRA service:

Somebody, usually referred to as a 'reliable informant' was providing the British intelligence services with detailed inside information on Volunteer and IRB planning at least from the autumn of 1916 to the end of 1919, and probably before the 1916 Rising. That somebody was male and was based outside of Dublin – though he was still able to provide useful information on matters pertaining to republican headquarters in Dublin. There are reasons to believe from the intelligence he provided that he may have been based in Cork.

On the day before Tomás MacCurtain's murder, a 'trustworthy informant' who was 'above reproach', informed the military authorities that MacCurtain had been at the Phoenix Park at the attempted

---

[20] Statement of Justin McCarthy, O'Donoghue Papers, NLI, Ms 31,327.

[21] Jim Herlihy, *The Royal Irish Constabulary Officers List*, p.258 (Dublin, 2005). Eunan O'Halpin, who tracked down Price's family in the 1970s, has an interesting story on Price's last years in the RIC. Price returned to full-time work as Assistant Inspector General in the Castle from October 1920 to his retirement in July 1922. According to his grandson, he received a warning that he was about to be shot and was advised to walk out of his office and go straight to England, leaving his hat on the door so that the IRA would not be aware that he had gone. This he did. He died in England in 1931. O'Halpin, endnote on p. 259. Eunan O'Halpin, 'British Intelligence in Ireland, 1914-1921', in Andrew and Dilks, *The Missing Dimension* (London, 1984).

assassination of Lord French in December 1919. The military were also aware that MacCurtain was about to go 'on the run', something that could have been known only to someone close to him.

Neither informant – if they were indeed two different people – reported through the RIC system, since their evidence is not in the County Inspectors' monthly reviews but seemed to find its way directly to the desk of the Inspector General in one case and the military on the other. This suggests that this agent, or agents, was being run by some branch of military intelligence and that military intelligence was passing on the information to Joseph Byrne, as well as to the War Office.

The 'reliable informant's' information ceased with Byrne's removal. Byrne may have brought him with him in 1916 from his previous job in the legal department of the Adjutant General's department in the War Office where he had served from 1914 to 1916. He is likely to be the same man who was providing intelligence directly from Ireland to the War Office through MI5 before the 1916 Rising so that Military Intelligence was able to predict the timing and planning of the Rising almost two months in advance.

The British military authorities in Cork used underhand means to have Seán O'Hegarty appointed as Commandant of the Cork No. 1 Brigade, a situation that suited the military 'exceedingly well'. Clearly, they wanted O'Hegarty or someone close to him to be at the heart of republican activities in Cork.

There is no good reason for suspicion to fall directly on O'Hegarty himself, other than the fact that the British authorities claimed he was not a brave man and that he was largely concerned with saving his own skin. He may, however, have been compromised.

From the arrest of Terence MacSwiney to the abortive attempt to import arms from Genoa, from the kidnapping of Reggie Brown to the evidence of Pat Margetts there are many reasons for believing that O'Donoghue in his published and unpublished accounts was being economical with the truth.

According to O'Donoghue himself, he did not join the Volunteers until the spring of 1917 and was not inducted into the IRB until 1918. Given this, he could not possibly be the same person as the 'reliable informant' who was providing information to Joseph Byrne from August 1916 and probably to the War Office from before that. This, however, is predicated on O'Donoghue having told the truth about himself and how and when he got into the movement.

In short, we have a conundrum. A 'reliable informant', a person with inside information on the IRB and the Volunteers, was reporting to the War Office, perhaps as early as 1914. O'Donoghue stated that he joined the Volunteers only in the early spring of 1917. So they could not possibly be the same person. Or could they? The rest of the book will concern itself with attempting to solve this conundrum.

But before we do that, we first have to look at something O'Donoghue seemed to have very little involvement with, yet it is something about which he had much to say and, since what he had to say was largely an attempt to overturn the evidence of reliable witnesses, it is worth looking at. This was the German attempt to land arms in Tralee on Good Friday 1916.

12

Our Gallant Allies in Europe

What can be said about the British approach to what they called the 'Irish Question' – how do you satisfy the demands of nationalists and unionists at the same time? – is that it vacillated on an almost weekly basis between repression and concession. The government's policy could be draconian one day, with many arrests, and the next day all those arrested might be let go. So, *inter alia* the British government's policy in Ireland was for much of the campaign one of confusion. But an increasingly active campaign by the IRA could never be completely stamped out short of using the most brutal of methods.

However, what could be controlled was the IRA's supply lines. And so one of the key elements of British military strategy on Ireland was to prevent, if possible, the landing of arms on a large scale into Ireland. The considerable focus of British intelligence, the Foreign Office, the Royal Navy's domination of the high seas, and a complex network of spies in ports and railway companies and agents placed in a variety of countries, all worked together in an effort to prevent the smuggling of arms. As we saw in the case of the planned importation of arms from Italy, the British were successful in this. If a huge influx of guns, such as the Genoa consignment, had gone ahead, the IRA would have been able to fight on for a decade or more. An army may march on its belly, but without ordnance that marching is futile.

The RIC records of the Dublin Castle administration over the revolutionary period contain ten large files devoted to the illegal importation and distribution of arms.[22] The best known of these

---

[22] These can be found in TNA CO 904/28 and TNA CO 904/29.

attempts, however, was the failure of the German Navy to land some 20,000 rifles and ammunition in Tralee Bay for the 1916 rebellion. It is necessary for us to look at this in some detail because it was something on which Florrie O'Donoghue wrote several detailed articles, and what he wrote about it tells us more about him than a hundred contended accounts of events during the War of Independence, especially since he was not personally involved. Indeed, his interventions on this topic point firmly in the direction of his true allegiances.

The story of Sir Roger Casement and the ship, the *Aud*, are well known. On Good Friday 1916, a few days before the Easter Rising, Sir Roger Casement and two still technically serving British soldiers, Robert Monteith and Daniel Bailey, came ashore from German submarine *U-19* at Banna Strand near the village of Ardfert in north Kerry. Casement intended to go into Tralee and link up with the local Volunteer command whom he believed were ready to meet him and to accept the arms and distribute them through the South for the planned Rising which was to be nationwide.[23] Owing to a series of mishaps and misunderstandings, the arms landing never took place, even though *U-19* and the *Aud*, the ship containing the guns, arrived almost exactly according to plan, despite the substantial naval blockade of the British Isles on account of the war.

The plan was to land the arms at Fenit pier and move them inland. The Volunteers on shore, however, were not expecting the arms to be delivered until Easter Monday night when the insurrection was scheduled to begin. Karl Spindler, captain of the *Aud*, a German steamer flying under the Norwegian flag, was unable to make contact with anyone on land. After 24 hours in Tralee Bay, Spindler abandoned his plans and went back out to sea. He was intercepted by a flotilla of British warships and escorted to Queenstown (now Cobh, Co. Cork) where he scuttled the *Aud* in the mouth of Cork Harbour. Meanwhile back in Tralee, Casement had been arrested by the RIC and identified. The whole episode ended in ignominy. Casement was tried for treason

---

[23] This is what Casement stated in the last letter he wrote before he left the submarine. Letter to Captain Heydell, 20 April 1916. Appendix in Karl Spindler's book *The Mystery of the Casement Ship* (Tralee, 1965). However, some believe he was trying to prevent the rebellion taking place. Since this debate is outside the remit of this book, I will not deal with it.

and hanged at Pentonville prison. Spindler and his crew were held, first at Queenstown before being transferred by marine escort to Chatham barracks in Kent where the captain was held for interrogation before being moved to a PoW camp in Derbyshire.[24]

Most accounts of the fiasco suggest that it was Sergeant Daniel Bailey, one of the two men who landed with Casement, who identified him to the RIC. Bailey was charged, along with Casement, with high treason at Bow Street magistrates' court and remanded for trial at the Old Bailey. Casement was found guilty, condemned to death and executed on 2 August 1916. Bailey was found not guilty and was released, though compulsorily retained in the army under the Conscription Act. He subsequently served with the Wiltshire Regiment, the Royal North Lancashire Regiment and the Royal Engineer Transportation (Railways) service, serving with these units in East Africa and the Middle East.[25]

However, Casement had already identified himself to the RIC. Indeed, he had been charged with gun-running in Ardfert RIC barracks within hours of being captured – and 24 hours before Bailey was arrested. Once he was taken to the larger RIC barracks in Tralee, he was further identified by the Head Constable from newspaper photographs and again admitted who he was.[26] Bailey, who was captured at Abbeydorney the following afternoon, filled in the rest of the details and confirmed what the police believed about the planned rising and that the arms ship they were expecting was to land at Fenit.[27] While Bailey takes most of the blame for betraying Casement, it is clear that the RIC knew that the gun running was taking place well before Bailey was captured.

An enormous amount has been written about the Casement affair, about what was or was not known by the various participants and how the various mishaps occurred. Effectively what happened was that Room 40, the Admiralty's decoding office in London, had long been

---

[24] Karl Spindler, *The Mystery of the Casement Ship*.

[25] Daniel Bailey service record, regimental numbers 7483, 31447, 26418, 272845 and WS.143247, Ancestry.com. There is a useful summary of Bailey's service record on the website of the Royal Irish Regiment, available online. Also see Michael J. Kehoe BMH WS741 for Bailey's background in the Irish Brigade.

[26] T. Ryle Dwyer, *Tans, Terror and Trouble, Kerry's Real Fighting Story 1913-23*(Cork, 2001) p.78.

[27] T. Ryle Dwyer, op.cit.

able to intercept and decipher cables passing between the German Embassy in Washington and Berlin. (These went through Buenos Aires because the Germans believed this route to be more secure.) Casement, who had left the United States in 1915 and went by circuitous routes to Germany, was in turn compromised by his lover, a Norwegian sailor called Adler Christensen, whom he had picked up in New York and who accompanied him to Germany. The British Foreign Office and the Admiralty knew almost as much about Casement as he knew about himself – some might even argue that they knew more. They had been tracking his movements and his contacts for years. By the spring of 1916, in the words of Sir William James, the previous head of Admiralty intelligence: 'Hall [Captain W.R. 'Blinker' Hall of Room 40 fame] was able to follow every one of the plotters and during the week before Easter was watching eagerly for the message with the password that would mean that Casement and the arms had sailed.' 'The tracking of the submarine carrying Casement and his two companions was not difficult.'[28]

Furthermore, the mission was beset with mishaps from the moment it arrived off the Kerry coast. Submarine *U-19* failed to identify the *Aud* and the *Aud* for its part never realized that the sub was nearby, though they had made a rendezvous a few days earlier out in the North Atlantic. Both headed back out to sea in ignorance of each other. Three Volunteers on their way to collect a wireless transmitter from Cahirciveen in order to make contact with the *Aud*, drove off a pier near Killorglin and were drowned – even though that exercise was a waste of time since the *Aud* had no wireless facilities anyway. Casement himself was thrown into the sea when the boat in which he was landing capsized and, being of a delicate constitution, was badly shook up as a result. The controversy about what happened on Good Friday 1916 and who was to blame for the various mistakes ran on for decades. However, the release of the material in the Bureau of Military History allows us to put together a good picture of what happened.

When Casement landed, his intention was to go straight to Tralee to meet up with the Volunteers. Instead, after his drenching in the sea, he hid in an old fort, McKenna's Fort, to recover while he sent his two companions into Tralee. The police quickly discovered Casement hiding

---

[28] Admiral Sir William James, *The Eyes of the Navy*, (London, 1955), p.111.

in the fort and soon found out that two other men had landed with him because all three had been seen around dawn by a local girl when she was bringing in cows. Casement gave his name as Richard Morton, a writer from Buckinghamshire, and claimed he was engaged in writing a life of St Brendan the Navigator.[29]

In the meantime, Monteith managed to contact Austin Stack, the local Volunteer commandant whose responsibility it was to land the arms and begin the insurrection on the Monday. Stack then took one of the more bizarre decisions of a bizarre weekend: he walked into the RIC barracks in Tralee with a sheaf of incriminating documentation on him, against the advice of his colleagues – so that he would be arrested – which he duly was. This effectively presented the police with any details they had not known up to this point. Stack was arrested, charged and ultimately sent to Frongoch internment camp in Wales.

There has been much debate over the years whether Stack could or should have rescued Casement – it appears it would have been quite easy to do so. However, Stack claimed that his orders were that no armed action should take place until the Monday and, since he was sure Casement would not be identified, he did not see the need to do as he thought Casement could have been rescued once the insurrection began – not a very convincing argument. Stack's own arrest put paid to all that. When Bailey, an expert in signals and Morse, was arrested the next day, the game was up. The British now knew all they needed to know.[30]
[31]

---

[29] Constable Bernard Reilly, BMH WS549.

[30] So the question is, as has often been claimed, had Bailey been a British mole all along? His subsequent behaviour suggests that at the very least he was at one with the majority of his fellow PoWs in Germany, that is to say his first loyalty was to the British army. He was asked to join the expedition on the suggestion of Monteith who wanted him along for his experience in signals and Morse. Bailey had been a corporal of signals with his regiment. According to F. E. Smith, the Attorney General (later Lord Birkenhead), at Casement's trial, who surprised the court by dropping the charges against Bailey, he 'was a private soldier of humble origin' who had made a statement on his arrest when he said that he was not, and had never been, a traitor to his country or to the army. 'He had joined the Irish Brigade with one object only – namely to return by a subterfuge to the army. He wanted to escape from the hardship and inactivity of his captivity. It was impossible to know what the motives might be that actuated a man – inference and conjecture were the only guides.' Smith decided

What is of interest to us here is to compare what Karl Spindler, the captain of the *Aud*, who wrote about the events of that weekend – originally published in German in book form in 1931 – with what O'Donoghue said about the same events in the very detailed preface he wrote to an Irish edition of Spindler's book which was reissued on the run-up to the fiftieth anniversary of the 1916 Rising.

It is quite clear from Spindler's account that if Bailey had given Casement away, he was only the tip of the iceberg of what the British knew about the affair. Spindler leaves little doubt that the British Admiralty was well aware that an arms landing was about to take place on the west coast of Ireland and that the Navy knew what the *Aud* was up to all along, even if they did overestimate her ability to fight back. Spindler's account of his encounters with British gunboats in his round-about voyage from Lubeck to Tralee – he went as far north as the Arctic Circle at one stage – has an almost comical air to it. On several occasions British warships of various kinds pulled up alongside him, had a quick look and steamed away again. 'Our luck in this respect began to seem a little uncanny,' Spindler wrote. 'Could there be something behind it? Did the British know of our coming?'[32] In subsequent conversations with British officers after his capture, he was told that the British warships were afraid that the *Aud* was heavily armed and guarded by submarines – which accounted for their erratic behaviour; they tended to zig-zag around the ship for fear of torpedoes. But they knew what she was doing – and they knew there were submarines involved.

'to offer no evidence, so that the jury might enter a verdict of acquittal.' Jeff Dudgeon, Casement's War, *Dublin Review of Books*, Issue 31, March 2013.

[31] If Bailey was an agent, he would have to been recruited from within the PoW camp in which he was held, which seems unlikely, though not impossible. He claimed in the statement he made to the police that he did not know in advance what was going on. He did, however, state that 'I heard that Dublin Castle was to be raided', so he had some foreknowledge. In any case, he was acquitted either because Smith decided he did not want to dilute the case against Casement by too much debate over the issue of Bailey or because he did not want to bring before the court evidence that might suggest that Bailey had been working for British Intelligence all along. Dudgeon, *op.cit.*

[32] Spindler op.cit., p.86.

Unfortunately, it became quite clear to me in the course of the examination that the British not only had got wind of the arrival of the *Libau* [the *Aud*'s German name], but that they possessed exact information. Their information on the preparation for the expedition was particularly accurate. There were traitors and spies at work! I cudgelled my brain in vain to think where they got their information. From what the British told me of my sojourn in the different German ports and in Berlin I concluded that a spy was following every step I took at that time. It was a complete mystery to me.[33]

So it is clear that British intelligence had been very active in Germany during the preparation for the voyage.[34] Bernard Reilly, one of the RIC constables who arrested Casement, got a statement from a crew member of a Royal Navy sloop who boarded the *Aud* in Tralee Bay – to the effect that they knew all along what the vessel was up to.[35] However, they played along with Spindler's claim that he was a Norwegian sailor, though he was told by the petty officer that 'we were sent here a couple of weeks ago from Aberdeen, mainly in order to intercept a German steamer which is expected to arrive here at any moment . . . . You Norwegians are good fellows, so there is no harm in telling you. Well, the naval authorities have discovered that the Germans want to join the Irish in bringing about a revolution. That is why we are here, in order to capture the auxiliary cruiser which is to come in here and bring arms for the Irish.'[36]

Spindler's first edition of his book was something of a success, being translated into English, Russian, French, Italian and Spanish. In the new edition, published in 1965, O'Donoghue in his preface 'presents a new and impartial study of the attempt to land the arms from Germany, based in part on materials not hitherto available. . . . It gives an illuminating interpretation of the events connected to the negotiations for the importation of the arms and the reasons for the failure of the enterprise.'

---

[33] Spindler, op.cit., p.138.

[34] There is a fascinating account provided to MI5 by an Admiralty agent working undercover in Germany in 1915. 'I have a good plan by which the whole operation can be rooted out and shall be pleased to lay it before the Admiralty, but I would like to be the principal actor in the business.' 'Confidential letter, copy to V.F. Hay', 15 May 1915, Sir Roger Casement intelligence file, TNA KV2/6.

[35] Appendix to Bernard Reilly, BMH WS 549.

[36] Spindler, op.cit., p.110.

Far from being new and impartial, however, O'Donoghue's effort achieves only one thing: it goes to extraordinary lengths to downplay the role of British Intelligence in the affair. His conclusions were that:

Apart from a single espionage report, probably from the continent, British intelligence appears to have no knowledge of Captain Spindler's mission. That isolated report was regarded with scepticism. On the basis of any known evidence it seems probable that the *Aud* masqueraded successfully as a Norwegian tramp steamer and that it was only her enforced wait in Tralee bay combined with the suspicions aroused by Casement's landing and arrest, which alerted the British authorities and led to her capture. . . .
. . . These observations are not made in any spirit of criticism but rather in an effort to present the facts fairly and readjust the unbalanced picture which Captain Spindler conveys.[37]

It is clear from O'Donoghue's foreword, which smacks of the factoid-seeking pedantry you find in 'contested history', that he is trying to muddy the waters in an effort to play down the amount of knowledge that British authorities had in advance of the attempted landing. For instance, he informs us that: 'Although a few British writers have stated, with a fine show of assurance, that the *Aud* was under continuous observation by naval patrols from beginning to end of her voyage' that this information, based on a British publication *Documents Relative to the Sinn Fein Movement* could have been culled after the event from German archives, which would have been available to British intelligence once the war was over. However, that does not negate the fact that Spindler was effectively told that the British were onto him, nor does it negate the entire trust of Spindler's book which practically says the same thing. Nor does it negate the *Documents Relative to the Sinn Fein Movement*, published in 1921 and the product of HM's own Stationery Office, which are accurate transcripts of the 30-odd telegrams that passed between Washington and Berlin, and along with the evidence of the 'very reliable informant' in Ireland, which predicted the Rising down to the very day it was to take place. It is clear that in this instance O'Donoghue was engaged in a doubt-creating exercise.

Not only that, but it is clear from O'Donoghue's private notebooks that he had done significant research into the circumstances of the

---

[37] O'Donoghue, Foreword to Spindler, op.cit.

landing and had even carried out a detailed analysis of Admiral Sir William James's account of these events, which show in unambiguous detail just how much the Admiralty and Foreign Office knew in advance about Casement's plans.[38] Yet he ignores this entirely. Instead, he focuses on the fact that Dublin Castle was not aware of the impending rebellion in Dublin almost until it took place, to suggest that they knew nothing about the gun-running either. He quotes from the evidence given at the Royal Commission into the Rising to the effect that Dublin Castle effectively ignored a warning from the Admiralty, given to them through the G.O.C. Dublin, that the Admiralty was aware that a German ship, equipped as a neutral, was heading to Ireland laden with arms. 'The information had been given to General Stafford by the Admiralty in Queenstown who had received it from the Admiralty, London. And the Admiralty was sceptical of its reliability.' Not so sceptical, though, that they did not send out navy vessels to keep a watch on the *Aud* across half the North Atlantic or that the Navy was put on warning along the Kerry/Clare coast on 14 April to watch out for submarines accompanying a steamer intent on landing arms and ammunition 'expected to be in connection with a rising which will take place around Easter'.[39] Naval officers were instructed not to go on land in pursuit of the weapons, since clearly the RIC and military were already on their guard in the south and south-west in anticipation of the expected landing. Just because Dublin Castle ignored the warning did not mean that the Admiralty or the military based in Queenstown ignored it, as O'Donoghue suggests.

He also endeavours to undermine the account given by a 'Mr A. Cotton', as O'Donoghue calls him, in *Kerry's Fighting Story*, published in 1949. Cotton stated, according to O'Donoghue, that he and Austin Stack had visited Patrick Pearse in St Enda's in Rathfarnam 'in the fall of 1915' and that Pearse had outlined to them that a Rising was planned for Easter 1916 and that arrangements had been made to land arms at Fenit. 'It is a matter of historical fact that the date of the rising had not been fixed 'in the fall of 1915'. How then could Pearse have given it?' O'Donoghue asks. 'The proposal to land the arms at Fenit was not made

---

[38] O'Donoghue Notebook, O'Donoghue Papers, NLI Ms 31,421(2).
[39] Orders dated 14 and 16 April 1916 to SNO Galway and Berehaven and to CO HMS Safeguard. TNA ADM 137/1187.

until March 23.' O'Donoghue dismisses Cotton's article on the basis that the decision to land at Fenit was not made until the latter date. He then goes on to rubbish the entire Cotton account: 'The absurdity of these claims very much discount the value of many other similarly improbable statements made by Mr Cotton in his article.'[40] 23 March was the very day that the Director of Military Intelligence, General George Macdonogh, informed Prime Minister Asquith that 'he had received information from an absolutely reliable source that a rising in Ireland was contemplated at an early date' – 22 April 1916. Or that two weeks earlier similar information had been received by the military from an informant in Ireland to the same effect? So not only was the date set before 23 March, but even the Director of Military Intelligence in London was aware of it by then.[41]

So who was 'Mr A. Cotton' and what were the 'absurd' and 'improbable' statements he made? Alf Cotton was a Belfast Protestant and IRB organizer. He was a civil servant in the labour exchange and was moved to County Kerry in 1914.[42] As captain of the Tralee cycle corps of the Volunteers, he went around the county carrying out work for the IRB and appears to have been an effective organizer and drill master.[43] Threatened with being dismissed from his post as a result of his Volunteer work, he was 'deported' by the authorities to Belfast in early 1916, which is where he was based by the time the Rising broke out in Dublin. Austin Stack also tried to smear Cotton by suggesting that he should have returned to Tralee at the time of the arms landing. But Seán MacDiarmada had ordered Cotton not to return to Kerry since his identity, which was known to the RIC, could jeopardize the entire operation. Cotton opted instead to make his way to the GPO in Dublin and the Rising itself. It is clear that Stack was trying to blame Cotton for his own incompetence.[44] As Cotton put it:

---

[40] Foreword to Spindler's book, p19-20.
[41] See Chapter 1.
[42] Alfred Cotton, BMH WS184.
[43] Sinead Joy, *The Fight for Independence in Iveragh, 1914-22*. In John Crowley, John Sheehan, and Mike Murphy, *The Iveragh Peninsula, A Cultural Atlas of the Ring of Kerry* (Cork, 2009).
[44] Una Stack, BMH WS214.

Some time in the fall of 1915, I accompanied Austin Stack who was the commandant of the Kerry Volunteers to an interview with P.H. Pearse at St Enda's, Rathfarnam. Having impressed on us the need for absolute secrecy Pearse informed us that a Rising had been planned for Easter 1916. He then stated that arrangements had been made with Germany to send rifles, machine guns and ammunition to Tralee Bay. We would make the local arrangements for the reception and distribution of the armaments. The plans decided upon for the Rising were not given to us in detail but merely a general outline of what was intended. [45]

Cotton subsequently updated this in his Bureau of Military History account because he said he had checked out some minor details and that the BMH statement should now be regarded as the 'authoritative document'. However, in its essentials the account remains the same. What's more, Cotton gives significant extra details of the meeting with Pearse in the BMH account which make it more convincing, and it reads as if he was telling the truth.[46]

Pearse told Stack and myself that night, under promise of absolute secrecy that:
The date of the Rising had been fixed for Easter.
That a cargo of arms would arrive at Fenit pier from Germany and that we were to make arrangements for their reception and distribution, and
That we were to arrange for a message to be sent from the Cable Station at Valentia that the Rising had taken place, so as to broadcast the news through America.

The main change from the *Kerry's Fighting Story* version is the date of the visit 'which I am unable to fix definitely but may have been at the end of 1915 or early 1916'. So Cotton's mistake was that he may have got the date of the meeting with Pearse wrong. Yet O'Donoghue uses this to rubbish Cotton's entire article. Common sense suggests that Pearse would have had to meet with Stack on this matter at some point, so the meeting would have to take place anyway, though later than Cotton initially remembered.

Cotton goes into more detail on this in his BMH statement:

Stack and I returned to Tralee . . . I accompanied Stack to Caherciveen where he interviewed some persons in connection with the task of having a cable announcing the Rising sent from Valentia Cable Station. I cannot, however, at present state who

---

[45] A. Cotton in *Kerry's Fighting Story* pp. 46-53 (Tralee, 1949).
[46] Alfred Cotton, BMH WS184.

the men Stack saw were – I think it was Ring or Keating – or the result of their conversation beyond the fact that everything was arranged.[47]

In other words, Kerry-based Volunteer officers knew a lot about the proposed landing and they knew of it well in advance of the Rising. Even the attempt to broadcast the news to America took place. Tim Ring, an operator at the Cable Station in Valentia and a Volunteer, did broadcast news of the Rising to America and was subsequently sent to Frongoch for his trouble.[48]

However, it is on the subject of the troubled journey by the wireless operators to Cahirciveen, in which three of them were drowned, that O'Donoghue shows himself at his most disingenuous. It appears that Mac Diarmada and Joseph Plunkett, the IRB leaders in Dublin, were concerned to try to contact the *Aud*, so they sent five men to Cahirciveen to steal a wireless transmitter from the Wireless College run by radio engineer Maurice Fitzgerald, to bring it to Tralee and use it to contact the *Aud* – a futile exercise since, as we have seen, the *Aud* had no wireless. In O'Donoghue's account:

For the purpose of making contact with the arms ship a group comprising Denis Daly, Con Keating, Dan Sheehan, Charles Monahan and Colum O'Lochlainn was sent from Dublin to Kerry on Good Friday. Its mission was to commandeer a wireless transmitting and receiving set from Maurice Fitzgerald's Wireless College in Caherciveen, take it to Ballyard near Tralee where it was to be set up and operated by Con Keating. He was the only wireless expert in the group, although Sheehan and Monahan may have had some experience . . . .

At Killarney the party was met by two cars sent from Limerick and they set out for Caherciveen. Daly and O'Lochlainn travelled in the leading car, Keating, Monahan and Sheehan in the other which was driven by Tom MacInerney. On the way to Killorglin they lost touch. The occupants of the leading car assumed the other had taken the Beaufort road which Keating, a native of Caherciveen, would have known. The first car went to Caherciveen but when the second car did not arrive, Daly and O'Lochlainn were helpless. Neither was a wireless expert. After waiting a long time they returned to Killarney and caught the morning train to Dublin.

The second car had unfortunately taken a wrong turning in Killorglin and in the darkness went over the pier at Ballykissane into the sea. Keating, Sheehan and Monahan were drowned; MacInerney managed to struggle ashore.

---

[47] Alfred Cotton, op.cit.
[48] Sinead Joy, op.cit.

119

This account is broadly true. However, O'Donoghue conveys the impression – without actually saying so – that the cars travelled towards Caherciveen by different routes, Keating taking 'the Beaufort route' because, 'as a native of Caherciveen', he would have known the road. However, Denis Daly was also a native of Caherciveen and he would also have known it. Besides, the Beaufort route is the most feasible way to Cahirciveen from Killarney, apart from going the other way round the Ring of Kerry which is much longer and at that time involved traversing difficult mountain passes on bad roads. In fact, both cars were travelling together and were supposed to stay within headlight distance of each other.[49]

O'Donoghue states that there were six men in the cars, two in the car that got to Cahirciveen and four in the one that went over the pier. However, there were seven in total, five IRB men and two drivers. O'Donoghue mentions only one of these, Tom McInerney, the driver of the car that went into the sea. The driver of the other car, one Sam Windrim, O'Donoghue, oddly, does not mention. Since O'Donoghue's account is based on the Bureau of Military History statement of Denis Daly, taken by O'Donoghue in 1948, and since Daly mentions Windrim as the driver of the second car, it seems rather odd that O'Donoghue would not at least name him as being one of those involved.[50] This is not mere pedantry. Rather, it may be related to the fact that Windrim himself left a detailed account of the events of that evening.[51]

Windrim, who was from Limerick, left a convincing account, and the impression it conveys is that the RIC were out in force and were aware both that important IRB men were arriving in Killarney by train on the Good Friday and that cars from Limerick were coming to collect them. Windrim was told that his orders were that he was to help in a gun-running venture but no specifics were given – he received no further information and his account suggests that he never even learned the

---

[49] T. Ryle Dwyer, op.cit.

[50] Denis Daly, BMH WS 110.

[51] Windrim's account is given as an appendix to James A. Gubbins, BMH WS 765, and was in response to 'criticism' Gubbins received for a paper he delivered on Limerick's part in the Rising. Gubbins was setting the record straight by including Windrim's paper with his own.

names of his passengers or the passengers in the other car or what their real purpose was.[52]

He paints a picture of very significant surveillance though, especially given that rural Ireland in 1916 was a sleepy place and security cordons were rare occurrences. Windrim states that there was a large cordon of RIC armed with rifles blocking the road at Newcastlewest and another group holding up traffic at Abbeyfeale. Both sets of police waved the cars from Limerick through after taking their (false) details. Once Windrim met Daly and O'Lochlainn at Killarney station he noticed a railway porter attending a lamp watching them and moved away so that they would not be overheard. Before the two cars set off for Caherciveen, he noticed something else: 'I remarked that it was strange we did not see a policeman in Killarney considering their activities all along the road from Limerick.' The reason for this became apparent when Windrim returned the following day and was told by a shop owner he knew that 'two loads of police had followed us out of the town the night before'.

As for the ill-fated journey to Caherciveen, both cars travelled together on the Beaufort route, with Windrim leading. Windrim made a slight detour on coming into Killorglin, but, other than that, the cars were in tandem. Two policemen standing at the door of the RIC barracks at Killorglin made an attempt to stop them but Windrim sped past. 'This incident made all in the car feel that should Tommy's car be still behind us that it would in all probability be held up.' (Windrim thought that while he was taking the slight detour the other car might have gone ahead of him through Killorglin.) He was also afraid he might be followed by the RIC, but that did not happen.

Later, coming into Caherciveen, they were held up by two RIC men with revolvers drawn who questioned them but let them through without searching the car. Then, to his surprise, Daly and O'Lochlainn ordered him to drive on to Waterville. At some point along the country road they asked Windrim to stop and they threw the materials they were carrying, including a long coil of wire, over a ditch. Eventually, lost in the darkness of the countryside – it was a grim rainy night – they decided to try to make their way back to Killarney without having completed the task they had set out to accomplish. After some mishaps, Windrim got

---

[52] James A. Gubbins, BMH WS 765.

his passengers back to Killarney and onto the Dublin train. Before they left, they gave him some money and he went for something to eat. While eating, he was questioned by yet another RIC man. The next day the car broke down and Windrim had to return to Limerick by train; he read in the *Cork Examiner* about the drowning of the men in the second car. He was arrested on the Sunday by the RIC in Limerick on a charge of gun-running 'by Order of the Naval Officer Commanding Queenstown'.

This tells us the on-land equivalent of what Spindler's book tells us: that the authorities – in this case the RIC doing the Admiralty's bidding – had advance and detailed notice of the arms landing. The authorities in Dublin Castle may have been tardy when it came to the Easter Rising but the Admiralty and military in Queenstown were not and this is something that, for whatever reason, Florrie O'Donoghue does not want us to know. As for the fate of the men in the second car, it was almost certainly an accident. Tom MacInerney, the only man to escape, told the car owner that it was a girl who directed them over the pier in the dark.[53] Yet the RIC in Killorglin were out; the cars were being followed by two other 'loads' of policemen according to Windrim. The RIC arrived on the scene soon after the car went over the pier. Con Keating was a native of Caherciveen and would have regularly passed through Killorglin. Would he have taken a wrong turn? There is no direct evidence for police involvement in the drowning, yet all the RIC would have had to do was block the Cahirciveen exit from the village after the first car passed and the second car would have been directed straight to the pier.

Taken altogether, O'Donoghue's 'new and impartial study', which strives to tell us that British intelligence knew next to nothing in advance about the landing of arms from the *Aud* and that they stumbled upon it only as a result of Casement's capture, is in fact the direct opposite of what happened. There is a clear intention to discredit the account of Alf Cotton and to cast doubt on Spindler's book, Admiral Oliver's memoirs and Windrim's BMH account, which deal with how much was known in advance about the matter. It is now accepted that British Naval Intelligence had cracked the telegraphic code between the German Foreign Office and its embassy in Washington and had been

---

[53] John J. Quilty, BMH WS516.

122

tracking Casement for many months, something that Spindler was even able to establish to the extent of publishing some of the telegrams.[54] The Director of Military Intelligence, General Macdonogh, also knew about it. Yet O'Donoghue is trying to tell us that the Admiralty, 'except for one espionage report' – the Admiralty was 'sceptical of its reliability' – knew very little about the landing and that the RIC knew nothing about it until they more or less accidentally stumbled upon Casement near Banna. This is obviously some sort of cover-up. But the bigger question is why O'Donoghue, who, according to his own accounts, did not join the Volunteers until at least nine months later, should pen such a statement and pass it off as definitive. Why would he even bother to put out such a denial of what, even then, were known truths, especially when he evidently could have had nothing to do with the affair himself.?

It is clear that O'Donoghue's motivation in writing about the Casement landing was to play down the role of British intelligence in the affair and that this is part of his overall attempt to convey the impression of British intelligence incompetence – an impression that has taken in the majority of historians. In the process, he manages to point the finger of blame at Alf Cotton, a Protestant and an outsider, while leaving no hint of Austin Stack's far more serious breach of security in walking into RIC custody with a sheaf of Volunteer documentation. As a doubt-creating exercise, it is a model of its kind. There are things O'Donoghue does not want us to know, and the success of British Intelligence in tracking down Roger Casement is one of them.

---

[54] Eunan O'Halpin, 'British Intelligence in Ireland, 1914-1921' in C. Andrew and D. Dilks (eds), *The Missing Dimension* (Illinois, 1984). Christopher Andrew, 'The Irish Debacle' in *Secret Service: The Making of the British Intelligence Community* (London, 1985). Paul McMahon, *British Spies and Irish Rebels* (London, 2008) pp. 17-22.

Part II

Some Unexpected Answers

13

'The *Sayonara* will be leaving the coast at the end of the month'

There are a number of documents in O'Donoghue's papers which strongly suggest a connection to British Intelligence. One of the oddest items is a list of alleged loyalist 'spies' operating around the Irish coast and reporting to the authorities through the Governor of the Bank of Ireland. This has been used by several Irish historians as 'proof' that there was spy ring amongst Protestant loyalists during the War of Independence who were supposedly spying on IRA activities and passing information on to the British. However, this interpretation is, to say the very least, wrong-headed, since it should be clear, from a cursory examination of the document, that was written in the winter of 1914/15 rather than in 1920/21, as these writers claim. In other words, it was written at a time when the IRA did not even exist.

The list of alleged 'spies' was real enough in its time though. It details an organization of loyalists calling itself the Irish Coast Intelligence Corps, which took upon itself the monitoring of Irish coastal waters for German naval activity during the early years of the Great War. Considering that Britain was at war with Germany and the damage inflicted on shipping by German U Boats was severe, the activities of the Irish Coast Intelligence Corps amounted to nothing more sinister than helping the war effort.

But what is the document doing in O'Donoghuc's papers? Because what its presence implies – and the document is almost certainly genuine – is that either O'Donoghue himself or someone very close to him was involved with, or reporting to, British military or naval intelligence in the winter of 1914/15.[1] The document consists of two pages of correspondence between the Admiralty in Queenstown (Cobh) and Captain Reginald 'Blinker' Hall, the Director of Naval Intelligence at the Admiralty in London. The correspondence arises out of inquiries about the activities of this unofficial intelligence-gathering organization. It claims that such a group operated and gives a list of those involved, stating that they reported through the Governor of the Bank of Ireland, who at the time was a member of the Guinness family – all perfectly patriotic at the time, one might think.

The document is an epitome of correspondence between the Admiralty in Queenstown and 'Blinker' Hall:

Queenstown:

Persons are going around the coast stating they belong to the Irish Coast Intelligence Corps. Please inform me if there is such a Corps and is it acting under your orders?

Admiralty:

I do understand there is a private organization around the coast but it is not under my orders and has not Official status. The organization has at times sent me certain information which has proved accurate and useful. I can, if you wish, supply you confidentially with a list of names.

Queenstown:

The organization overlaps somewhat with the Military Patrols and representations on the subject have been made to me. I should be glad of their names though I possess some.

Admiralty:

Herewith is a list so far as I know it. I don't think you'll find they call themselves anything. I understand they very much wish not to be known. I confess that in England and Scotland the civilian help has been most useful, and I have found the same in Ireland. You may feel assured that I have satted [*sic*] no official organization in Ireland, and am only making use of their services through a third party. You know that the Admiralty commanding Coastguards and Reserves is starting a coast watch in certain parts. I am afraid the *Viknor* has gone down. She had some very important prisoners on board and I badly wanted their papers. The *Saymara* [*sic*] will be leaving the coast at the end of the month.

R.W. Hall

Secret

---

[1] Correspondence re. 'Irish Coast Intelligence Corps' O'Donoghue NLI Ms 31,223 (1).

128

In the counties of Donegal, Derry, Antrim and Down the officers of the Ulster Volunteer force are at our disposal but are not aware of the objects or details of the scheme.

In the counties of Cork and Waterford there are several Agents who write to me through the Governor of the Bank of Ireland – **who do not wish their names disclosed** [bold in original].

The document can be dated precisely because it mentions in passing that the 'Saymara [sic] will be leaving the coast at the end of the month' and that 'the Viknor has gone down'. HMS Viknor sank in heavy seas off County Donegal on 13 January 1915, with the loss of all 406 passengers and crew. [2] The Sayonara, a British yacht being used for spying, left Irish coastal waters in February 1915. This means the document was written around the end of January 1915.[3]

What follows is a list of some 55 names of those civilians involved in the Coastal Intelligence Corps around Ireland. All were prominent loyalists, many of them Justices of the Peace, Deputy Lieutenants and some clergymen, living around the coast – what might be called the core of late Edwardian Irish loyalism. Among the names is one very interesting one: Rodger [sic] Hall of Narrow Water, Warrenpoint, County Down. Roger Hall was a brother of Frank Hall, who ran Kell's MI5's 'g' section and who had responsibility within MI5 for Ireland.

'I believe the 'Saymara' [sic] will be leaving the coast at the end of the month'. The Sayonara was a steam yacht, sent by 'Blinker' Hall of Naval Intelligence and Basil Thomson of the Secret Service, to sail casually around the coast of Ireland with a fifty-man crew posing as Americans looking for evidence of German submarine activity. Its captain was one Frederick Murray Simon, an officer of the Royal Naval Reserve, who could do a passable American accent from his time working on Cunard liners.[4] Simon found little evidence of German naval activity and had nothing to do with the tracking of Casement or his capture, which took place over a year later, though that did not stop Hall from claiming that it did.[5]

---

[2] It is said there was an important German spy on board the Viknor, along with six 'stowaways', perhaps the men guarding the spy.

[3] O'Donoghue Papers, NLI Ms 31,223(1).

[4] Christopher Andrew, Secret Service, pp.177-78.

[5] See Andrew, pp.177-80 for a hilarious account of the 'outing' of the Sayonara.

129

The pages contain several other useful pieces of information. The Admiral in Queenstown writes: 'The [loyalist] organization overlaps somewhat with the Military Patrols and representations on the subject have been made to me.' 'Blinker' Hall replies: 'You know that the Admiral commanding Coastguard and Reserves is starting a [similar] coast watch in certain parts.'[6] This tells us two things: that the military were running patrols and that the Admiralty was about to do the same, using the coastguard and the naval reserves. It appears that the Irish Coastal Intelligence Corps was simply the Irish branch of a civilian 'Observer Scheme' that Kell's MI5 was developing in Britain to watch out for German activity.

The army in Ireland, however, also ran a coastal intelligence operation. The Southern Coastal Defence was already being run by the Royal Engineers and Royal Artillery which both had a number of depots around the coast. On the outbreak of war, full-time Royal Engineers were withdrawn from Coastal Defence and moved to the various front lines; their domestic functions now being carried out by local reservists. In Cork, for instance, up to 1914, Coastal Defence had been run by 33 Fortress Company of the Royal Engineers.[7] These were transferred to Salonika during the Greek campaign, their role in Cork now being assumed by the Special Reserve. The Navy was soon carrying out its own patrols, using disguised 'trawlers' and coastal patrol vessels to gather information, several of which were involved in the tracking of Casement. What all this amounts to is that, in addition to the RIC, there were at least three other organizations gathering intelligence along the coast of Ireland by the middle of 1915.

But the real question is: who transcribed the *Sayonara* correspondence and who was he or she working for? It is found among a batch of so-called 'captured documents' which O'Donoghue claimed dated from 1920/21.[8] The usual interpretation is that it was smuggled

---

[6] Correspondence re. 'Irish Coast Intelligence Corps' O'Donoghue NLI Ms 31,223 (1).

[7] *Guy's Postal Directory* Cork, 1913.

[8] O'Donoghue stated that the document was 'a rather interesting document which has come into my hands' around September 1921. 'I believe the thing is old because of reference to certain ships which have gone down but anyway the names are useful.' I/O 1st S. Division to Intell, GHQ, 23 September 1921. Collins Papers, IE/MA/CP/5/2/6. What is interesting about this disclaimer is that it implies familiarity

out of the Admiralty in Cobh in 1920/21 by one of O'Donoghue's agents. While it is clear from IRA intelligence records that the Cork Brigade did manage to place an agent in the Admiralty, this did not happen until the autumn of 1921 when the war with Britain was over.[9] Of course the agent, one Roger Creighton, could have picked it up then. But if that were the case, what was a highly secret and confidential document – a list of actual agents – doing lying around the Admiralty for seven years before it was picked up? And why was no equivalent documentation from 1920/21 found? Creighton was indeed looking for lists of spies but, apparently, 'there was little chance of getting [them].'[10]

The most obvious and likely explanation is that O'Donoghue had the correspondence from the time it was written, that is to say from the winter of 1914/15. If so, how did he get it? According to his own accounts – which we will accept at face value for the moment – he did not join the Volunteers until early 1917 and was not an IRA intelligence officer until 1919.

There is one very strong hint in the document on who the author was working for. Writing of one of the members of the Irish Coastal Intelligence Corps, one Charles Stanley, the author notes: 'See report by Military Intelligence officer attached as to this man's unreliability and drunkancy [sic].'[11] This suggests that the writer was an agent or an officer reporting to military intelligence and that he was working with, or reporting to, a military intelligence officer. Interestingly, the author of the document also appears to have been mildly dyslexic. He spells *Sayonara* incorrectly; he refers to Admiral Coke as Admiral 'Cooke', he refers to 'Blinker' Hall as 'R. W. Hall' rather than W. R. Hall, Roger as

with the *Sayonara*, which was top secret and which had sailed almost seven years earlier. The *Viknor* also had an intelligence connection and included Queenstown based officers among the dead.

[9] Report of interview with Roger Creighton, 8 October 1921. O'Donoghue, NLI Ms 31,207(2). This is a fascinating interview and details how Creighton managed to get information out of the Admiralty in Cobh, though he did not manage to get important material at this point. But it is seven years out of date as regards the *Sayonara* document.

[10] Report of interview with Roger Creighton, 8 October1921. O'Donoghue, NLI Ms 31,207(2).

[11] Correspondence re. 'Irish Coast Intelligence Corps', O'Donoghue Papers, NLI Ms 31,223(1).

131

'Rodger' and coins a new word 'drunkancy' above. [12] There is ample evidence that O'Donoghue was similarly dyslexic.

However, we cannot exclude the possibility that he may have been involved with Naval Intelligence. There are two significant references in Admiralty documentation to the Navy running agents within the Republican movement in 1916. The first concerns reports from Commander, later Admiral, William J. Hicks, who was operating off the County Kerry coast: 'My friend is in touch with the leading Sinn Feiners. I consider this information important . . . .' 'I have the honour to report that I have again come in contact with my friends and they say that the present quietness is only temporary. . . .'[13] 'My source of information is most reliable, as my informant is in the know.'[14] It is clear that the informant was bringing his information directly to Hicks who was patrolling the waters off the south-west of Ireland as commander of HMS *Safeguard*.

The second reference may be more significant. Over a year earlier, on 12 May 1915, in a file entitled 'Securing the Services of an Agent to Obtain Information . . . re Sinn Fein or Pro-German party in Ireland' Admiral Coke, the Vice Admiral commanding the Navy at Queenstown, requested permission and funding for his head of intelligence, William V. Harrel, to take on six agents to penetrate the 'Sinn Fein' movement. They were to be paid at a rate of two pounds and ten shillings a week. Permission and funding were both granted, subject to Harrel informing the Inspector General of the RIC of what he was doing. (The Under-Secretary for Ireland, Sir Matthew Nathan, objected to the proposal on the basis that it would be a waste of time and work on the part of the RIC which spent several months earlier investigating the *Sayanora*, believing it first to have been a German ship, only to be informed later that Hall it had run it from London. Nathan, however, gave in when he was told Harrel would keep the Inspector General informed.)

Moreover, Harrel had somebody specific in mind when he put in his request: 'I am in the position to secure the services of an agent who can

---

[12] Hall's full name was Admiral Sir William Reginald Hall (1870-1943.)

[13] Correspondence in 'Sinn Fein Movements in Ireland', 22 May 1916. TNA ADM 137/1187.

[14] W.J. Hicks, Commander, HMS *Safeguard*, to Vice-Admiral, Queenstown, 12 October 1916. TNA ADM 223/671.

give me reliable information regarding the Sinn Fein or pro-German party at various points around the coast. He has *peculiar facilities* for doing so and has before now done important work in that direction for me.' Harrel suggests that the agent be sent on a few weeks' 'business' tour to gather information.[15] Vice Admiral Coke, 'Blinker' Hall and Sir Matthew Nathan (with some reservations in the last case) all ended up approving of the scheme, and funding was provided, first for the 'reliable' agent and presumably, thereafter, for five others as well.

It is possible that the 'reliable' agent with the 'peculiar facilities' was the same person as the 'very reliable informant' who began reporting to Inspector General Byrne from the autumn of 1916. Harrel did have a significant contact with Cork. His brother, A.G.W. Harrel, was Resident Magistrate for Cork during those years after a career in the RIC – and was to die in Bandon in 1926.[16] It is also interesting to note that William Harrel's own peregrinations to gather information both before and after the 1916 Rising took him over much of the West of Ireland and as far south as Kerry. He did not seem to have had the need to visit Cork, however, suggesting that he already had a source of intelligence there. However, what Harrel was able to gather in advance of the impending Easter Rising was limited. Indeed, he seemed to have been as surprised as anyone else when it took place, while the 'reliable informant' was able to tell the military in London a month earlier of the day and date the Rising was planned to take place. In short, Harrel was doing a lot of huffing and puffing but he did not have the level of detailed information that the Director of Military Intelligence in London had. [17]

In summary, it is not possible at this point to establish for certain whether the writer of the *Sayonara* document was working for military or naval intelligence or whether Harrel's man and the 'very reliable informant' reporting to the Inspector General of the RIC might be one and the same person. It was not uncommon – to the dismay of the intelligence community – for one agent to be paid twice for the same

---

[15] W.V. Harrel to Vice Admiral Commanding Queenstown, 5 May 1915, TNA ADM 223/671.

[16] *Thom's Directory* of 1914 and subsequently.

[17] Harrel was in Kerry the day the *Aud* went down. 'I was in Kerry yesterday. . .' Harrel to Hall, 23 April 1916. Notes by Harrel to Admiralty, 24 October 1917. Both in TNA, ADM 223/671. Also see report of Harrel to Vice Admiral, Queenstown, 3 August 1916. TNA, ADM 137/1187.

information by the simple process of reporting simultaneously to two different branches of the intelligence services. The obvious drawbacks of this kind of thing – the duplication of evidence and its mirror-image multiplication, as well as the waste of money – is something that is regularly commented on in surviving records of the intelligence services.

What we can say, though, is that it is highly likely that O'Donoghue, because he possessed these papers, was either their creator in 1915 or was close to whoever created them. It suggests that O'Donoghue was involved at some level with British intelligence as early as 1915 – if only in the business of being on the look-out for German submarines – and on the look-out for those who were on the look-out for German submarines. It is said that before he died, O'Donoghue conveyed a huge amount of documentation to the flames. What was this documentation? Did it concern IRA matters or perhaps British matters? It is likely that the *Sayonara* document was simply overlooked in O'Donoghue's literary auto-da-fé. Its value was not that it contained a list of so-called Anti-Sinn Féin League spies. Its real value is that he was in possession of such a document in the first place.

14

The Leaked Intelligence Report

Most of those shot in Dublin as spies were actual spies and there is no question that in Dublin, as the cliché has it, Collins was winning the intelligence war. While there were certainly some spies among those shot in Cork, many of them were probably not – or at least there is no evidence that they were and, despite O'Donoghue's claims to the contrary, it is clear that in Cork the IRA was losing the intelligence war. British Intelligence failed to penetrate Collins's circle in Dublin. Collins, Mulcahy and most of the Dublin leadership, despite having huge prices on their heads, survived the War of Independence and managed – just about – to avoid arrest. In Cork city, on the other hand, beginning with Tomás MacCurtain, most of the leadership were gradually whittled away, either killed or arrested over a twelve-month period, apart from O'Donoghue himself and Joe O'Connor and, of course, Seán O'Hegarty, who became Brigade O/C because the British wanted him in this position. British Intelligence – and its undercover hit squads who carried out the actual dirty work – was very effective in Cork. Far from being 'bad, very bad', as O'Donoghue put it, this has all the signs of being a very effective operation. That this blindingly obvious deduction has not been made by historians of the revolution in Cork – with the honourable exceptions of William Sheehan and to a lesser extent Peter Hart – is rather astonishing.

As we saw in the first part of this book, O'Donoghue, like Banquo's ghost, is in the background of many of these operations. He was close, in turn, to MacCurtain, MacSwiney and O'Hegarty, being nearby when the first was shot, the second arrested and the third made commandant with British help. He had been with MacCurtain at Wallaces only an hour before MacCurtain was murdered; he was sharing a bed with

Terence MacSwiney and detailed as part of MacSwiney's security when MacSwiney 'forgot' to bring along the key to the secret passageway in the City Hall which would have allowed him to escape on the night he was captured. He may even have been captured with MacSwiney and then released; he was also nearby when Seán Moylan was captured in north Cork in June 1921 – he ended up with the papers found on Moylan when he was captured, as well as with the letter found on Diarmuid Hurley when he was shot dead by the RIC that indicated which David Walsh had been executed as a spy.[1] Then there is the strange delay over Mick Leahy's passport on the eve of his departure to Genoa, the cover-up that followed, and the fact that British Intelligence was aware of the Genoa project almost from its inception and were in all likelihood tracking Leahy. Why was Wallace's shop not raided and shut down until O'Donoghue went off to west Cork after being allowed to operate as IRA headquarters for the previous two years?[2] Then there are the parallels between what the British knew about the IRB in 1916-19 and O'Donoghue's membership of it, and the fact that the British subsequently stated that they had placed a spy in its ranks. It is possible of course to dismiss all these as mere coincidences, but they mount up. There must surely come a time when a series of coincidences accumulate to the extent that they can no longer be regarded as coincidences.

But is there any specific decision O'Donoghue made – and that we can prove that he made – while in effective charge of the IRA in Cork which we can point to categorically and say that this was in the interests

---

[1] David Walsh, an itinerant ex-soldier, was executed as a spy in Glenville, Co. Cork in May 1921, allegedly for betraying the East Cork column at Clonmult. All the available evidence suggests that, despite the fact that he confessed to the crime – when faced with the choice between an open grave and deportation to Australia – he could not have been present in the Clonmult area around the time of the affray (also see Chapter 3). A photostatted copy of the confession can be found in O'Donoghue's papers, NLI 31,207(2).

[2] This is not strictly true – though the reality was actually worse. Na Fianna member P. J. Murphy recalled how: 'Towards the end of July 1920, information was received that the shop was to be raided by the British just before curfew hour which was 10pm. An ambushing party was detailed to cover both entrances to the street. . . This detail was carried out for three consecutive nights and no sooner withdrawn the third night when the raid took place. No arrests were made. P. J. Murphy, BMH WS 864.

of the British security apparatus? There is one and it sheds a lot of light on how O'Donoghue managed to invert the history of the revolution in Cork to suit his own agenda. In a chapter entitled 'Intelligence and Counter Intelligence' in *No Other Law*, his biography of Liam Lynch, O'Donoghue writes of IRA intelligence: 'In estimating the factors which contributed to the success of the IRA in its operations against Crown Forces, the admitted superiority of its intelligence services, particularly in the eighteen months before the Treaty, must be taken into account.' By contrast, 'quite suddenly, and with shattering finality, the mainstay of British espionage in Ireland [the RIC] had become worthless. Political intelligence and that falling normally within the security sphere had once been its exclusive province. Now there was a gaping void.[3]' This is partly true: RIC intelligence was greatly diminished as a result of the campaign of assassination and intimidation waged on the police, and in particular by the decision of the RIC to close down many of its rural barracks. It is also true that the intelligence apparatus was almost shut down by the end of 1919. But if this is true and the British were getting no information on IRA movements, then why was the IRA in the city and surrounding area practically on its knees at the Truce? In this game of attrition, why were most IRA officers in the area either dead or in jail and why were arms dumps being discovered on an almost daily basis?

As evidence of the alleged 'failure' of British intelligence in 1921, O'Donoghue devotes eight pages to an analysis of a British military intelligence weekly report of 17 May 1921, the only one of its kind to fall into the IRA's hands during the War of Independence.[4] For somebody now married to a forewoman clerk working, as she claimed, in an intelligence office in Victoria Barracks, it would seem extraordinary that she did not manage to get out even one of these reports. Such reports were produced weekly and circulated to no fewer than 61 army units and police throughout Ireland, though mostly in Munster. There is no greater indication of the essential lie in O'Donoghue's and wife's account of events during the War of Independence than that she did not manage to smuggle out even one of

---

[3] O'Donoghue, *No Other Law*, Chapter 10.

[4] Though three others were to leak out, one during the post-Truce period and two during the Civil War. In these cases, the leaks may also have been deliberate.

these weekly intelligence reports which were in every intelligence mail bag (or equivalent) to every unit in Munster and beyond over the two-year period in which she was ostensibly supplying the IRA with intelligence from Victoria Barracks. Nor did this copy come out through Josephine, something O'Donoghue himself admits. He published the report in full (or at least his version of it) as an appendix in *No Other Law*. All in all, the document itself and his commentary on it take up no fewer than 30 pages of his book – in what might be called a classic exercise in pedantic overkill.

In O'Donoghue's disingenuous account, he states, with not so subtle irony – present day propagandists are only trotting after him: 'The extent to which British Intelligence had succeeded in delineating the IRA, its organization opposed to its forces in the South, its knowledge of IRA personnel, and its information on IRA methods and intentions, may be judged from an official document captured by the East Limerick Brigade Column in May 1921 and made available through the courtesy of Lieut-Col. J.M. McCarthy.'[5] In an extensive exercise in sophistry, O'Donoghue dismisses the report, picking up on minor details of phraseology and the inevitable errors that will be found in any intelligence report trying to come to grips with an enemy in real time, especially one based on information that, because it is no more than a few days old, is bound to be full of flaws.

He begins by mocking the beginning of the report: 'Its general tendency is propagandist rather than factual.' 'The long expected rebel offensive took place on Saturday,' claiming that the IRA did not engage in pitched battles. Yet the 'long expected rebel offensive' did take place that weekend, the weekend of 14-16May 1921, which was one of the bloodiest few days of the entire War of Independence in Cork because reprisals for the execution of Dan O'Brien took place all over the county.[6] He then takes issue with the statement that 'no military skill or courage was shown by the rebels who find it more profitable to shoot down unarmed men – and women, than to take to the field', stating that 'no woman had been shot by the IRA in the period referred to'. Yet that

---

[5] O'Donoghue, *No Other Law*, p.120.
[6] For details of this see *The Year of Disappearances*, p.311. The document also shows signs of having been severely censored, the activities of the Cork No. 1 Brigade being mostly left out.

week saw the shooting of Winnie Barrington, in Co. Tipperary, one of the most prominent women to be killed in the entire period, a killing which is also notable by its absence from his version of the published document.

After eight pages of this kind of nit-picking O'Donoghue comes to the conclusion that the report 'had no particular value except in a propaganda sense' and that British Intelligence in the Martial Law area had come down to 'a confused hotch-potch of rumour, gossip, inaccuracies, plain untruths and mendacious reports' and that as a result, 'had failed utterly to obtain such information of the Volunteer Army opposed it as would enable the British forces to make effective use of their immense superiority in strength and arms'. He told Ernie O'Malley: 'It is a farrago of rumour, nonsense and inaccurate intelligence. This would seem to suggest that Connors ['Cruxy' O'Connor] had not given the information he was supposed to have given. It proves to me that the Intelligence System of the 6th Division was bad, very bad.' 'It mentioned Hegarty and myself but is quite wrong about us.'[7] The surviving copies of the document make no reference at all to O'Donoghue and only a passing reference to Seán O'Hegarty, stating that he was in Kanturk which is probably incorrect, though O'Donoghue himself was not too far away, being on the County Limerick border on 13 May.[8] And his published version makes no reference at all to 'Cruxy' O'Connor.

O'Donoghue states that the source for his copy of the document was Lieutenant Colonel John M. MacCarthy, formerly East Limerick IRA Brigade commandant and later senior National Army officer. MacCarthy, a shrewd, intelligent man, had a different view of the report: 'Its contents, while wildly inaccurate in some instances and highly coloured by propaganda in others, were factual in general, and were a notable sidelight on activities in the South in 1921.' MacCarthy noted that the document suggested that British intelligence, far from having no particular virtue, was improving, especially 'in relation to the movements and billeting areas of the IRA', something he had good

---

[7] Florrie O'Donoghue, O'Malley Notebooks, P17b/96.
[8] Borgonovo, p.158.

cause to believe in view of its accurate account of IRA activities along the Limerick/Tipperary border.[9]

But it is the provenance of the intelligence report that is most damning of O'Donoghue. According to MacCarthy, it was captured when an RAF plane carrying dispatches was downed in east County Limerick in 1921.[10] O'Donoghue implies that the first time he saw it was when editing the Bureau of Military History in the late 1940s. This is almost certainly another lie. For one thing, the downing of the plane occurred in February 1921. Considering that the report was the Intelligence Summary for the week of 17 May, it could hardly have been on that plane.[11]

The real story of how the document found its way into IRA hands, though, did not involve anyone smuggling it out of a barracks, or capturing it from planes, or intercepting dispatch riders. Though it did involve O'Donoghue. It was actually given to the IRA in Cork by the British themselves at the end of May 1921 in an effort to initiate peace negotiations.

David Kent, Sinn Féin TD for East Cork, was in prison on Spike Island in Cork Harbour. Towards the end of May 1921 he was put on a navy launch and brought for an interview to the office of General Strickland, Commander in Chief of the British army in Cork. Kent, two of whose brothers had died as a result of a stand-off with police in Castlelyons in 1916, was in good standing among republicans and was regarded by the British as one of the figureheads of republicanism in Cork.

In his office, Strickland – in one account accompanied by Captain Kelly, the British army intelligence officer for the Cork region – asked Kent if he would carry a message to de Valera and Michael Collins with a view to finding a peaceful solution to the conflict. While Kent

---

[9] John M. MacCarthy, BMH WS 883. The 'original' copy can be found as an appendix to one of MacCarthy's BMH witness statements.

[10] John M. MacCarthy BMH WS 1147.

[11] Letter, dated 13 February 1921, written by Flying Officer Mackey, RAF, the pilot of the plane, MA CD/29/5/6.

suspected Strickland's motives, believing that this might be some kind of trap, he agreed eventually to try to pass on the message that the British were interested in talking, and he was released on condition that he be given free passage and would not be followed. As proof of his bona fides and, presumably, to convey the impression that the British were in possession of a lot of detail on the movements of the IRA in Munster, Strickland handed Kent a copy of the 6th Division Intelligence report of that week – the very document that O'Donoghue used so much ink in disparaging – on condition that he return it the same day. Strickland presumably hoped that the wealth of information that he believed was in the report would nudge the IRA in the direction of the negotiation table, leading them to believe the game was up.[12]

Upon being released, Kent made contact with Seamus Fitzgerald, fellow East Cork TD and IRA man on the run, who at that time was engaged full-time as an engineer at the bomb-making factories in Knockraha. Fitzgerald brought Kent out to Ovens on the west side of the city to meet the only senior officers of the Brigade they could make contact with, namely Joe O'Connor and Florrie O'Donoghue.[13] The plan backfired because, when told about the offer, O'Connor and O'Donoghue dismissed it as a joke and sent Kent on his way. They never bothered to send the message on to Dublin that the British were putting out peace feelers. But they did have the intelligence report copied – the Brigade had the document for three hours, according to Fitzgerald. It was then censored, and redacted copies sent to the various brigade areas in Munster where it was used to identify several IRA informers.

So O'Donoghue *did* see the 6th Division intelligence report in 1921 and was the man responsible for the redacted copies that were circulated to the various IRA commands. His own letters to Josephine confirm that

---

[12] Seamus Fitzgerald, O'Malley Notebooks, P17b/111. In his BMH submission, Fitzgerald gives a truncated version of this in which he states that Kent refused to cooperate with the British and met the Brigade leadership only afterwards to inform them of his decision. Seamus Fitzgerald, BMH WS 1737. However, the version of events he gave to Ernie O'Malley, because it contains more details, is likely to be the more accurate.

[13] Though technically, of course, with the 1st Southern Division at this point. O'Connor was partly standing in for O'Donoghue as Brigade IO.

he was in Cork city that week.[14] It did not fall out of the sky in County Limerick, nor was it captured. Yet O'Donoghue never bothers to mention this in his writings, though his letters to Josephine during those weeks confirm that he knew that peace negotiations were in the air.[15] One would have thought that the possibility of a cessation of violence would have been one of enormous importance for an army fighting for political independence. After all, if the aim of political violence is to effect political change, then negotiating your way out of the conflict is an important part of it. In fact, given that the IRA claimed to be answerable to the Dáil, his prime responsibility on the matter should have been to ensure that the message reached Dublin. Instead, that particular peace initiative fell through. 'I doubt if David Kent ever got his story to Dublin,' as Fitzgerald put it.[16]

Too right. O'Donoghue buried it because the military in Cork believed it had the IRA almost defeated at that point. Strickland's message came from his political masters in England, not from the army. Peace was not what the military wanted. When this attempt to contact de Valera failed, they tried again within the week through Patrick Moylett, a Galway-based businessman and one of Collins's IRB contacts. This was more successful and ultimately led to the talks that led to the Truce and the end of the Anglo-Irish conflict. But O'Donoghue's (and O'Connor's who was with him) refusal to pass the message up the line can only mean that he did not want to pass it on. Communication channels between Cork and GHQ were fully open. O'Connor was in almost daily contact with Michael Collins's intelligence department during those months. The jubilation with which the Truce was received by IRA men and by the people of Ireland some weeks later, with its implication that the British had come to the negotiation table and that the IRA had won, which in a way they had – simply by surviving – suggests that O'Donoghue's refusal to pass on that message was not just a dereliction of duty, it was in direct opposition to the IRA's *raison d' etre*. Because, after all, what was the point of fighting if it were not to bring your enemy to the negotiating table?

---

[14] Borgonovo, pp.160-61.
[15] Borgonovo pp.160-70.
[16] Fitzgerald, O'Malley, P17b/111.

O'Donoghue gets just one mention in RTE's documentary *The Irish Revolution*, a three-part series based on UCC's *Atlas of the Revolution*, and it is to say that he was one of the IRA leaders who believed the fight should have been carried on at the Truce. He also went to a lot of trouble subsequently to try to scotch the idea that the IRA, especially in Munster, was on its knees at the Truce and was low on arms and ammunition.[17] Yet, as Liam Lynch put it in March 1921: 'We will soon be in a bad way for .303 as we have been in hard luck for capture of some recently. . . . Also a few rifles at once. . . About 1,000 rounds even will be appreciated.'[18] It was his duty to pass the above information up the line. To do otherwise, with something of such vital importance, was in itself a treasonous act. And who would have benefited from this? Certainly not the IRA, which was struggling to hang on. And not the British government which was by now looking for a way out of the conflict. The only people it benefited were the military mandarins of the War Office who wanted the war to continue so that they could snuff out the IRA. (Or who thought they could.) There are enough memoirs available of former British officers involved in Ireland, both published and unpublished, to show that the view of the military establishment was extreme annoyance that 'the frocks', i.e. the politicians, pulled the rug out from under the army just at the time they believed themselves to have got on top of the IRA, particularly in Cork. If proof is needed as to what side O'Donoghue was working for, this is surely it.

---

[17] Piaras Beaslai in a letter to Richard Mulcahy in the 1950s said O'Donoghue wrote to him claiming that Beaslai's comment in his biography of Collins that Liam Lynch had contacted Collins about the lack of munitions was not just wrong but it was a slight on the character of Lynch. Piaras Beaslai to Richard Mulcahy (n.d), Beaslai Papers, NLI, Ms 33,930(13).

[18] Liam Lynch to Director of Information, 8 March 1921. Collins Papers, IE-MA-CP-05-02-08. Collins replied that he would do his best to send some munitions south.

15

A Boy on a Mission

We saw in Chapter 13 how O'Donoghue was in possession of British intelligence documentation dating from the winter of 1914/15. We also saw that the 'reliable informant' was supplying information from the late summer of 1916 and probably before that. Yet in almost all his published accounts – and most accounts published about him – it is stated he did not join the Volunteers until early 1917. So is there any evidence that O'Donoghue was active in Republican matters before 1917? To get to the bottom of this, we need to look at what he wrote about himself and how this fits – or does not fit – with external documentation.

Because, ironically, of all those who fought with the IRA during the War of Independence, Florrie O'Donoghue was probably the longest-serving. Indeed, despite his own claims to the contrary, there is very significant evidence that he was serving for quite a while before 1917. While he states in his IRA pension application form that he did not move to Cork until the winter of 1916, he says in his memoir, written for the benefit of his children, that he left his home in Rathmore, County Kerry, in 1910 to take up a position as apprentice draper at the shop of his cousin Michael Nolan at 55 North Main Street, Cork. He would have been sixteen at the time. As he left on that 'fateful' day, he says he remembered his father saying to his mother ' "don't call him back when we start" ' and to me he said "don't look back".'[19] Yet, rather than

---

[19] John Borgonovo, *Florence and Josephine O'Donoghue's War of Independence* (Dublin, 2006), p.9.

accompanying his son on the train to Cork, Patrick O'Donoghue left him in the charge of someone who was to the boy a stranger.

To his relief he found a man whom he introduced as a friend. My father occasionally referred to men, widely scattered in parts of Kerry and Cork, men who I had never seen, as 'friends'. They were not relatives. Thinking about it later I supposed that they were men with whom he had associated in the Land League and Plan of Campaign struggles. He had served a term of imprisonment in Tralee Jail, but when he spoke of it the humorous aspects were the only ones to which he referred, so that I had then no understanding of what the land struggle was about. As the train moved off I looked shyly at my temporary guardian. I never knew his name. I remember him as a solid, silent man with a grey moustache, dressed in a suit of dark tweed. I had never been on a train and the novelty of the changing scene precluded any thoughts of loneliness or homesickness. These were to come later.[20]

O'Donoghue's erstwhile guardian did his job well. He located 55 North Main Street and 'refused to part with me until he had been assured that he was handing me over to Michael Nolan in person'.

Some of this is probably true, but it seems rather strange that with a nervous wife and a nervous son, Patrick O'Donoghue would not himself accompany his son to his destination. On the other hand, if you had a sixteen-year-old son – or in this case a seventeen-year-old, since, as we shall see, O'Donoghue actually came to Cork in 1911 – would you not be more relieved that he was going on to gainful employment rather than being overly upset that he was leaving?

The area in which O'Donoghue was brought up, from Castleisland in the west to the border with County Cork in the east and including areas in County Limerick and around Bantry in County Cork – over 500,000 acres – had for centuries been in the possession of the Kenmare estate. Lord Kenmare, who at the time had an enormous mansion in Killarney, which was accidentally burnt down in 1913, moved in the highest circles of British society. Various Earls of Kenmare counted members of the Royal Family as friends – the 3rd Earl was Comptroller of the Royal Household and later became Lord Chamberlain in 1880. Royal visits were not uncommon to Killarney House in the latter half of the nineteenth century. It is not for nothing that Kerry is referred to as 'The Kingdom'. What was odd about the scene in Killarney, though, was that

---

[20] John Borgonovo, *Florence and Josephine O'Donoghue's War of Independence* (Dublin, 2006), p.11.

visits from the Papal Nuncio and various other prominent Catholic churchmen were also common, because, unusually for an Anglo-Irish family, the Earls of Kenmare, the Brownes, were Catholics. Pugin's impressive cathedral in Killarney is a lasting monument to the munificence of the family. The irony of this is that doyens of Rome and Windsor Castle could rub shoulders in Killarney. There was something catholic with a small 'c', in the sense of diversity and inclusiveness, about the visitors' book at Killarney House.[21]

In his memoir, O'Donoghue also states that the only education he received was at Rathmore National School under a Master O'Leary and later on at Cork School of Commerce which he claimed he attended from 1913 to 1916. These two institutions, he said, gave him all the education he needed 'until I was privileged to join the best university in those days, the national freedom movement'.[22] If this was the case, it meant that he was in primary school until the age of sixteen or seventeen. Or perhaps he left primary school at thirteen or fourteen and spent several years working at home with his father?

According to the Rathmore National School rolls for the 1901-10 period O'Donoghue started First Class in 1901 and left the school in May 1908 – when he was thirteen years of age.[23] So the question is where did he spend the intervening three years? Because if he spent it working with his father, he is curiously reticent about it in his memoir. It is hard to envisage that someone with the poetic instinct of O'Donoghue would not recall at least one frosty morning out working under the shadow of the Paps Mountains or that that idyllic and mythological place would not have made a stronger impression on him. Did he never make-up a cock of hay or lead a horse to water on a summer's day? Considering his ability to record the beauty of the world around him, which is palpable in his letters to Josephine written in 1921, it seems strange that these years – the early teenage years are perhaps

---

[21] For a visit of the Papal Nuncio and for Kenmare's son, later gossip columnist, Lord Castlerosse as an altar boy, see George Malcolm Thomson, *Lord Castlerosse: His Life and Times* (London, 1973).

[22] John Borgonovo, *Florence and Josephine O'Donoghue's War of Independence* (Dublin, 2006), p.14.

[23] I am grateful to Paul Horan, Headmaster of Rathmore National School, for granting me access to these records and for being generally very helpful and generous with his time.

the most memorable in anyone's life – appear to have left no impression on him. Moreover, how was it that later on he was able to get into the Cork School of Commerce in 1913 with no hint of secondary education?

The release in 2010 of a British Army service record from the records of the Chelsea Hospital pensioners database goes some way to answering this and indeed answers a good many other questions.[24] Because in May 1911, a month after he is recorded in the 1911 census as living over Nolan's shop in Cork, a young lad called Florence O'Donoghue made his way to Ballymullen Barracks, the headquarters of the Royal Munster Fusiliers in Tralee, and signed up for to that regiment, having already been a member of the 3rd Battalion, the Special Reserve of the RMF, the reserve force to the regular army whose members were liable to be called up for full-time military service in the event of war. Its commanding officer was Honorary Colonel Valentine Charles Browne, the 4th Earl of Kenmare.[25]

Within a few weeks of joining he found himself attached to the 2nd Battalion, that is to say, one of the two full-time battalions of the regiment. The 2nd Battalion of the RMF was then stationed at Tidworth in Wiltshire where he found himself for most of the latter half of 1911. Tidworth Barracks on Salisbury Plain was a major training centre for the army. (Robert Graves found himself training there the following summer.[26]) When he joined up, O'Donoghue was not quite seventeen years old, though he stated he was eighteen in order to join since he was still underage – shades of Dinny Lehane here. He was also – at five-foot-three inches tall – equally the smallest man in the British army. Apart from his age, all the other details in the attestation paper

---

[24] Florence O'Donoghue Royal Munster Fusiliers, Regimental No. 9553 Attestation Papers, 12 May 1911. TNA WO97/5616. Accessed at Findmypast.com.

[25] Most reserve battalions in different parts of the country were under the honorary command of members of the local gentry. Kenmare, in the words of his son's biographer: 'tall, handsome, a superb horseman who carried off countless prizes at the Dublin Horse Show and was renowned as a dandy … all an Irish aristocrat was expected to be' was later to become Colonel in the King's Own Liverpool (Irish) Regiment and on the outbreak of war in 1914 a temporary major in the 9th Battalion of the Munster Fusiliers. See Thomson, p.7 and *London Gazette*, 6 November 1908 and 23 December 1914.

[26] Robert Graves, *Goodbye to All That*, revised edition, p.59 (London, 1960).

147

correspond to what we know of O'Donoghue. He says that he was living out of his father's house for more than three years and, while he called himself a farmer's labourer, he stated elsewhere on the form that he was an apprentice, which he was – at Michael Nolan's drapery shop. It is stated that his father's name was Patrick; that he was born in or near Killarney, that he was five foot three in height, 118 lbs, with blue eyes, brown hair and a fair complexion, which is an exact description of O'Donoghue. Handwriting analysis of his signature and comparing it with what Florrie O'Donoghue submitted in his IRA Pension application in the 1930s suggests that they are very likely the hand of one and the same person.[27]

The attestation papers also tell us where O'Donoghue spent the intervening three years between May 1908 and March 1911. It states that he got a third class certificate in education from a school in Tralee, graduating on 15 March 1911 – a few weeks before he was to go to Cork to join his cousin in the drapery business.[28] In other words, he was an apprentice and had been over three years out of his father's house at the time of enlistment because he had been away at school in Tralee. So in the description in his memoir of how he left home, O'Donoghue seems to be conflating two different departures. When his father told him 'don't look back' as he was leaving Rathmore, and his heartbroken mother was advised not to call him back, this most likely happened in

[27] According to Denis Sexton, of Graphology Ireland, who analysed the handwriting in detail, the signatures are a probable match. While the word 'O'Donoghue' is virtually identical in both samples, he changed his way of writing 'F' and 'r' between 1911 and the mid-1930s. It is not unusual for the handwriting of teenagers to evolve significantly on entering adulthood. I could find no signatures of O'Donoghue in War of Independence documentation, where he usually signed himself by his rank in the IRA or occasionally by a scribbled 'FoD'. Interestingly, when he submitted supporting statements for his intelligence operatives in Cork for IRA pensions in 1936, he sometimes signed these with the same 'f' that he had used as a teenager, not the reverse 'f' that he used in most of his adult correspondence. See O'Donoghue to Minister for Defence, 18 September 1936. MA-MSPC-RO-27. The reason they are not High Probability is because of the 25-year gap. (Denis Sexton, handwriting analysis report, 27 November 2017.) I am grateful to Denis for carrying out this analysis.

[28] There were several secondary schools in Tralee at this time, including St Joseph's (CBS) which included an industrial school used as a recruitment source for the army, a private college, Jeffers Institute, a school run by the Dominicans, and a technical school. I have not been able to establish which one O'Donoghue attended.

148

1908 when he was thirteen and was boarding the train for Tralee with his father, since his father was able to tell him 'don't look back'. And the business about the strange 'friend' of his father guiding him to his destination in Cork referred to his later move to Cork in 1911 when he was almost seventeen.

As to his father's role in the Land War, this may be a piece of fiction too, though the evidence is ambiguous. O'Donoghue stated that his father had spent time in jail in Tralee for Land League activities during the early 1880s.[29] However, while there was a Patrick O'Donoghue arrested, there is no record of his name among the lists of prisoners held for Land League activities in County Kerry in the early 1880s – nor is he listed as a prisoner in Tralee Jail during those or later years.[30] On the other hand, his land at Rathmore, all 18 acres, 3 roods and 18 perches of it, was occupied by the family and leased from Lord Kenmare only from 1891, some three years after the alleged incident.[31] O'Donoghue also mentioned in his memoir that the family had a sheepdog, 'a big collie Dot', that his father had got as a gift from Lord Kenmare[32] – who at this time was on the staff of the Lord Lieutenant in Dublin. Were the mysterious 'friends' of his fathers, whoever they were, not so much former Land League colleagues as their opponents? This is likely to have been the case because, when the family home was burnt down by

---

[29] According to reports of land agitation on the Rathmore part of the Kenmare Estate, a Patrick Donoghue was sentenced, along with a few others, to a fortnight in jail (February 1888) arising out of an illegal assembly on Sunday, 4 December 1887. On 28 October, a plan of campaign was adopted by tenants of the Kenmare Estate and was proposed by Patrick Donoghue at Mounthorgan, to the west of Rathmore. This is probably another Patrick Donoghue, since Florrie O'Donoghue's father became a tenant of Lord Kenmare only in 1891. I am grateful to John Stephen O'Sullivan for much of this information.

[30] An index with the names of those taken into custody as a result of Land League activities in Munster can be found in Vol. 5 of the records of the Protection of Persons and Property Act 1881. NA. CSO/ICR/5. There are no O'Donoghues or Donoghues listed. The prisoner lists for Tralee Jail are now available at Findmypast.com. While there are several Patrick Donoghues named in the lists for late nineteenth century, on the basis of their ages, none of them seem to be O'Donoghue's father.

[31] Valuation Book: Rathmore Vol. I, Book III, 1894-1905 and Book IV, 1884-1894. Records of the Valuation Office Dublin. Kenmare Estate Rent Books, Rathmore Division November 1886-May 1894. It should be noted that not all the Rathmore ledgers appear to have survived. Kenmare Estate Papers, available online.

[32] Borgonovo, p.10.

149

British forces in May 1921, the British government gave a loan of £375 to cover the cost of its rebuilding.[33]

So the evidence points to the fact that Florrie O'Donoghue spent three years, between the ages of thirteen and sixteen, at secondary school in Tralee and that he joined the Special Reserve as soon as he was able to. Tralee, a loyal garrison town, was the headquarters of the Royal Munster Fusiliers. The regiment was in good standing in the area, Ballymullen Barracks being the town's biggest employer. The implication of this is that O'Donoghue was recruited into the Special Reserve while still at school – and then joined the army proper within a few months of leaving, after two months at Michael Nolan's. But it is when we look as his service record in detail that it becomes really interesting. Because, if we are to take the attestation form at face value, O'Donoghue lasted no more than six months in the army and was back at the counter at Nolan's shop by the end of the year. But that is almost certainly not the entire story.

---

[33] This was part of the first batch of property compensations agreed between the Compensation (Ireland) Commission and the British government. 'The question of by whom the injury was committed had been disregarded altogether. I mean that no question of who is ultimately responsible has weighed with the Ministry of Finance at all.' Compensation (Ireland) Commission to Lionel Curtis, 18 September 1922. Compensation Awards Lists TNA CO 739/13.

16

Discharged for 'Misconduct'

For anyone chancing upon the attestation form of Florence O'Donoghue to the Royal Munster Fusiliers, it is likely that he or she would be forgiven for dismissing it pretty quickly. It would, on the face of it, appear to be a minor episode, one that, because of its brevity, could have little influence in his subsequent life – a teenage experiment that went wrong. What the attestation form merely tells us is that he joined the Munsters in Tralee on 13 May 1911, served at the Tralee depot until 26 June when he was moved to the 2nd Battalion at Tidworth in Wiltshire. While in England, he was 'awarded detention by his commanding officer' twice over the next few months before being dismissed for misconduct on 21 November 1911. Maybe the boy was just homesick and wanted to go back to Ireland?

If that was all that was to his attestation form, then we would have no further interest in it. But what is it doing among the files of the Chelsea Hospital pensioners, seeing as that the form states that he got no pension from his six months in the army, especially when all it led to was a dishonorable discharge? (It should be pointed out that Chelsea Hospital pensioners were not just confined to patients or inmates of the hospital but that the hospital processed the pensions for the broad ranks of the British army – the so-called 'out-pensioners' – up until 1955.) This suggests that O'Donoghue received a military pension of some kind at a later stage.

Then there are the two periods of detention. These were for twenty-one days and fourteen days respectively, the first from 20 September to 10 October and the second from 10 to 23 October. In other words, he was given five straight weeks' detention with no gap between them and did not return for duty even when the detention was over.[34] If the misconduct that led to the first detention was genuine and serious, he would hardly have had time to commit it again before being detained a second time. What is also odd is that no reason is given for either period of detention. In most army service records, such misdemeanours are stated, along with their associated punishment. Initial punishments are small, such as the docking of a day's pay or a few days confined to barracks – or even a few days in detention. In fact, such punishments usually have CB written after them, meaning 'confined to barracks'. This is not the case here. Far from having his pay docked, he was fully paid for every day he was on service, something which was signed off by the very officer who 'awarded' him detention, Captain H.A. Carroll.[35] But to be given five weeks in lock-up for a first strike which is not even detailed suggests that his misdemeanour must have been something out of the ordinary. Was this a boy who was so clearly unsuited to army life that he spent one-fifth of his time in the army locked up? Given that he was a goodie two-shoes who had proudly stated that he was 'still serving with the Special Reserve' when he joined the Royal Munster Fusiliers and presumably knew what to expect – how likely is that?

So there must be another explanation for all of this. When you read the small print, a few things become apparent. O'Donoghue is described as being discharged for misconduct, but the words 'for misconduct' are in inverted commas, suggesting that the misconduct was not real. Also the discharge is on the authority of a brigade major of the 7th Infantry Brigade, the brigade at Tidworth of which the Munsters were part and the discharge confirmed by Captain Carroll. In cases such as this, genuine orders for discharge are invariably given with the official reason for the discharge and the appropriate King's Regulations code that apply. In the case of misconduct, the code would be KR Para 392 xi, or its equivalent.[36] In this instance, however, the order for

---

[34] The 10 October date is crossed out in the form and replaced with 10 November, but that makes no sense because he had 'left' the army within the fourteen days.

[35] Henry A. Carroll was a native of Fermoy and died during the First World War.

[36] There were seven classes of misconduct that merited discharge from the army, according to Paragraph 392 of King's Regulations, 1912. While this case slightly predates the 1912 King's Regulations there was a similar system in operation prior to 1912. *King's Regulations, 1912*, Harvard University Library. Accessed online.

152

O'Donoghue's discharge was signed, citing an Order Number 925, DI, on 18 November 1911. This appears not to be an actual discharge at all. Rather, King's Regulations, Paragraph 925 refers to one regimental duty taking precedence over another: 'An officer detailed for one duty will, in addition, be detailed for such other duties as he can perform consistently with the proper discharge of the first duty.'[37] One of the principal ways of recruiting operatives into the secret services during World War I – and indeed since – was to identify promising candidates from various branches of the armed forces, get them either 'discharged', or if they were officers, to resign their commission, so that they could slip quietly into the reserve where they could be paid for their membership of the secret army whose existence for many years was known to only a small number of people. In other words, O'Donoghue was being detailed for another duty – in this case an invisible one. Stepping back into the reserve, which was what O'Donoghue was in effect doing, was standard practice in the recruiting of intelligence personnel by the secret services. This was simply how things were done.[38] As a member of the Special Reserve he should have been liable for call-up on the outbreak of war in 1914. The fact that he was not called up says that he was already serving, albeit in a less visable role.

But probably the most significant detail here are the letters 'DI' appended to the 'discharge' order. DI in all likelihood refers to District Inspector, one of the senior ranks in the Royal Irish Constabulary. The significance of this is that during this period there was a semi-official arrangement in place between the army and the constabulary in Ireland whereby military personnel were being quietly trained in intelligence techniques by local district inspectors.[39] This is even more interesting since two of the RIC's district inspectors serving in Munster in 1911 were to go on to play very significant intelligence roles on the British side during 1916 and the War of Independence. These were District Inspectors Ivon Price, whom we have seen before, and Henry Toppin,

---

[37] *King's Regulations, 1912*, Harvard University Library. Accessed online.

[38] Kell's staff transferred to 'the Reserve of Officers on undertaking this work'. *History of the Military Intelligence Directorate*, TNA, WO 32/10776. Phil Tomaselli, *Tracing Your Secret Service Ancestors* (Barnsley, 2009), p.14. They were still receiving full pay, however. See Chapter 21.

[39] Elizabeth A. Muenger, *The British Military Dilemma in Ireland* (Kansas, 1991), p.113.

both of whom were later 'loaned' to the military for intelligence work in Ireland during the Great War.

Price was the more important of the two since he was the head of military intelligence in Ireland during the war years – and 'singlehandedly' saved Dublin Castle during the Easter Rising (see below). In the context of O'Donoghue, however, Toppin may well be equally important since he was DI for Queenstown at the time O'Donoghue joined the services.[40] Originally from County Tipperary, he had become a DI Grade 3 in 1891 and was promoted to resident magistrate in February 1913. He then served as Resident Magistrate for County Leitrim until 1917 when he was brought into the Irish Command (military) with the rank of Temporary Major at the instigation of Ivon Price and 'attached to Headquarters Irish Command and to various special military headquarters'.[41] He then served in the army until 1920, initially as a major and later as lieutenant colonel, acting as Assistant Adjutant General to the 6th Division in Cork until his retirement, on 19 October 1920.[42] Toppin's name signs off many of the arrest and transfer documents relating to IRA prisoners in Cork up to the time of his retirement – including the official account of the arrest of Terence MacSwiney. But he did not quit on his official retirement. Rather, he moved to the staff of Sir John Anderson, Under Secretary at Dublin Castle where he was still signing documents as late as 1 June 1921.[43]

There is no question that Toppin had a significant role in intelligence in Munster before he was moved into the Castle. He took over an office in the County Council building in Tralee from Tadgh Kennedy, the intelligence officer of the 1st Kerry Brigade of the IRA, to investigate the shooting of two RIC men. Kennedy got on well with him:

Topping [sic] was more or less on my side and could not justify the actions of the RIC. I continued to be friendly with him and we had many drinks together at the Grand and Central Hotels. I met him in Dublin after the Truce and we joined in a good laugh at the thing, but I did not tell him I was Brigade IO . . . . He was a nice fellow, a

---

[40] 1911 Census.
[41] Henry Toppin Service Record, TNA WO 339/90383.
[42] Jim Herlihy, *The Royal Irish Constabulary Officers* (Dublin,2005), p.300.
[43] For instance, see note of 1 June 1921 from Chief Secretary's Office in TNA, WO 35/129.

Protestant and a Mason and, of course, a Loyal Britisher whom it wasn't easy to get on the blind side of. He got a good account of me from his Unionist friends in Tralee and he found it hard to believe that I was mixed up with these murderous people. [44]

This does not mean that O'Donoghue was recruited by either Price or Toppin personally. It is unlikely that District Inspectors of the RIC would be aware of a little guy up from Kerry who was now working as a draper's assistant in a relatively large city like Cork. It is far more likely that he was recruited by someone closer to the cutting edge of RIC surveillance. It will be worth recalling that Ormonde Winter stated in his confidential report that the only agent to penetrate the IRB had been recruited by an RIC Crimes Special Sergeant. As we have seen, among regular visitors to the Nolan shop in North Main Street were Special Crimes sergeants T.J.Flynn and Jack Maliff, for whom Michael Nolan was working as an informant.[45] Maliff had a central role in British intelligence operations in Cork and was taking a special interest in republican matters at least from 1915 on and probably earlier.[46]

Given that he was already in England in the autumn of 1911, it is unlikely that O'Donoghue would have been brought back to Ireland for training under Toppin or anyone else in the RIC. Otherwise, why even bother to bring him to England? It is far more likely that, while the order for his 'discharge' may have come from Toppin, Price or from another District Inspector, the five weeks spent 'in detention' are more likely to have been spent at a spy school run by the Secret Service in London.

The British Secret Service, as we now know it, initially known as the Secret Service Bureau, was set up in 1909 as a result of a number of 'spy scares' that captured the imagination – though not the reality – of Edwardian England. The Secret Service Bureau was to greatly expand over the years of the Great War where it morphed into MI5, MI6 and a range of other services until by 1918 it was a vast bureaucracy, employing thousands of people. In 1915 it was divided into foreign espionage under former naval commander Mansfield Cummings, and domestic counter-espionage under Major Vernon Kell. These were ultimately to evolve, after several name changes, into MI6, otherwise

---

[44] See Tadgh Kennedy, BMH WS 1413.
[45] Murphy, *The Year of Disappearances*, Chapter 58.
[46] P.J. Murphy, BMH WS 869.

155

known as the Special Intelligence Service (SIS), and MI5, respectively. As Kell put it at the time: 'I was made responsible for counter-espionage within the British Isles. With this latter object in view, I was to work both for the War Office and the Admiralty.[47] Kell was also to liaise extensively with Special Branch of the Metropolitan Police as well as with the constabularies of mainland Britain and Ireland.

The first detective Kell took on was William Melville, who had officially retired in 1903 from the Special Branch of the Metropolitan Police, though he was still carrying on intelligence work for the War Office in the intervening years. Melville was a Kerryman, who still spoke with traces of a Kerry accent and retained an interest in Gaelic games. Born in Sneem, Co. Kerry in 1850, Melville was highly decorated for his work, including, among other things, foiling a plot to assassinate Queen Victoria.[48] By the time he started working for Kell out of an anonymous office on Temple Avenue in London, he was in his fifty-nineth year and, though technically retired, was still busy travelling around the world carrying out his investigations.

One of the many tasks Kell set himself was 'the earmarking of minor agents in important British Ports, who during the Precautionary Period [pre-war], would report anything of an unusual nature' and also 'the earmarking and training of our own agents in the Coast Counties, to set behind enemy lines in case of invasion'. Among the responsibilities of these agents would be to shadow 'known spies or highly-suspected persons, seeing who they associated with etc, thereby getting on the track of traitors'.[49] The priority was 'the collection of information in Home Ports and the selection of agents in those Ports, who would be useful during the Precautionary Period and afterwards in time of war' and also the 'dissemination of false or useless information at places where foreigners frequent, such as ports etc.[50] Kell, as we have seen, also put in place an 'Observer Scheme' in which the Chief Constables of the various areas were to earmark potential candidates to act as agents. By July 1911 the Chief Constables of fourteen counties had nominated agents for this scheme. These were by then busy gathering

---

[47] Kell's General Report, April-October 1910, TNA, KV 1/9.
[48] Andrew Cook, *M: MI5's First Spymaster* (Stroud, 2004).
[49] ibid.
[50] ibid.

lists of 'potential suspects'.[51] How much Kell had extended his interests into Ireland at this early stage is unclear. However, by December 1911 he was already receiving reports of a suspicious envelope picked up in Berehaven in west Cork containing maps of coastal defences, searchlight stations, submarine pier, rifle ranges and so on, and addressed to a German name in London.[52] From then on, Kell's reports themselves have very few references to Ireland. What is clear, though, is that, from his General Report of April-October 1913 onwards, the sections dealing with Ireland are heavily redacted.[53] War Office correspondence dealing with sedition in Ireland in the two years leading up to the 1916 Rising appear to be mostly the work of Kell's new department, MI5.[54] So while the Secret Service's own KV files show only limited engagement with Irish matters, the actual data from its various government customers, such as the military, the Admiralty and the Dublin administration, say the opposite.

The qualities Kell required for agents were 'mental alertness, elasticity, knowledge of men, intuition, an accurate and powerful memory combined with imagination, judgement to choose the right method of handling a case and moment to strike.'[55] In Kell's view, policemen were not ideal for this work: 'however excellent their [Chief Constable's] men's work may be as regards crime, they have not all got the necessary degree of tact to carry out such delicate enquiries. I have also had to rely to a great extent upon the services of Mr. Melville, who in view of his age and standing can hardly be expected to perform such work as the shadowing by night and day, a duty which in any case is quite impossible for one man alone.'[56] Besides, according to his biographer, 'Melville – Mr M – had another job to do, besides detection'. It appears it was he who ran the school in London where 'the right people must be picked and they must be properly trained'.[57] According to one 'graduate' of the spy school:

---

[51] Kell Report, 30 June 1911. TNA KV 1/9.

[52] Report on Counter-Espionage, December 1911 to 31 July 1912, TNA KV 1/9.

[53] Kell Report, April-October 1913, TNA KV 1/9.

[54] Some of this correspondence can be found at TNA in WO 35/69, WO 141/5 and WO 141/6.

[55] The Experiences of MI5 from 1909 to 1918. TNA KV 1/39.

[56] Review of the Work Done, October 1910 to May 1911.TNA KV 1/9

[57] Andrew Cook, *M: MI5's First Spymaster* (Stroud, 2004), p.232.

There was a medical doctor, taken in because MI5 reasoned that a doctor was 'the last person to be suspected of intrigue'. Together with him in that class of 1914 he later remembered ex-policemen, journalists, actors, ex-officers, university dons, bank clerks, several clergy and to my knowledge two titled persons.

That was what he described as a Spy School, starting up then to teach them all what is now called tradecraft. The training included lectures from ex-Detective Superintendent Melville on how to pick locks and burgle houses, followed by practical exercises; others on the Technique of Lying, the Technique of Being Innocent, the Will to Kill, and Sex as a Weapon in Intelligence; and (finally) Dr McWhirter's Butchery Class, which gave advice on how to top yourself if you were caught. . . . If we can credit this account, Spy School clearly gave these new wartime recruits an excellent grounding, especially on practical subjects.[58]

There is little doubt that the 'spy school' existed. Keith Jeffery, the official historian of MI6, states that when Sir Samuel Hoare was being trained for intelligence work in 1915 he was given 'an intensive course in the various war Intelligence departments over several weeks. One day it would be espionage or contre-espionage, another coding and cyphering, another war trade and contraband, a fourth, postal and telegraph censorship.'[59] O'Donoghue also seemed to be familiar with the south of England, since he wrote to Josephine in the summer of 1921 that the 'brightly-painted, ivy-clad houses' and the level countryside around the head of Dingle Bay reminded him 'somewhat of the South of England'.[60] For a young lad raised on Sexton Blake and other spy heroes, as O'Donoghue claimed he was, this must have been a veritable heaven – even if the last class mentioned above might make some recruits blanch. Other lecturers were Ewart, Cummings and barrister Douglas Hogg.[61] If O'Donoghue was a pupil in this school, he

---

[58] Bernard Porter, *Plots and Paranoia: The History of Political Espionage in Britain 1790-1988*, (London, 1989), p.136, quoted in Cook, pp232-33. Alan Judd also mentions the Spy School in his *The Quest for C: Mansfield Cummings and the Founding of the Secret Service* (London, 2000), p.377. As a former MI6 officer, Judd probably knows what he is talking about.

[59] Sir Samuel Hoare quoted in Keith Jeffery, *MI6: The History of the Secret Intelligence Service, 1909-1949* (London, 2010). Chapter 1.

[60] Borgonovo, p.157.

[61] This is likely to be a reference to Sir John Spencer Ewart, who as Director of Military Operations and Intelligence was instrumental in setting up the Secret Service Bureau. Jeffery, op.cit., Chapter 1. It may be that this refers to events before the spring of 1914 since Ewart was one of those who had to resign as a result of the so-called Curragh Mutiny in 1914. On the other hand, his interest in military intelligence

was in eminent company. This suggests that O'Donoghue was known to, and may even have been a pupil of, some of Britain's most famous spies. It was a long way from the Paps Mountains to Kensington – though maybe not so long when you consider that Sneem is even farther away.

---

followed him after his demotion. Nevil Macready mentions in his memoir calling on Ewart's expertise and wisdom during 1916, suggesting that he was at the very least attached to the War Office at this time. As a senior barrister, Sir Douglas Hogg would have been in a position at the time to provide legal advice to recruits.

17

The Fact of the Small Fair Man

Poster put up by the IRB in Wexford in February 1915:

> People of Wexford
> Take no notice of the police order to destroy your own property and leave your homes if a German army lands in Ireland. When the Germans come they will come as friends and to put an end to English rule in Ireland. Therefore stay in your homes and assist as far as possible the German troops. Any stores, hay, corn, or forage taken by the Germans will be paid for by them.[1]

One of the more bizarre events of the early war years in Ireland was the trial and acquittal of Seán O'Hegarty for sedition – for pinning the above notice to telegraph poles in County Wexford in 1915. O'Hegarty, who had been earlier dismissed from his job as a sorter at the GPO in Cork for his revolutionary activities and 'exiled' to west Cork, found himself in Enniscorthy in early 1915. During the small hours of the morning of 24 February, O'Hegarty was arrested at 8 New Street in the town.[2] The house was owned by Larry de Lacy, a sub-editor of the *Enniscorthy Echo* and an active local IRB man, and was occupied by de Lacy and Jim Bolger, a young journalist working at the same paper.[3] O'Hegarty faced a range of other charges, however, because when he was arrested, a quantity of explosives comprising '19 cartridges of dynamite, 3½ yards of blasting fuse, 15 percussion caps, 2 packs of rifle ammunition and leaflets of seditious literature' were found in his

---

[1] Notice placed on telephone poles in County Wexford by the IRB in February 1915. *Documents Relative to the Sinn Fein Movement* (HMSO, London, 1912).
[2] *Cork Examiner*, 25 February 1915.
[3] Thomas Doyle, BMH WS 104.

bedroom.[4] The trial, under the Defence of the Realm Act (DORA) is celebrated in republican lore because Tim Healy K.C. (and MP) defended O'Hegarty with a performance that amounted almost to genius.

It took several trials to decide the issue, however. On the matter of the explosives, Healy managed to persuade the jury that the dynamite and accessories were the property of de Lacy, who had inconveniently done a runner (via Cabra) to the United States and that they could not possibly have anything to do with O'Hegarty – even though fifteen automatic pistol cartridges and two letters offering him a position as organizer of the Volunteers were found on his person. The next charge – that four large parcels of leaflets, including copies of pamphlets written by Roger Casement and seditious literature containing phrases like 'In this war Ireland has only one friend. Let every Irish heart, let every Irish hand, let every Irish purse be with Germany' were found in the downstairs rooms of the house – was dismissed on similar grounds.[5]

On the charge of putting pro-German posters written, apparently, in O'Hegarty's distinctive handwriting up around Enniscorthy, which one would imagine was beyond all doubt, Healy showed his consummate skill at throwing red herrings at the jury. When several post office officials who knew O'Hegarty in Cork and who could identify his handwriting and even had samples to prove it were called as witnesses, Healy managed to insinuate that because they were Protestants, they must have had it in for O'Hegarty and that the latter was the real victim in all this.

If Hegarty having been driven out of County Cork, went to lodge with de Lacy in Enniscorthy it was a question of 'needs must when the devil drives'. He was driven out of his native county – like Adam from the Garden – with the fiery sword of the military authorities, and should go somewhere for a few months, thinking the war would be over. If they were all suddenly ordered to leave County Dublin – which was much smaller than County Cork – how many of them knew where they would sleep tonight? He did not complain of the military regulations, although sometimes they might not agree with all that was done, but Major Price was not a Pope – he could not issue bulls (*laughter*). In conclusion he asked the jury in light of conscience which they got from above and the light of common sense which they received from experience to send Hegarty a free man from the dock.

---

[4] *Cork Constitution*, 9 April 1915.
[5] *Cork Examiner*, 13 April 1915.

161

Justice Kenny, before whom the case was heard, while admitting that almost all the evidence suggested that O'Hegarty was guilty as charged, 'deplored that sectarian matters should have been introduced into the trial and that the prisoner should have instructed his counsel that there was animus against him in the Cork Post Office for religious reasons.' Justice Kenny then discharged the jury when they could not reach a verdict.[6]

A new trial, scheduled for 8 June 1915 before Justice Dodd, followed along similar lines, with the Salvation Army being dragged into it – one witness, a Mr Wallace, the Assistant Superintendent of Cork Post Office, being accused of going out on Sundays to deliberately hold Salvation Army meetings under the windows of Nationalists and that he got his promotion as a result of 'the most barefaced piece of jobbery ever perpetuated in Cork' and had it in for O'Hegarty because, as Healy claimed, O'Hegarty 'and his friends had made a strong protest against that favouritism'. This was news to Wallace, who said that O'Hegarty had made no protest to this effect. Besides, Wallace was only fourteen when the alleged Salvation Army meeting took place. Healy insinuated that Wallace 'hated Ireland and everything Irish' and that it was he who went to Major Price to procure the prosecution against O'Hegarty, something Wallace denied. This was of course eyewash. However, the one man who might have been expected to clear this up, Major Ivon Price, the head of military intelligence, was not called as a witness – after a short discussion between prosecution and defence lawyers – though the prosecutor suggested that he should have been called. O'Hegarty, after a trial that made a laughing stock of the legal system, walked free.[7]

The back story to this is that in August 1914, P.S. O'Hegarty, Seán O'Hegarty's elder brother, had been removed from his position as postmaster of the GPO in Queenstown when he came under suspicion of

---

[6] *Cork Examiner*, 13 April 1915.
[7] *Cork Examiner*, 8 June 1915.

subversive activities and was moved to a post office job in Montgomeryshire, Wales. The elder O'Hegarty, a lifelong IRB man had, it was alleged, been in contact with the German ambassador. As the head of the Post Office in Ireland, A.H. Norway, who was working for Price at intercepting the mails of 'known rebels', put it: 'It would be idle to attempt to recapture the impressions under which official life went on at the outset of the war. Embarkation was going on secretly and swiftly at many points in Ireland and, as it was of great importance that details of the units embarking should not leak out, the question of what dependence could be placed on the Post Office leapt into the front.' In other words, if the British military knew the value of intelligence as to what German units and supplies were going to the Front, then common sense dictated that the Germans would be interested in similar intelligence on British troop movements. As Queenstown was one of the principal ports in the UK for embarkation of troops and supplies from Ireland to the war zone there was an obvious need to stop any information leaking from Queenstown. 'Relations of any sort with the German Ambassador at that moment served to show unsuitability for control of the Queenstown [Post] Office in war.'[8] 'A high officer called to me to say Hegarty must not remain at Queenstown . . . (at which port many secret things were happening) . . . or indeed in Ireland'. Norway was none too happy to lose O'Hegarty, given that he had a good reputation and was well thought of by his bosses in England. Nonetheless, the 'exile' went ahead.

Seán O'Hegarty had for the previous dozen years been a sorter in the GPO in Cork city. Now Norway was requested to remove him as well. 'The evidence pointed clearly enough to association with dangerous and disloyal men but established no fact which could be said to justify punishment. Thus the case could only be met by transfer to an equivalent position out of Ireland and I notified to Hegarty that he must go and work in England for a time, retaining his pay, and receiving in addition a subsistence allowance of a guinea a week.'[9] In other words, in the tradition of many large bureaucracies O'Hegarty was being compensated for being so discommoded. He refused to go and so was

---

[8] Keith Jeffrey (ed.), *The Sinn Fein Rebellion as They Saw It*, Mary Louisa and Arthur Hamilton Norway, (Dublin 1999), p.22.

[9] Jeffery, op.cit. p.102.

suspended from his employment in the post office, 'dismissed for disobedience' as Norway put it.[10]

He was then ordered by Brigadier General Hill, the officer commanding the South Irish Coastal Defence at Queenstown to immediately reside outside the areas of Cork Borough and the urban districts of Queenstown, Midleton, Youghal, and the rural districts of Bandon, Kinsale, Midleton and Youghal. In other words, he was to remove himself from port areas and districts where military embarkation might have been going on, not an unreasonable order in wartime.[11] By June 1915 some forty-five persons, many of them IRB men, were given terms of imprisonment or banished from their homes. However, while many, including Liam Mellows, Ernest Blythe and Denis McCullough were exiled out of Ireland and others such as Seán Mac Diarmada were put in jail, O'Hegarty was exiled to Ballingeary, where his family and his wife came from and where he worked as a labourer. In other words, this was not exactly the chain gang or the Irish equivalent of a Siberian salt mine since he was also free to engage in his IRB work while safe in the hills of west Cork.[12]

He was under instructions to remain in the Ballingeary district and was there at the time of the Easter Rising in April 1916 where he attempted to mobilize the local Volunteer units amid the confusion of that week.[13] He returned to live in the city in the winter of 1916/17 when, it appears, the ban on him was lifted.[14]

So what was he doing in Wexford in February 1915? Some writers claim he was 'in exile' – based largely, it seems, on the histrionics of Healy's courtroom performance. Considering that he was supposed to be residing in west Cork and that he returned there immediately after the trial, it is clear that he was in Enniscorthy out of choice. According to

---

[10] Jeffery op.cit. p.102. Also see Kevin Girvin, *The Life and Times of Sean O'Hegarty, O/C First Cork Brigade,* MPhil Thesis, UCC 2003, pp.36-37.

[11] Order served on Seán O'Hegarty, 14 October 1914, Appendix 3 in Girvin, op.cit.

[12] Alice M. Cashel, BMH WS 366.

[13] He and his wife lived in a cottage owned by Alice Cashel, according to Cashel 'for some years restricted to a certain area'. Alice M. Cashel BMH WS 366. See also Girvin, op.cit. pp. 42-44.

[14] O'Hegarty appears to have been 'released' from Ballingeary at around the same time that other IRB leaders were released from Frongoch, that is to say about the end of 1916. Borgonovo, *The Dynamics of War and Revolution, Cork City, 1916-18*, p.83.

Robert Brennan, who was also on the staff of the *Enniscorthy Echo* and later married Jim Bolger's sister, O'Hegarty had simply come to Enniscorthy 'on a visit to de Lacy, a kindred spirit'.[15]

But there were other interesting questions arising out of the trial. While it is clear that it was military intelligence who instigated the case against O'Hegarty, at no time did military intelligence give evidence at the trial. The trial – O'Hegarty was able to opt for a civil trial rather than a court martial because his misdemeanours took place just before the Defence of the Realm Act came into force – was largely a civilian affair. When Powell for the prosecution suggested Major Price be called as a witness, Healy quashed it. It appears that it was Healy who raised the canard of O'Hegarty being exiled 'out of the County of Cork', rather than that he was simply exiled out of those parts of County Cork where military embarkation was taking place.

But there was another detail that emerged at the trial which appears to have been entirely ignored. Because there was another man arraigned for trial on the same charges as O'Hegarty. This was Jim Bolger, the young journalist also of the *Enniscorthy Echo*, and Larry de Lacy's young cohabitee at 8 New Street. Bolger, though brought before the court and charged, appears eventually to have been released.[16] When the police raided the house around 2.00am, they found O'Hegarty and Bolger in bed together in the front upstairs bedroom of the house.[17] According to Robert Brennan, there was a second bedroom occupied by an elderly caretaker, a Mrs. Carberry, who was described by Brennan as 'a tried and true friend of them. She always said she never heard or saw anything that happened in the house.' Nicknamed 'Ann Devlin', when Mrs. Carberry was asked at the trial had she seen the yards of fuse, 'she said of course she had seen it. She had cut off a length of it to tie the little dog to the bed post.'[18] What Brennan does not report is that Larry de Lacy was in another room and appears to have slept obliviously through the entire thing and managed to decamp to Dublin the following morning and thence to the United States.

[15] Robert Brennan, BMH WS 779.
[16] Seamus Doyle, BMH WS 315.
[17] *Irish Times*, 9 April1915 and 13 April1915; *Cork Examiner,* 9 April1915 and 10 April1915.
[18] Robert Brennan, BMH WS 779.

What is interesting about this instance of two men sleeping together is that it is emphasized in almost every internal report of the incident. Its only mention at the trial was that Healy drew attention to it in order to induce incredulity on the part of the jury: 'He was sleeping with a Mr Bolger, a newspaper reporter, and arrested on a particular charge which was not now before the court'.[19] If this was a reference to homosexual activities, it seems to have been quietly overlooked. The policeman who arrested them stated: 'Bolger was in bed with Hegarty and witness, on searching, found in the room a small brown paper parcel on a stretcher bed and found 19 cartridges of gelignite dynamite.'[20]

If this discovery had been made in 1920 or 1921, nobody would think to comment on it. Men 'on the run' were often found in bed together for the simple reason that the reality of guerrilla warfare meant you slept whereever you could lay your head. This led some British officers to comment that they regarded the Irish as a uniquely degenerate race – especially when they found entire families in the same bed – who were there in order to make room for their IRA guests. Florrie O'Donoghue for instance, remembered sharing a double bed with Terence MacSwiney at Hurley's in Sunday's Well for long periods in 1920 and neither he nor anybody else ever made anything of it.[21]

However, this was 1915; the country was not at war, other than the Great War, which was rather a long way away. O'Hegarty was not 'on the run'. O'Hegarty and Bolger were both living in the house. According to the 1911 Census, the house had nine rooms – and presumably plenty of beds. De Lacy was in one, Mrs Carberry in another, Hegarty and Bolger in a third. Even if they had to share a bedroom, they could have slept in different beds. There was the second bed on which the small brown parcel with the explosives was found. Robert Brennan, in his account of the events of that night, wrote that the reason they were in the same bed was because the room was so full of armaments they had almost to climb over them to get into the one space that was left in the room, the bed.[22] However, the amount of munitions

---

[19] *Cork Examiner*, 10 April 1915.
[20] *Cork Examiner*, 9 April 1915.
[21] John Borgonovo, *Florence and Josephine O'Donoghue's War of Independence*, p.94.
[22] Robert Brennan BMH WS 779.

actually found in the room would fit on the seat of a chair. Presumably, if they were capable of getting the dynamite into the room in the first place, they were capable of taking it off the bed and placing it on the floor. There is only one conclusion: they were in bed together out of choice.

But there is another fascinating addendum that calls the entire basis of the court case into question. It is clear from the transcripts of the case that it was ultimately being brought at the instigation of Price's military intelligence department, though Price was represented by his superior officer, General Friend. Because there was another person associated with events that took place at 8 New Street. It appears the police had been watching the house well in advance of the night of the arrest. A cattle fair took place in the town some days beforehand and another man was spotted coming and going. Local District Inspector R.R. Heggart of the RIC – though he made no mention of this at the trial – reported to Dublin Castle that 'the fact of *the small fair man* [italics added] being there at the time is also known to the police. The fair referred to was held on 22nd inst. His name and business here have not been ascertained up to the present. He is about 23 years of age, 5ft 3ins, fair complexion, fair hair (almost ginger), clean shaven, wore glasses, wore heavy dark grey overcoat, black leggings and grey cap. When leaving, went to Dublin. A special report regarding him is being made.'[23] This is as close a description of Florrie O'Donoghue as makes no difference. The main difference from his Royal Munster Fusiliers attestation form is that he had 'fair hair, almost ginger' which on a February night is surely very close to 'light brown hair'. Furthermore, O'Donoghue, who had significant eyesight problems in later life, sometimes wore glasses. Mrs Carberry also remembered him: 'On the night before the fair in February when a small fair man came and remained that night he left the following morning. To the best of my knowledge, he slept with de Lacy.'[24]

These accounts suggest two things of importance. First, the 'small fair man', who clearly was not known to the local police, made his way immediately to Dublin the following day, the morning before the raid. It

---

[23] Arrest of John O'Hegarty under DORA, Special Crime (Wexford) 27 February 1915. Laurence de Lacy file, TNA CO 904/198/011.
[24] Mrs Margaret Carberry statement, Laurence de Lacy file, TNA CO 904/198/011.

may be purely coincidental but a day or two later the RIC's Crime Special report for February 1915 noted that 'suspects T.J. McSweeney [Terence MacSwiney] and T. Barry [Tadgh Barry] were in Dublin on 27th inst where the latter visited suspect T.J [Tom] Clarke'.[25] Neither the Crime Special report of the arrest in Wexford nor the RIC intelligence file on Larry de Lacy makes any mention of seditious notices going on telegraph poles written in O'Hegarty's hand. While a large quantity of the notices were found in the house and policemen did give evidence of having found them on poles around Ferns, Co. Wexford you would have to wonder how likely it is that such notices could have been written in O'Hegarty's handwriting, seeing as it is almost indecipherable to anybody who has not spent half a lifetime studying it. Was the business of the notices on the poles a diversion, to cover up the real background of the surveillance that was placed on the house? Was the real reason the visit of 'the small fair man' who had conveniently departed before anything happened? The implication is clear: that 'the small fair man', though unknown to the local police, was Price's man in the camp, and the source of the information that led to the raid.

And attaching himself to someone like O'Hegarty was going to yield results sooner or later. In the latter half of 1914 O'Hegarty was sent by Tom Clarke to Kinsale and Tralee to meet with the local IRB men – Austen Stack in the case of Tralee – to establish the suitability of these ports for submarine landings, contact with the Germans being well established at that point. Clearly O'Hegarty was 'in the know', at least to some extent, about such developments.[26]

Events subsequently even add to the strangeness of the case. Larry de Lacy was able to escape by the simple expedient of having slept in a different room.[27] He was not deliberately let go since the authorities went to considerable lengths to try to track him down afterwards. The British government even managed to have the US authorities arrest de Lacy in San Francisco a few years later. Dublin Castle placed a censorship warrant on the mails of his fiancée, Mary Hayes and also on those of Seán O'Hegarty's wife – in the expectation de Lacy would be

[25] RIC Crime Special Report for February 1915, TNA CO 904/164/2.
[26] Interview with Seán O'Hegarty, O'Donoghue Papers, NLI Ms 31,364(7).
[27] *Century Ireland*, 10 April 1915. Available online.

in touch with both. (Seán O'Hegarty was, of course, in prison at this time awaiting trial, so his mail would automatically be examined anyway.) Both the censorship of Mary Hayes's mail and that of Mrs. O'Hegarty was lifted after a few months when the authorities found nothing of importance.[28]

The above account suggests there may well have been homosexual activities going on in the house in Enniscorthy – though this is unprovable. There seems to have been no good reason for all these men to have been in bed together. It is not possible, nor will it ever be possible, to be definitive about something like this, since evidence is always thin on the ground, but a few relevant observations can be made.

As we saw in Chapter 7, there was something very strange about the British military's attitude to Seán O'Hegarty during the War of Independence in Cork. We saw how they went to considerable lengths to undermine the candidacy of rivals for the position of commandant of the Cork Number 1 Brigade when the post came up on the death of Terence MacSwiney, so that O'Hegarty would get the job – 'an appointment that suited the Crown forces exceedingly well'. This was unlikely, as they claimed, because O'Hegarty was 'not a brave man and was chiefly concerned with his own safety'. O'Hegarty was described as a 'fearless and courageous man' when he was appointed storeman at Cork Workhouse in 1917. Even among his critics, O'Hegarty is portrayed as a highly intelligent and capable background operator who outmanoeuvred all his supposedly more moderate colleagues, an *éminence grise*, as Peter Hart called him. For those who served under him, he was regarded as a man of great integrity, 'thoroughly honest and thoroughly genuine', as Mick Leahy described him.[29] This is not to portray him as a saint since the epithet 'surly', as he was described by Richard Mulcahy is also more than justified from some of his correspondence. But a coward? Hardly.

Perhaps he was compromised. One of the interesting things about the entire period from 1914 to 1920 is that neither the RIC nor the military appear to have any file on O'Hegarty, despite the fact that he was clearly of utmost importance to them – or if they had, it has not been released. (Most senior republicans had files, some of them very

---

[28] HQ Irish Command to Under Secretary 4 March 1915, TNA CO 904/164.
[29] Michael Leahy, UCD, O'Malley P17b/108.

169

detailed).[30] He was allowed to live quietly and unobtrusively in Ballingeary and back in Cork city later, even though throughout all that period he was organizing for the IRB and later for the Volunteers. He was not arrested or deported in 1916, though it appears that he was briefly arrested in 1917. Nor was he arrested during the War of Independence – except the one time when he was caught up in the group taken when Terence MacSwiney was arrested and, as we have seen, immediately released – even though the authorities knew well who he was. It is clear from this that Pat Margetts's assertion that O'Hegarty needed to watch his command because there were more British spies in it than just 'Cruxy' O'Connor was correct. It now seems incontrovertible that the real reason why the British wanted O'Hegarty to be in the top position in Cork in both the IRB and the IRA was that he had the most important British intelligence asset – O'Donoghue – under his wing.

O'Hegarty had been married since 1912, though he and his wife had no children. His wife, Maghdalen (known as 'Mid'), a niece of the well-known novelist an tAthar Peadar O'Laoghaire, was herself a strident and determined political activist, deeply involved in Cumann na mBan and often on the verge of going to jail herself for her own activities.[31] Could it be that the British military description of O'Hegarty as 'not a brave man' was a veiled reference that he may have had a weakness, in this case a weakness for young men? There are grounds for thinking this may have been the case.

For instance, at the time he went to Enniscorthy, his wife had apparently left him a few months earlier and had moved in with her sister.[32] It is interesting to note that the police report that noted this is annotated that 'Major Price wished Mrs O'Hegarty's address to be given as Inchimore, Ballingeary, Co. Cork and Charlotte House, Queen Street, Cork City.' Clearly, notwithstanding the lack of a file on O'Hegarty, Price was keeping a close eye on him. From 1911 onwards, O'Hegarty was a history teacher and instructor to a 'sluagh' of Na

---

[30] It should be pointed out that by 1922 Military Intelligence did finally have a file on O'Hegarty, but its contents are minuscule, considering O'Hegarty's role in the IRA.

[31] Girvin, op.cit. pp.10-12.

[32] Crime Special Report, Cork City, 3 March 1915, TNA CO 904/164. The sister's name was a Mrs E. O'Leary. *Guy's Postal Directory* 1916.

Fianna, the republican boy scouts organization set up in Cork by O'Hegarty himself, Tadgh Barry and Tomás MacCurtain.[33] However, the most suggestive evidence that O'Hegarty may have had homosexual tendencies and that these made him vulnerable to exploitation comes from British efforts to infiltrate the 1st Brigade.

Michael 'Mickeroo' Walsh, the ex-British army spy who infiltrated the IRA from 1919 and who was rescued by the British army from Cork Workhouse where O'Hegarty worked was close to O'Hegarty and was actively homosexual.[34] In November 1918 at Kent Assizes, Walsh had been 'charged with gross indecency with a male person' and spent two weeks in prison.[35] Indeed, 'Monkey Mac' McDonnell, a hairdresser/barber – to judge by the comments made by many IRA men about him, may also have been so inclined. When 'Cruxy' O'Connor managed to attach himself to the top echelons of the Brigade, many of the officers had their suspicions of him and could not understand how O'Hegarty allowed O'Connor to be 'in' on everything. The only conclusion they could come to, according to Jamie Moynihan, was that he was O'Hegarty's 'white-haired boy'; in other words, that he too had come under O'Hegarty's wing and that O'Hegarty was protecting him.[36] Was it any wonder they had Walsh shot and sent a hit team to New York to try to have O'Connor assassinated?[37]

---

[33] Girvin, op.cit. p.27.

[34] Walsh was abducted in the summer of 1920 from his place of employment at Fords motor works. Michael V. O'Donoghue, BMH WS 1741. He was tried by the IRA for spying, along with a Mrs Marshall, and sentenced to death. Before being killed, however, he was rescued in August 1920 from the Cork Workhouse by the British army. 'We sent him to England but he returned and was shot by rebels'. JO'C Kelly to AA QMG, 27 February 1921. O'Donoghue Papers, NLI Ms 31,223(1).

[35] Michael Walsh, Regimental Number 600617, Royal Engineers, Inland Waterways and Docks. Available at Findmypast.com.

[36] Jamie Moynihan, O'Malley, UCD, P17b/112.

[37] Interestingly, while there is an RIC file on almost all the 1916 leaders who also at one time or another had their respective mails censored, there is no file on the Pearse brothers nor was their mail intercepted. This is surely odd because it is clear from Dublin Castle correspondence that Patrick Pearse and his brother Willie were known to be leaders of the IRB. Was this also because Pearse was gay and there may have been a more direct route to him? One way or the other, it seems an extraordinary oversight. See Ben Novick, 'Postal censorship in Ireland, 1914-16', *Irish Historical Studies*, XXXI, no.123 (May 1999).

171

This suggests that the British may have been only too well aware of O'Hegarty's weaknesses in this regard and were more than happy to exploit them. After all, if they could place Adler Christensen in Sir Roger Casement's path in New York, they could find equivalents in Cork. O'Donoghue would have been ideal: '[my] innocent and harmless-looking appearance, which I thought was my proud possession and passport to salvation.'[38] Presumably, the classes on 'Sex as a Weapon in Intelligence', given by MI5 in London did not confine themselves to heterosexual activities. Compromising targets because of their homosexuality is one of the oldest of all tricks employed by intelligence agencies. If this is the case, this makes O'Donoghue one of the most extraordinary of all the players in the Irish revolution. And he almost got away with it.

---

[38] Borgonovo, *Florence and Josephine O'Donoghue's War of Independence*, p.153.

18

A Pearl of Great Price

Ivon Henry Price was one of the more interesting and capable military intelligence officers to see service in Ireland during World War I. The son of an engineer, he was born in County Dublin in 1866 and received a degree in Law from Trinity College in 1890. His greatest claim to fame was that, on the Monday morning of Easter Week 1916, while he was discussing the deportation of known agitators with Sir Matthew Nathan, the Under-Secretary in Dublin Castle, he heard the firing of the rebels as they shot dead a policeman on guard duty outside the Castle. He rushed downstairs, pulled out his revolver and fired on the group of rebels, who fled. Thus, he claimed, he saved the Castle singlehandedly, a claim that, it turns out, was, bizarrely, more or less true.

But Price was a much more important figure than this. In the early years of the century he had been one of the principal figures in intelligence gathering for the RIC. After receiving the King Edward VII Medal in 1903, he served as a District Inspector in the RIC's main intelligence centre, the Crimes Special Department in Dublin Castle until near the end of 1908. The 1911 Census finds him in residence as a DI in Nenagh, Co. Tipperary. It is fair to assume that he was still carrying out intelligence work while on this posting because as soon as war broke out in August 1914 Price was immediately appointed by the War Office as chief intelligence officer for the Irish Military Command, with the rank of temporary Major. (It should be pointed out that it was standard practice to appoint military officers to senior commands in the RIC – Neville Chamberlain had been a colonel and had seen service in the Boer War. It was less common for personnel to move in the opposite direction, though, as we have seen, it also happened in the case of Henry Toppin.) Price, 'who had wide experience in dealing with advanced nationalist agitation, was given the rank of major and immediately placed in charge of military intelligence in Ireland'.[1] As Chamberlain put it to the 1916 Commission: 'At the commencement of the war, I placed the services of an experienced officer of the Royal Irish Constabulary at the disposal of the military authorities in Ireland to serve in their intelligence branch. He had previously been employed for some years as the District Inspector in the 'Crimes Special Branch' and he had a thorough knowledge of its working.'[2] Thus Price effectively became head of military intelligence for Ireland, collating police as well as military intelligence.

One of his first tasks, in parallel with that set up in England by Vernon Kell, was a system of postal censorship – though his operation was only a pale shadow of that put in place in England. While MI5 had 1,453 men working in its postal censorship bureau by the end of 1915, Price had to make do with a staff of less than five in Dublin and the same in Belfast. A plan to set up a similar operation in Cork was abandoned at the end of 1915 when it was felt that the staff to be employed there were more urgently needed in London.[3] Price was in close contact with Kell throughout the war and appears to have been reporting directly to him or through MI5's officer dealing with Ireland, Major Frank Hall, who ran MI5's (g) Branch – later to become D Branch.

With a dual rank as RIC County Inspector and army Major in 1916, Price ran his operation out of army headquarters in Parkgate Street, Dublin, with a network of motorcycle couriers bringing him messages from his agents in various parts of the country. He remained in this role until the intelligence services were (rather short-sightedly as it turned out) wound down in 1919, when he reverted back to his role in the RIC. He was promoted to Assistant Inspector General of the RIC in October 1919 before being pensioned off with the disestablishment of the police force on 8 June 1922. But for almost twenty years from around 1900 to

---

[1] Ben Novick, 'Postal Censorship in Ireland, 1914-16', *Irish Historical Studies*, Vol. 31, No.123 (May 1999), pp. 343-56.

[2] Sir Neville Chamberlain, Inspector General of the RIC. Evidence given to The Royal Commission on the Rebellion in Ireland. Minutes of Evidence and Appendix of Documents, HM Stationery Office, 1916, pp. 43-51.

[3] Ben Novick, 'Postal Censorship in Ireland, 1914-16', *Irish Historical Studies*, Vol. 31, No.123 (May 1999), pp. 343-56.

174

1919, Price was a key man in police and army intelligence operations in Ireland. It appears that in the run-up to the 1916 Rising, however, the War Office kept Price in the dark regarding the impending rebellion, and it is clear that they were getting at least some of their core intelligence directly from Ireland rather than through Price.

Price's *modus operandi* can be seen from the account of Robert Brennan, a journalist with the *Enniscorthy Echo* and a member of the IRB and later Irish Ambassador to the United States. Brennan recalled his encounter with Price when he was trying to negotiate on behalf of Jim Bolger, his brother-in-law, who had been arrested with O'Hegarty and was facing trial – with potentially deadly consequences.

The discovery and the arrests caused a sensation. The Dublin newspapers gave the event big headlines. The two prisoners were kept incommunicado and they were whisked away in the dead of night to Arbour Hill barracks in Dublin. We learned that the opinion of the police was that they would be courtmartialed and shot. I got orders from the Supreme Council of the IRB that I was to go to Dublin to try and secure an interview with Bolger, and Una [Brennan's wife and Jim Bolger's sister] came with me. After many futile calls on various officials we were directed to see Major Price, the Chief of the British Intelligence Service in Ireland. He had a very sinister reputation and all our Dublin friends warned us that we were to be very careful about what we said to him as he was dangerous. I was surprised to find that he was child's play. We saw him at the Headquarters of the Irish Command near the entrance of the Phoenix Park. He was a tall handsome man with suave and polished manners and he was even polite to the orderly when he told him he wished to be alone with us.

I said to him that we had come up to see Bolger and told him of the relationship. He replied that the young man was in great danger and might be executed. He had been found sleeping in the house which was, undoubtedly, the headquarters of the rebels in the Wexford area. I protested that I was sure Bolger had nothing to do with any rebel movement, and that he was a most law-abiding citizen and that he knew nothing of what was going on in that house.

'He's in bad company,' said the Major.

'I'm sure he was not aware of that,' I replied.

'Very well,' said the Major. 'If that is so, you can see him. Get him to write down the names of all those who frequented that house. If he does that, he can go home with you. Will you promise me that you will ask him that?'

'Sure I will,' I said.

So we saw Bolger and when I had conveyed to him the information that the Dublin men were raising a defence fund for him and that they were going to move heaven and earth to have them tried by jury, I said loud enough for anyone who might be listening to hear:

'Major Price says that all you have to do to get out is to write down the names of all those who frequented that house.'

175

He did not laugh though he knew my own name would be the first one on the list.

I couldn't do that,' he said. 'The only ones I saw there were ourselves. I always left early in the morning and got back late at night.'[4]

It is safe to say Price was not as ignorant of who was coming and going from the house as he let on to Brennan. But clearly he was a perfectly mannerly and civilized man looking for as much information as he could find. Since it was almost certainly Price who ordered Seán O'Hegarty's arrest, it is likely that the presence of O'Hegarty and the (literally) explosive contents of the house were notified to him by 'the small fair man' who went to Dublin with his information the previous morning.

As we have seen, there is a link between Price and O'Donoghue through Jack Healy, Price's army intelligence courier, and his membership of O'Donoghue's IRA cycle company in Cork.[5] Was he the conduit of messages gathered by O'Donoghue as a result of his work as officer in charge of the cycle corps and elsewhere until Healy – and Price were retired from the service in 1919? The very fact that O'Donoghue neglects to mention Healy in his lists of the cycle company membership, though he was a member, suggests that this may well have been the case.[6]

---

[4] Robert Brennan, BMS WS 779.
[5] See Chapter 11.
[6] Membership of Cyclist Company Cork No.1 Brigade 1917-1920. O'Donoghue Papers, NLI, Ms 31,340(10).

19

Rising without trace

You are coming to the time when you will have to choose one of two roads in life. One is going to bring you a lot of crosses and trouble. I don't know which you are going to take.[1]

These are the words a fortune teller spoke to Florrie O'Donoghue around 1917. It is clear that at this stage O'Donoghue was trying to travel two roads at the same time. But if he was any of the things implied by the last few chapters, he would have to have been a member of either the IRB or the Volunteers before 1916. He claimed himself that he did not join the Cork Volunteers until February 1917. So he could not have been 'out' in 1916. Or could he?

O'Donoghue's account of how he joined the Volunteers is full of inconsistencies. Notwithstanding the fact that in his IRA pension application he claimed that he did not come to Cork until the winter of 1916, he says: 'On Easter Sunday 1916, when I was very busy in the shop, a first cousin of mine Pat O'Conner called.' Pat O'Connor, a member of the Volunteers and the IRB, was on his way from his brother's funeral to Dublin to take part in the Easter Rising where he would be killed a few days later. O'Donoghue claimed that he did not know his cousin was a Volunteer, let alone a member of the IRB, even though it is clear they were close. It is also strange that he should say he was busy in the shop, it being Easter Sunday, since he states elsewhere in his memoir that Sunday was the only day in the week when he was not working and so was free to carry out his Volunteer work. Would a

---

[1] A fortune telling lady to O'Donoghue, probably sometime in 1917. Borgonovo, p.28.

177

man of religious convictions like O'Donoghue have been working in his employer's shop on Easter Sunday?

He says he joined the Volunteers in the spring of 1917, that is to say some nine months after the Easter Rising, when he states he and Leo Murphy went to the Volunteer Hall in Sheares Street, Cork to join up. He claims he first met Tomás MacCurtain and Terence MacSwiney in the spring of 1917 after they had been released from prison, though he did not get to know them well until later since 'their minds were completely out of reach'. Yet, remarkably, he claims it was in the first months of 1917 that he joined the Cycle Company and in April or May of that year he was invited to join the IRB.

In April or May of 1917 I was sworn into the Irish Republican Brotherhood. This was a secret, oath-bound society, small in numbers but comprising only carefully selected personnel. Its previous existence was known since the Rising, but this was the first indication I had that it was being reorganized. The pre-Rising strength in Cork did not exceed twenty, and at the time of my invitation it was still under twenty, though there were over one thousand Volunteers in the city.[2]

What this is telling us is that, within months of joining the Volunteers, this unprepossessing young fellow just up from Kerry had become one of a 'carefully selected personnel' who were invited to join an ultra secret, oath-bound society. He claims he was soon allowed to attend Brigade Council meetings and that it was at one of these meetings that he met Sean O'Hegarty for the first time – notwithstanding the fact that it appears he was almost found in the same bed as O'Hegarty two years earlier: 'In some ways he [O'Hegarty] was a more forceful character than Tomás, he had a fine intelligence and a faith and determination that literally blazed in his eyes when he was moved. He was then slight, sallow, with a heavy moustache, magnificent eyes and an intellectual forehead. He had not MacCurtain's genial imperturbability, nor half his humorous tolerance and understanding of human frailty.'[3]

In February 1918 MacCurtain asked O'Donoghue if he would be happy to take on the role of Brigade Adjutant. After some hesitation – according to his own account – O'Donoghue agreed. The appointment

---

[2] Borgonovo, p.31.
[3] Borgonovo, p.37.

was unanimous. Nobody stood in his way. 'I was in that post until I went on promotion to the Division in April 1921, and it was a liberal education. Everything administrative and much besides came into my hands. Soon there was not the smallest aspect of Brigade activity into which I had not poked my nose.'[4]

The obvious question here is how did O'Donoghue, in little more than a year, rise from knowing nothing about the Volunteers or caring less about their activities, to being a member of the Brigade Council, officer commanding the Cycle Company, which at MacCurtain's urging was now a proto-intelligence and communications system, member of the IRB and now also Brigade Adjutant? Given that the rank of adjutant is probably the most important role in any military organization since he is the one who deals with the detail, this could only be described as an astonishingly rapid rise to prominence. It might be explained in 1916 by the fact that many of the senior Volunteers were in jail. But O'Donoghue's elevation into all these roles came about after the imprisoned Volunteers had been released. Clearly there must be something he is not telling us. In Chapter 17 we saw how a young man with the same characteristics as O'Donoghue was sharing a house in Wexford with Seán O'Hegarty. So the question is: is there evidence that he had more background in the insurgency movement than he let on in the above, almost universally accepted, account? The answer is almost certainly yes.

In the blurb of his first book, his 1955 biography of Tomás MacCurtain, O'Donoghue is described as follows: 'Major O'Donoghue, a member of the pre-1916 IRB, joined the Irish Volunteers in Cork in 1914'.[5] When the book came out, the Cork 1916 Men's Association produced a substantial pamphlet correcting the faults they had found in the book. This is a scrupulous examination from the men who were members of the Volunteers in Cork in 1916. One of the many things they picked up on was O'Donoghue's assertion that the Royal Navy became aware of the *Aud* only when it reached Tralee Bay, correctly pointing out that: 'The capture was not the result of suspicions. The British officially claimed that they were aware of the voyage of the *Aud*

---

[4] ibid.
[5] Back cover of Florence O'Donoghue: *Tomás MacCurtain: Soldier and Patriot*, 1955 edition, Anvil Press, Tralee.

from start to finish, and that the arrest was made as soon as it was expedient.' As we have seen in Chapter 12, this is essentially correct, and points to O'Donoghue's habitual practice of downplaying British intelligence successes. The booklet points out over thirty errors in O'Donoghue's book, some of them relatively minor but others that give an entirely distorted picture of what happened in Cork in 1916 and later.

The important point is that it is extremely unlikely that the Cork Men's Association would have failed to spot such a blatant, double error on the cover of the book, stating that O'Donoghue was involved pre-1916 in both the IRB and the Volunteers if he was not. I think we can take it that the view of the committee of the Cork 1916 Men's Association was that he was indeed a member of the IRB and the Volunteers before 1916, which would mean of course that, instead of knowing little or nothing about it until afterwards, he had been 'out' in 1916 and had been a member of the Volunteers and the IRB as far back as 1914 and that the 'small, fair man' in Enniscothy was indeed O'Donoghue. It is also highly unlikely that there would be such a blatant error concerning his career on the cover of his own book. In his last year, 1967, O'Donoghue wrote the foreword and contributed several articles to a book on IRA jailbreaks. The book did not come out until 1971. When it did, it contained brief biographical sketches of the contributors. According to this: 'A member of the pre-1916 IRB, O'Donoghue joined the Irish Volunteers in Cork in 1914'.[6] If this was an error in 1955, it is probably fair to suggest that there would have been adequate time to correct it by 1971. O'Donoghue was to go to considerable lengths in the 1950s to try to track down copies of the 1916 Roll of Honour which had been compiled by the committee of those who were members of the Cork Volunteers in 1916, to see whether he was on the list or not. He was not on it, and therein lies another story, in this case a tale of profound mistrust.

The context of this was that 1916 was remembered by Cork city Volunteers as an ignominious climb-down. The confused orders and counter-orders issued from Dublin was what created the chaos. MacCurtain and MacSwiney were subsequently court-martialed for the failure of the Cork Volunteers to rise. They were both exonerated since

---

[6] *IRA Jailbreaks*, Foreword by Florence O'Donoghue, (Tralee, 1971, reissued Cork, 2010), p.305.

the circumstances they found themselves in were outside their control. The point is that nobody wanted to talk too much about it afterwards. (One of the outcomes of this was that MacCurtain and MacSwiney both resigned from the IRB, allowing O'Hegarty and O'Donoghue ultimately to take control of that organization in Cork.)

While trying to track down the 1916 Roll of Honour in the late 1940s, O'Donoghue received a letter from a veteran of the 1916 Cork Volunteers. Referring to himself only as 'Dick', he gave an interesting account of the events of Easter Week in Cork, in which he states categorically that O'Donoghue had indeed been a member of the Volunteers in 1916:

There was a stand-to from [Good] Friday and the official messenger was a chap with a bicycle with a bunch of cabbage plants tied to the carrier. I think his name was Sullivan. He lived in Horgans Buildings.

Sat night [Easter Saturday night 1916] you were both on duty in the Vol[unteer] Hall whilst I was left in charge of the guns with a revolver and orders to shoot anyone who came into the house without the pre-arranged signal. You marched off from Sheares Street to Macroom to fight & returned at night weary, dispirited and wet to the skin. You were the youngest armed man to march out to fight – there were some Fianna boys but they were unarmed.[7]

This is clearly stating that O'Donoghue was involved in 1916, that he was on duty along with the cyclist with the cabbage plants at the Volunteer Hall on the Saturday night, that he went to Macroom on Easter Sunday and that he returned 'weary, dispirited and wet to the skin'. This tallied with most accounts of that day: the dejected state the Volunteers were in, having 'marched' to Macroom and returned to Cork sodden and demoralized without having fired a shot. The dreadful weather conditions are also regularly commented on.[8]

---

[7] Undated letter from 'Dick and Dolly', O'Donoghue Papers NLI Ms 31,338. 'Dick' may have been Dick Murphy, although Dick Murphy of 'A' Company died in the United States in 1934. There were several Dick Murphys in the Cork Volunteers then and later. There was also a Dick Henchion and a Dick O'Neill in 'A' Company and at least a dozen other Richards in the Cork City Volunteers.

[8] They did not actually march. Some went by bicycle, others by train and the senior officers by car. They all met up at Crookstown and then marched to Macroom. See Gerry White and Brendan O'Shea, *'Baptized in Blood': The Formation of the Cork Brigade of the Irish Volunteers 1913-1916*, (Cork, 2005) pp. 93-109.

181

'Dick' then goes on to say how, after Easter Week, many of the Cork Volunteers disobeyed the order from the British to hand in their rifles to the Lord Mayor on the advice of Dr Cohalan, the Bishop of Cork, and how they spirited them away – only about 20 percent of the guns were handed in. It is clear that Captain Dickie, the chief military intelligence officer in Cork, was aware that most of the usable rifles were not handed in.[9] The houses where the guns had been kept were then raided by the military – suggesting that the military were privy to where the remainder of the guns might have been hidden: 'Our house was one of the first to be raided. I think you should remember that since you were in bed when it was raided.'[10] Referring to some of the Volunteer officers' roles in 1916 'Dick' also appeared to remember O'Donoghue's role during Easter week: 'Yes, Jack Scanlon was [there] (Capt Jack), as was Christy Gorman and the Cotters. Har was Batt[alion] Quartermaster and you were Aide de Coy [*sic*] to Tomás.' The intimate tone of the letter suggests that it is likely that 'Dick', 'Har' and O'Donoghue were all members of the same company of the Volunteers in 1916 – that is to say, A Company – under the command of 'Captain Jack' (Seán) Scanlon. The 'Har' referred to is almost certainly Harry Varian, who was company quartermaster of A Coy since he is referred to as 'Harry' elsewhere.[11] If 'Dick' is correct, then Florence O'Donoghue was aide-de-camp to Tomás MacCurtain in 1916, in other words, two years before he said he was. Several Vounteer officers cite him as witnesses for their service during 1916 – something they would hardly have done were he not serving himself.[12]

The Cork 1916 Men's Association had been established at Easter 1946 on the thirtieth anniversary of the Rising: 'The first task was to compile a record of all those who paraded under arms on Easter Sunday

---

[9] See correspondence between Moirin Chavasse, O'Donoghue and Wallace Dickie. NLI, Ms 31,282(1).

[10] 'Dick and Dolly' letter, O'Donoghue Papers NLI Ms 31,338.

[11] ibid. O'Donoghue refers to Varian as 'one of the tough men of my old G Company.' Borgonovo, p.59. So they appear to have been members of the same company. However, it was called A Coy rather than G Coy in 1916. See the 1916 Roll of Honour for the Cork City Volunteers in Seán Murphy *et al*, BMH WS 1598. The officers listed for A Company were Seán Scanlon, Paddy Corkery, Seán Hurley and Harry Varian.

[12] Martin Corry, MSP34REF4079. Joseph O'Connor, MSP34REF1878.

1916 which is now embodied on a specially designed commemorative certificate ... which took two years to compile.' The Roll of Honour was printed on 5 June 1948 and can now be found on a commemorative monument put up by the descendants of many of the men and unveiled on the centenary of the Rising at Parnell Bridge in Cork.[13]

O'Donoghue's name is not on it – despite the evidence above that he was a member of A Company. The inside story was that O'Donoghue was detested by the Cork 1916 Men's Association. It has not been possible to establish the exact details of the falling out but they appear to date back to the attempts by the IRB under O'Hegarty to put all the Volunteers' arms under their own control in 1918. Quartermaster Seán Murphy was effectively forced to resign from the IRB as a result, though he carried on as Volunteer quartermaster. His family recall O'Donoghue regularly visiting their house when they were young and Seán Murphy's wife being sent to the front door to send him packing by telling him that Seán was not in. The words used to describe O'Donoghue at the time were not complimentary.[14] The reasons for this are hinted at in Murphy's Bureau of Military History witness statement made in 1957 where, along with three other veterans representing the 1916 Committee, he alleges that there was a 'whispering campaign' against MacCurtain and MacSwiney from within the Volunteers: 'it was alleged that they made an abject surrender to the British Military Authorities, and that they handed up all the guns and ammunition in their possession to the enemy without a struggle. Nothing could be further from the truth than gossip of this kind.' As we have seen, the Volunteers handed up only a fraction of their weapons, something the British were only too well aware of. The British raided for the rest – in a house in which O'Donoghue was sleeping. Murphy confirms the broader picture when he quotes Bishop Cohalan: 'Monday, May 8th. The police are searching the city for the remainder of the arms, which would have been given to the Lord Mayor if the military party had kept

---

[13] The original certificate is in the possession of Johnny McCarthy, grandson of Seán Murphy who compiled it.

[14] I am grateful to Tara Breen and Johnny McCarthy, Seán Murphy's grandchildren, for this information and also for granting me access to the family's documentation on those years.

183

faith with me and the Lord Mayor'. So clearly the truth appears to lie on Murphy and his colleagues' side, rather than on O'Donoghue's.

Would that have been enough to drop him from the roll though? Riobárd Langford was also accused of putting out false allegations about MacCurtain and MacSwiney that they prevented an engine driver from derailing an armoured train on its way from Cork to Dublin with troops during Easter Week. Yet he is included in the roll as 2nd Lieutenant of C Company, which indeed he was. O'Donoghue's crime must be greater than being a mere rumour-monger.[15] The interesting thing about the Roll as printed is that there is a precise role into which O'Donoghue would have slotted had his name been included. The membership of all four of the city companies, plus the officers and the Na Fianna members who were out in 1916 are listed. Most of the companies have five officers named. All have a captain, 1st and 2nd lieutenant, three out of four have a quartermaster and all but one has an adjutant. The missing adjutant is from A Company, the company of 'Dick' and 'Har' and 'Captain Jack' Scanlon. Was O'Donoghue actually adjutant of A Coy and at the same time aide-de-camp to MacCurtain – and thus at the very centre of things? This is highly likely to have been the case and that he adjusted what he wrote afterwards to suit his agenda. Clearly the surviving members of A Coy must have had their suspicions too.

In 1947 the Bureau of Military History began its work of collecting the accounts of veterans of the revolutionary years. The early submissions for Cork Volunteers begin with 1916. By the end of 1947

---

[15] Seán Murphy et al, BMH WS 1598. Langford was to stick to his story, including it in his own Bureau submission. Riobárd Langford BMH WS 16. There was an armoured train sent to Dublin during Easter Week. But it was sent from Belfast. See report on armoured train, TNA, ADM 137/1187. There was one brief mention of the train in the newspapers, in the *Meath Chronicle* of 6 May 1915 to be precise. It is highly unlikely this would have been read in Cork however. On the matter of the armoured train you would have to wonder where Langford got wind of such a story. This was a joint army and naval operation and was commanded by a naval officer, Lieutenant Colin Campbell. It travelled from Belfast to Amiens Street Station in Dublin and back again. Its function is unclear, though it appears to have been bringing reinforcements from the 10th Royal Irish Fusiliers, as well as naval personnel. The important point is that his was not publicly known at the time, suggesting that Langford may have been told of it by someone with knowledge of naval or army matters.

some ninety submissions were in – the last one of these for Cork was that of Con Collins, witnessed on 30 December of that year. All the Cork statements up to this point were taken and witnessed by Florrie O'Donoghue. What is interesting about this is that not a single member of A Coy is listed as having given a statement during those early years. In fact, the only member of A Coy who ever gave a BMH statement was Patrick Canton and he gave it in 1957 as part of the Seán Murphy group, long after O'Donoghue had been removed from his role in the BMH. So either the A Coy members were the most reticent company in the Volunteers or they were not asked to give submissions. Maybe O'Donoghue ignored them in 1947 or they gave submissions but these were not passed on to the Bureau. The latter may indeed have been the case.[16] A page with a list of personnel has been removed from Con Collins's statement, which had been witnessed by O'Donoghue and is accurate in all other respects.[17] Con Collins is another one of those whose reliability was questioned by O'Donoghue in correspondence with the Bureau.[18] It does appear, though, that O'Donoghue was using the Bureau to clean up the record of Cork in 1916. It is now becoming obvious why he was doing so.

Something else that becomes apparent from the accounts of Cork veterans of 1916 is that the cycle company of the Volunteers was in existence well before 1917 when O'Donoghue claimed he helped set it up.[19] In fact, the cycle company was one of the groups that travelled to Crookstown and thence to Macroom on Easter Sunday morning 1916. From 1914 to 1916 the cycle company was commanded by Fred Murray, though on Easter Sunday morning it was under Seán O'Sullivan. The messenger boy with the cabbage plants and O'Donoghue on their bicycles almost certainly played a role in events in Cork in 1916, but did O'Donoghue play a bigger role? MacCurtain was the head of both the Volunteers and the IRB in Cork in 1916. In the latter role he was aware of the upcoming rising well before it took place.

---

[16] A case in point is the submission of Diarmuid Ó Donnabháin, which is in O'Donoghue's papers but not in the Bureau records. NLI, Ms 31,334(7).

[17] Con Collins, BMH WS 90. The document is stated as consisting of six typed pages. Only five survive. The list begins on the page before the missing page, page 2 – so we know it existed.

[18] O'Donoghue Papers, NLI 31,368.

[19] Liam de Roiste, BMH WS 1698 and Fred Murray, BMH WS 15.

The question is: how much of this did his aide-de-camp know and when did he know it, and did he pass that information up the line? Is this why he was so busy creating a smokescreen about what the British did or did not know in the run-up to 1916?

Is this why he pretended he was not 'out' in 1916? Is this why he is missing from the roll of honour and held in extremely poor regard by the compilers of the roll? Being coy about the success of British intelligence in tracking the *Aud* and predicting the 1916 Rising with perfect accuracy all appear to be part of the same story.

Could it be that O'Donoghue played some role in the search for the missing weapons? Did he play a bigger role in tipping off British intelligence about the forthcoming rising, something he would have picked up from Sean O'Hegarty, one of the few Corkmen, along with Tomás MacCurtain and Terence MacSwiney, who knew about it well in advance? Was he the 'very reliable informant' whose information led to the prediction of the Rising by the Director of Military Intelligence and whose information, probably passed through MI5, was of such use to Joseph Byrne during his three years as Inspector General of the RIC? Given that O'Donoghue was attached to the intelligence services from 1911 the evidence points very strongly in that direction.

And there is a corollary to this. By the time of the War of Independence, A Company of the original Cork Brigade of the Volunteers had became G Company of the 1st Battalion in a reorganized Volunteer structure. It still retained some of its old members, men like Harry and Paddy Varian, and Dan, Dick and Joe Murphy. Along with its Nominal Roll submitted to the IRA Pensions Board in 1936, the Company Captain at the time of the Truce, Tadgh Twohig, sent a note to the Pensions Board, 'an 'explanatory note re Officers of G/Comp, 1st Batt'. Explaining the various roles played by the company officers at various stages and the fact that a great number of the members of the company had been jailed during the War of Independence, Twohig wrote: 'The word "Interned" in enclosed Roll covers both sentenced & interned prisoners. 10 were sentenced & 25 interned. (The unusually large number of prisoners in this Company *was due to the fact that one member of the Comp [sic] was in the pay of the British & was not discovered until a short time before the Truce* [italics added], when he paid the penalty of his crime.)'[20]. In fact, it was documentation from A/G Company that was 'found' in Terence MacSwiney's dest at Cork City Hall that led to his conviction.

Is it possible that this refers to O'Donoghue? The last part of the sentence would suggest not, that the informer in question was probably executed.[21] Yet this is all very odd. Because in his list of members of the company, which is extremely detailed and accurate, Twohig includes many of the original members. Yet he neglects to mention O'Donoghue, who was certainly a member since he says so himself in his pension application form and elsewhere and is detailed in the Brigade activity series as having taken part in several actions with the company, such as the attack on Blarney RIC barracks and the raid on Clarke's of Farran, of which he took such a dim view.[22] Other officers who had long since left the company, O'Donoghue stalwarts such as Joe O'Conner – mentioned as 'Staff of 1st S. Division', Matt Ryan, who was O'Donoghue's secretary during his months with the Division in the summer of 1921, and Paddy O'Reilly of Youghal are all listed. Yet O'Donoghue, who served longer than any of them – in fact well before 1916 if the above evidence is to be accepted – is not mentioned at all. Maybe some of the surviving members of A/G Coy had more than mere suspicions and that the 'penalty for his crime' was that he was blacked by the Company members for ever and excluded from the rolls of honour, having being saved in the first instance by the Truce and subsequently by his senior position within the IRA.

It is interesting that in this context another member of the company, Dubliner Stephen Foley, who was First Lieutenant, mentions two

---

[20] List of members of 'G' Coy and Note re Officers of 'G' Company, 1st Battalion, Cork No. 1 Brigade. April 1935. IRA Nominal Rolls, MA/MSPC/RO/28.

[21] It is possible that this may be a reference to the killing of Denis O'Donovan as an alleged spy in April 1921. However, this was not shortly before the Truce and O'Donovan was not a member of the company and certainly not an officer. Besides, O'Donovan appears to have been blamed for a specific incident, information reaching the police on the killers of Sergeant O'Donoghue of the RIC in late 1920. This is a particularly murky tale.

[22] IRA Brigade Activities Series MA/MSPC/A/(G)1. O'Donoghue states in his own IRA pension application that he was a member of 'A' Company of the city Volunteers from early February 1917. MSP34REF2091.

meetings with O'Donoghue in his BMH witness statement. In the first he remembered encountering O'Donoghue in Parnell Square in Dublin while part of a group on their way to shoot District Inspector Swanzy in Lisburn. O'Donoghue appeared out of the blue, from a hotel doorway, to inform the group that the job had been called off – which it had not. In the second, Foley, again in Dublin, was on his way to do a job in England – the plan to shoot members of the British cabinet is mentioned – when he was again waylaid by O'Donoghue. 'I thought you'd be over in England already.' O'Donoghue told him[23]. It should be pointed out that this 'job' also came to be known to the British authorities.

And almost as if he had a sixth sense that Twohig and Foley might have passed on some home truths, O'Donoghue goes on to cast aspersions on their service and their reliability in subsequent correspondence with the Pensions Board. 'We would like to point out that "G" company committee have been working without the aid of Tadg [sic] Twohig or Stephen Foley, both being away from the City, consequently their efforts were seriously handicapped.'[24] This was despite the fact that Twohig had already send in a full list of the membership of G Company and it was more comprehensive than that sent in by 'the committee'. Stephen Foley got his wings clipped as well: 'We would further point out that Stephen Foley did not act as an officer of the company during the Truce or subsequently, at the same time he was never officially informed that his rank was withdrawn, since the matter did not arise.'[25] In point of fact, Twohig had already told the board: 'On the outbreak of the Civil War, Timothy Twohig was sent in charge of a Column to Limerick & 1st Lieutenant Stephen Foley was in the same column.' Clearly somebody was lying. This is all too typical of the kind of whitewashing that O'Donoghue carried out throughout his life. Maybe the reactions of members of A/G Company is simply proof you cannot fool all the people all the time.[26]

---

[23] Stephen Foley, BMH WS 1669.

[24] Old IRA Men's Association, Cork County to the Referee, Military Pensions Board, 29 February 1936. The letter is signed by O'Donoghue, Tom Crofts and Liam O'Riordan. IRA Nominal Rolls, MA/MSPC/RO/28.

[25] ibid.

[26] The question of how much was known in IRA circles about O'Donoghue's undercover activities is a topic that will be examined in more detail in the third volume of this series.

20

Florence and the Machine

One of the more intriguing questions in all this is which part of the British Secret Service machine O'Donoghue was working for. This is not easy to establish. Secret Services tend to keep their secrets – especially where their agents are concerned. All the evidence suggests that he was part of military intelligence, rather than the Special Branch, Scotland Yard or RIC operations in Ireland. Even within military intelligence, there are no shortage of permutations, from field intelligence to the Intelligence Corps – as represented in Ireland by Ivon Price – to MI5. And there is even a possibility that, at least for a time, O'Donoghue may also have been involved with naval intelligence.

What we can say is that having been recruited as an agent in 1911, he was likely to have been part of the Secret Intelligence Bureau almost from its inception. This suggests that, *inter alia*, he must have been in some way associated with MI5's operations. Which means that from 1914 onwards he was reporting either directly to Major Frank Hall who ran 'g' section – later to be renamed 'D' Section – the part of MI5 with direct responsibility for Ireland, and that later he was working though Ivon Price and the Irish Command.

It is quite clear from even a cursory examination of the early SIB files that they are coy when it comes to Ireland. Yet, as we have seen, even as early as 20 December 1911, just after O'Donoghue joined the service, Kell was receiving information from Cork, when a large envelope containing a sketch map of coastal defences and addressed to a

German in London was picked up in Castletownbere.[27] This suggests at the very least that the recently conceived plan for 'the earmarking and training of our own spies in Coastal Counties' was working.[28] It should be pointed out that this was well before Kell got around to setting up a liaison with the RIC through its Inspector General. This he only managed to do in April 1913.[29]

In April 1915, part of MI5, named section A3, was set up under Hall. 'To section A3, Major F. Hall, General Staff, were allocated all cases of suspected espionage, sedition or treachery in Ireland.'[30] 'The importance of Irish affairs is proved by the formation of a special section to deal entirely with them.'[31] The *Sayanora* correspondence found in O'Donoghue's papers seems to have come out of this surveillance. The Irish Coastal Intelligence Corps mentioned in the document was almost certainly part of the 'civil intelligence service' set up as part of a civilian 'Observer Scheme' by Kell in 1910.[32] It is clear that information on the main suspects accused of sedition, people like Ernest Blythe, Herbert Pim, Liam Mellows and Denis McCullough, was being sourced through MI5 in 1915 and early 1916. As Kell put it: 'There is no doubt in my mind that these sort of men are among the most dangerous we have in our midst and nothing short of internment will stop the mischief.' Kell sent Hall to Dublin in July 1915 to personally 'explain the whole case to the GoC in C. Ireland'.[33] Interestingly, there is no mention of extending this courtesy to Dublin Castle. Hall and Kell's fingerprints are all over the case against Roger Casement. Indeed, it is now believed that it was Frank Hall rather than Reginald 'Blinker' Hall who suggested that the separatist movement was a festering sore that needed to be lanced: 'better let this festering sore come to a head'. If this reflected the view of his commanding officers, Kell and the Director of Military Intelligence, it effectively

---

[27] The German in London could not be traced. Kell Bureau Progress Reports 1910-1914, TNA, KV1/9.

[28] Kell Bureau Report, April-October 1910, TNA KV1/9.

[29] He established contact with the 'Director General' of the RIC to this end on 9 April 1913. Kell Bureau Progress Reports, TNA, KV1/9.

[30] German Espionage, MI5g Branch Reports, TNA KV1/42.

[31] ibid.

[32] Kell, General Duties, 1909-1910, TNA KV1/35.

[33] Notes from Kell, 17 June 1916 and 6 July 1915. Cover file notes, TNA 141/5.

nudged the British into allowing the Rising to go ahead in the knowledge that it would be crushed.[34] The question of whether the information flow was being processed through Price becomes largely academic from October 1915 when 'a further gap in the co-ordination of home defence was filled by the instructions of District Intelligence Officers to link up the armies in the United Kingdom with the Directorate'. These officers were trained by MO5g (MI5g).[35] This suggests that by 1916 there was something approaching a unitary command system for intelligence and that what was being picked up in a provincial city like Cork was at the very least being shared with the Irish Command in Parkgate Street in Dublin.

This system appears to have worked relatively well up until the Easter Rising of 1916 when Hall still had his 'reliable informant' operating in Queenstown. As we have seen, the Director of Military Intelligence, George Macdonogh, got warning of the Rising, down to the very date it began and, with the help of NID's Room 40 telegraph interceptions, the military in Queenstown were able to throw a cordon around Munster on Good Friday when Spindler and the *Aud* were expected to arrive in Tralee Bay. Hall claimed he had informed Dublin Castle of the imminent arrival of Casement in Tralee Bay on Good Friday 1916, but that was ignored.[36] By the end of 1916, however, Hall seemed to be getting his best information via Price's operation in Dublin. In mid-October Price passed on an extremely accurate portrait of how things were operating within the IRB in Munster – 'information supplied from a well-informed source which has hitherto been found reliable'. This details the visits of Seán Ó Muirthile ('John O'Hurley') to Waterford and Cork, 'to consult with the leaders there and to find out the cause of the activity in military and police circles during the past week'.[37] This suggests that by now the 'well-informed source' may have been reporting to Price, though he was still probably based in Cork.

---

[34] Jeffrey Dudgeon, *Roger Casement: The Black Diaries* (Belfast, 2002), p.485. Also Gerry Doherty and Jim Macgregor's Hidden Histories series: Ireland 1916, 7: Who Knew What … and When? First World War Hidden History. Available online.

[35] G Branch Reports on German Espionage 1916. TNA, KV1/43.

[36] Jeffrey Dudgeon, *Roger Casement: The Black Diaries* (Belfast, 2002), p.483.

[37] F. Hall, MI5D to DID 15 October 1916. TNA, ADM 223/761.

Thereafter, however, MI5's usefulness when it came to Ireland went into decline. Whether this was due to the exigencies of war or simply because of overwork on the part of Hall and his staff is unclear. Certainly, the charge of hubris can be made, the view being that the wound had been lanced by allowing the Rising to go ahead and the leaders executed or jailed. Did Kell and Hall – and indeed Byrne for a while – believe they had achieved 'victory' against the separatists by crushing their rebellion and locking up the leaders from around the country? With Kell and Byrne being decorated, perhaps the military felt it had won. Besides, the War Office had more than enough on its plate with a world war going on.

Overwork is probably the main reason though. Because this also coincided with Hall's section, now renamed G3, getting responsibility for processing intelligence on enemy agents from nearly all foreign countries outside of Scandinavia, Holland and the belligerent European states. Hall had just one secretary – with additional help from Major Sidney Welchman and two of his secretaries – but it was surely an overwhelming task to process intelligence emanating from all corners of the globe but most particularly from British colonies and dominions. 'In September 1916 the work in Ireland and in the Dominions had grown to such dimensions that G3 was constituted into an independent branch known as D.'[38] And so the permutations and combinations kept changing.

Direct intelligence was still dribbling in of course. For instance, German American spy George Vaux Bacon was seen to meet with Sinn Feiners in Cork in December 1916 and also in Belfast.[39] As late as September 1917 Hall still retained his 'reliable informant' in Queenstown.[40] At the end of the war MI5 wrote up a report detailing its activities in Ireland. 'Special report on Ireland touching on connections of espionage and sedition.'[41] Unfortunately, this has not been released, and the likelihood is that it may never be released.

---

[38] G Branch Reports, TNA KV1/43.

[39] Bacon was subsequently convicted of treason and sentenced to be hanged. However, as a result of American pressure he was reprieved and repatriated to the United States. Note of 13 December 1916, G Branch Reports 1916, TNA, KV1/43. TNA KV2/5.

[40] Note by Hall to DID, 29 September 1917. TNA, ADM 223/761.

[41] 'D' Branch Report sheets, p.83. TNA, KV1/68.

A summary of the work of D Branch has however recently been released. While short on specifics, it does paint the overall picture. 'Since the discovery of the help given to Ireland by Germany in connection with the Rebellion of April 1916, the Irish work of MI5 had become much more important. By February 1917, in addition to the investigation in consultation with G, cases of espionage and sedition in Ireland which had considerably increased in number, D Branch had now become responsible for the examination of intercepted correspondence relating to Colonial or Irish-American affairs, and co-operated with the Home Office and other Government Departments on matters connected with German-Irish-American intrigues; it also dealt with Irish Intelligence reports in co-operation with GHQ H[ome] F[Forces].'[42]

There is no doubt that after the end of the war and the general winding down of MI5 and MI6 Hall had another reason for neglecting Ireland. In 1919 and 1920, while he successfully 'carried on the collection and distribution of information about Sinn Fein activities in England and the USA. He was [now] unable, however, to get good informants in Ireland, and in April 1920, in compliance with Lord Curzon's Committee, his work in Ireland was handed over to Sir Basil Thomson.'[43] Thomson's efforts did not turn out to be a whole lot better.

Hall continued to be involved in Irish affairs, however. In addition to his work in MI5, from 1916 he had taken over a small agency known as 'Q' which was run by the Home Office and involved itself in gathering information on Irish Republican activities in England and the United States. In 1919 he was also forced to hand that office over to Sir Basil Thomson.[44] But all was not all plain sailing with the new structures because there were a group of agents who refused to work under the police in the new set-up – and who presumably refused to work for Thomson, who was regarded by military men as a shyster and a careerist. 'In May 1919, the services of a group of agents, who refused to work under the police, were placed at the disposal of the intelligence officer at GHQ. From this group a considerable amount of information

---

[42] MI5 D Branch Summary Report, TNA, KV1/19.
[43] The Home Office Secret Service: Historical Note, 28 November 1921, TNA KV4/151.
[44] Memo by the Home Secretary, 23 January 1919, and Home Secretary's Historical Note, 28 November 1921, TNA, KV4/151.

about Sinn Fein and the Irish Volunteers was obtained.'[45] The question is who was this group working for before May 1919 – MI5 or GHQ Ireland? The former more likely, seeing as they were *now* placed 'at the disposal' of GHQ.

But these gains were quickly lost with the winding up of much of the military intelligence apparatus in 1919, with Price returning to the RIC and Byrne increasingly side-lined by unionist elements both within cabinet and in Dublin Castle. The irony is that the repressive measures put in place during the Lord Lieutenancy of Lord French and encouraged by unionist cabinet ministers, such as Walter Long, was to result in the effective collapse of the intelligence system in Ireland.

But this does not mean that it was completely wound up. Price and Byrne might be gone and British intelligence in Ireland had almost to start from scratch again in early 1920, but it is clear that some elements of the old system were kept in place.

Towards the end of 1919 it was decided by the Irish Government that the secret service in Ireland should be controlled from London and directed from the office of Sir B. Thomson, in Scotland House. It was believed that agents could be collected in England and sent to Ireland more easily and safely than if the head office were in Ireland where it was difficult to ensure safety. The military authorities agreed that *with the exception of any agents already employed by the Intelligence Branch at GHQ*, all agents should be controlled by Scotland House and an officer from Scotland House was attached to GHQ for liaison duties.[46]

This tells us is that agents already in the field before 1919 – presumably those agents who refused to work for the police – were retained and still continued to be run by GHQ in Parkgate Street. This is where we are likely to find O'Donoghue at the beginning of 1920 when the 'reliable informant' was passing on his information in Cork that Tomás MacCurtain was present at the attempted assassination of Lord French and that he was about to go 'on the run'. We have already seen how the vast majority of those arrested in the army swoop of 31 January 1920 came from the 6th Divisional area, indicating that their prime intelligence source was in Munster. Indeed, it was probably in Cork

---

[45] *A Record of the Rebellion in Ireland, Vol II (Intelligence)*, TNA WO 141/93.
[46] A Record of the Rebellion, quoted in Julian Putkowski, 'The Best Secret Service Man We Had, Jack Byrnes, A2 and the IRA', *The Lobster, Journal of Parapolitics,* Vol. 94, No. 28, pp.4-15.

since 'only persons suspected of complicity in an outrage' might be arrested'. This, of course, was to also include Tomás MacCurtain.[47]

The history of the performance of British Intelligence in Ireland during the War of Independence has been well documented elsewhere and there is no space to go into it here. But the numbers say it all. In 1913/14, the British Treasury had spent £870 on intelligence gathering on Ireland. By 1921/22 this had ballooned to a staggering £160,000, only to drop back to £10,000 the following year.[48] Most, if not all, that money went to waste, since even with effective informers the Irish problem was a political one and could not be fixed by military intelligence methods. General Strickland might have what he called a perfect machine, but it was the wrong machine in the wrong field mowing down the wrong crop of hay.

So what was O'Donoghue's true role during the War of Independence? Was he a straightforward British agent who had penetrated the Cork republican movement almost from its inception, or was he a double agent? The balance of evidence suggests that he was different things at different times and that he was working more or less unambiguously for the British up until March 1920. Then – possibly as a result of the murder of Tomás MacCurtain whom he clearly admired, or of the shabby treatment meted out to Byrne, who was also an honourable man – he threw his lot, at least for a time, in with the IRA. His letters to Josephine in the summer of 1921 suggests that both saw themselves at that stage as being on the Irish side – though there are also other far darker hints in the correspondence. As he clearly admitted when he was leaning on Father Dominic for spiritual advice, O'Donoghue was conflicted and did not necessarily find it easy to play both sides at the same time. He may have worked mostly for the IRA

---

[47] *A Record of the Rebellion in Ireland, Vol I (Operations)*, TNA WO 141/93.

[48] The £160,000 can be divided into £60,000 for clerical staff and ancillary facilities, and £100,000 to pay informants, spies and intelligence officers. Initially it was all coming out of the Secret Service Vote but it was decided in March 1921 that the £60,000 could safely be provided for by public money. Report of the Cabinet Intelligence Committee, 22 March 1921 and Memorandum by the Chancellor of the Exchequer, January 1922, TNA, KV4/151.

for much of 1920, only to revert back to his British role in 1921 – most likely as a result of the necessity to cover up the fate of Reggie Brown, which, reading between the lines, British intelligence almost certainly knew about. After Reggie's kidnap, the British had him over a barrel. Certainly, 1920 appears to represent largely a gap year in what might be called the 'British' documentation in his papers.[49]

British Intelligence – not unsurprisingly – has always gone to considerable lengths to hide the identity of its agents. As the official historian of MI5, Christopher Andrew put it in the context of Roger Casement: 'Details of several Irish agents who also provided intelligence on Casement to British intelligence agencies still remain classified in order to maintain government policy of neither confirming or denying the names of former intelligence agents.'[50] The best chance of identifying intelligence agents, if you are lucky enough, is to see if they gave evidence at court cases. In the case of Casement's trial, it is possible to identify likely agents and indeed the MI5 officer who attended the trial.[51]

The other way is to see how they were paid. As we have seen, agents were usually recruited from the forces and they would have to have been paid through some agency within the forces. If O'Donoghue was working up to 1916 for what became MI5, or even up to 1919, he would have been paid through his membership of the Special Reserve. While no official salaries or pensions were paid from Secret Service money,[52] British intelligence officers and soldiers acting as agents received their normal salaries – plus suitable pay allowances from secret service funds

---

[49] See Appendix 1.

[50] Christopher Andrew, *The Defence of the Realm: The Authorized History of MI5* (London, 2009), endnote 13, p.882.

[51] Likely agents, certainly informants, can be established from those who received expenses to attend the trial and the sources of these expenses. Several were funded by the Special Branch, others by the Crimes Special section at Dublin Castle. The MI5 officer in question was Captain Cecil George Leslie (1879-1919). TNA, MEPO2/10671. As we have seen, MI5's fingerprints are all over the Casement trial. Frank Hall controlled the evidence: 'Major Hall read out the names and J.B. identified most of them.' TNA, MEPO2/10669. Interestingly, when I first came across Leslie's name a number of years ago, I was able to find quite a lot about him using online searches. Nowadays, there is very little (May 2019), suggesting that some material may have been taken down.

[52] Secret Service Blue Notes, TNA, T165/445.

to defray expenses.[53] Those deemed to have given 'Special Service' could receive an additional Royal Bounty for their efforts, which was entered in a book kept by the Treasury for that purpose. Despite the generally held view that agents received no pensions, 'if the Royal Bounty was to be given for longer than three years it was deemed to be regarded as a pension.'[54]

O'Donoghue stated in his attestation form for the Royal Munster Fusiliers in May 1911 that he was already serving in the Special Reserve. He must have joined the Reserve in the summer of 1910 so as to have availed of their summer training camps to get his basic training. The standard length of service for the Special Reserve was six years. This would have brought him up to the summer of 1916. After this, a new method would have to be found to pay him.

What evidence we have suggests that the 'very reliable informant' came with Joseph Byrne when he moved from the War Office to take up his role as head of the RIC. Since he was not an RIC informant, he must have remained under the military and probably in MI5. As we have seen, Hall still had his 'reliable informant' in Queenstown at the end of 1917. So either his membership of the Special Reserve would have to have been renewed or he would have been paid through some military agency engaged in intelligence work in Cork.

There exists a World War I medal card for one Florence Donoghue, who is described on the card as a sapper in the Inland Waterways and Docks section of the Royal Engineers.[55] Sapper Florence Donoghue has two regimental numbers, 178529, the Royal Engineers' regimental number he was given, and WR/502824, the IW&D number. [56] Neither of these correspond to the other Florence Donoghues or O'Donoghues who served with British forces during the war.[57]

---

[53] Pensions of Secret Service Agents, TNA, T161/177.

[54] Secret Service Blue Notes, TNA, T165/445.

[55] O'Donoghue's family used the name 'Donoghue' up to and including 1911. 1901 and 1911 Censuses.

[56] Florence Donoghue Medal Card, RE Sapper, Reg Nos 178529 and WR/502842, Medal Roll RE/104/B11, p3110. Accessed on Ancestry.co.uk.

[57] Florence O'Donoghue Royal Munster Fusiliers Reg No. 7651 was from Newcastlewest, Co. Limerick and was aged 23 in 1908 – his service record is available on Ancestry.co.uk. Florence O'Donoghue Royal Munster Fusiliers Reg No. 9517, transferred to the RASC with the collapse of the 10th Irish Division in 1918 and was

197

Inland Waterways and Docks was set up in 1914 by the Royal Engineers as a facility for supplying the army in the field with all the materials that an army needs, from arms and ammunition, from fuel to food. IW&D was largely concerned with the sourcing of materials and transportation. From humble beginnings, by the summer of 1916 it was a vast logistics organization, operating mainly cross channel but also up the canals and rivers of the Netherlands and farther afield in Mesopotamia, Egypt and the eastern Mediterranean.[58] What the card

discharged on 24/2/1919 and was wounded at the Front. WWI Medal Roll, accessed on Ancestry.co.uk. The latter was a Cork city native. Source: British Army Pension Cards. Both these men have pension cards. Sapper Donoghue has none.

[58] The date of joining can be estimated by cross-checking against the service records of IW&D personnel that do exist. I first came across the card quite a number of years ago and it was the first intimation I had that O'Donoghue might have been a British agent. However, for a long time afterwards I could find no other evidence. I decided to check if an as-yet unreleased army service record might exist. The Historical Disclosures of the Army Personnel Centre replied immediately that they had no records of him. I had no reason not to take their reply at face value. A few years later, however, I discovered that the IW&D section of the RE had been taken over by the Admiralty in 1918. Perhaps if a service record existed for Sapper Donoghue it might be with Naval Records. I contacted Naval Records at Swadlincote in Derbyshire with the same request. The reply took several months to arrive and when it did, it was rather strange and convoluted. Again, they could find no record of Mr Donoghue, yet on the back of the cheque I sent them somebody had scribbled in pencil the name and service number of yet another Florence Donoghue who had served in the Navy and had died in 1915 – six months before my man joined. Were they trying to put me off the scent? They attached several non-sequiturs to the letter: If I was not happy with 'this response' or if I had 'any wish to complain about any aspect of the handling of the request' I was to contact the person who signed the letter 'in the first instance'. Furthermore, if I was 'still dissatisfied', I could apply for an independent internal review by contacting the 'Information Rights Compliance Team' at the MOD Main Building at Whitehall. If I was still dissatisfied with this internal review, I could take it up under Section 50 of the Freedom of Information Act – which 'would not investigate my case until the MOD internal review process had been completed.' Was this just a box-ticking exercise, or was it an effort to put me off? I asked a friend of mine who had an ancestor in the IW&D in an identical position, who also had no service record, to put in an identical request. The Navy got back to him right away. There was no box-ticking. (Nor is there any pension card available for either Sapper Florence Donoghue or Royal Munster Fusilier Florence O'Donoghue 9553, even though the latter must have received something like a pension since his SR came from the Chelsea Pensioners database.)

tells us is that Sapper Donoghue joined the IW&D branch of the Royal Engineers in late June or early July 1916.[59] The card is problematic though, from our point of view, because what its very existence means is that Sapper Donoghue must have done some service overseas, or he would not have been entitled to the medals in the first place. (Sapper Donoghue received the British War medal and the Victory Medal but not the 1914 or 1914/15 Star, since his service began after 1915.) The only thing in Florrie O'Donoghue's papers that suggests a link to the Great War is his collection of newspapers. What his copies of the *Cork Examiner* from 1915 and 1916 tell us is that he was concerned, not with events in Ireland, such as the Easter Rising, but matters farther afield, particularly those concerning the Royal Munster Fusiliers who were at that time engaged first in the Dardanelles campaign and then in Salonika. This might seem odd when looked at from a republican point of view. It is not odd, however, from the point of view of a former – or still possibly serving – member of the Munsters.[60] Furthermore, the IW&D was heavily involved in the war effort in Greece – where O'Donoghue's great friend, Father Dominic, was serving at that very time. Greece in 1916/17 was also the nexus of one of the war's most elaborate espionage operations.[61]

---

[59] The card as such contains no record of his service, other than that he received a Victory and a British War medal. It is possible, however, to date his attestment from the odd service record of other Royal Engineers IW&D members with numbers on either side of his.

[60] The kind of things O'Donoghue decided to keep clippings of: lots on the Dardanelles, the sinking of the *Lusitania*, Royal Munster Fusilier heroes, Irish military medals, especially to the RMF, various Admiralty operations, particularly those involving Queenstown and, on 24 June 1916, the death of Bishop O'Callaghan of Cork. British Intelligence was particularly interested in the death of the bishop since they were wishing to influence the choice of his successor. Their hope was that he would be replaced – as he was – by Bishop Cohalan rather than by Canon Sexton, who was seen as having more pro-separatist leanings. O'Donoghue Papers, NLI, Ms 31,516.

[61] The history of espionage in Greece in 1916/17 is far too complex to go into here. MI1c, that is to say MI6, ran a major intelligence operation from Athens under Compton Mackenzie, using what were technically called RNVR officers, while the British army in Salonika also had a large intelligence corps. Mackenzie's memoir *Greek Memories*, gives a surprisingly unguarded account of these operations – and he nearly went to jail for writing it.

If O'Donoghue served abroad, this service most likely took place in the summer of 1916 since his war newspapers are mostly related to this time. This is also the period – from Easter 1916 to late August of that year – when the 'reliable informant' seemed to provide no information. Was O'Donoghue removed from Ireland in the wake of the Easter Rising for his own security and then returned when things had settled down – and all the leading separatists were in jail? This may well have been the case.

In its account of the rebellion in Ireland, the 6th Divisional 'Record' describes the intelligence operations in Cork during the 1916-19 period:

An Intelligence Branch existed at the Headquarters of the Southern District, which afterwards became the 6th Division, but during the latter part of the war it was chiefly concerned with matters concerning with enemy aliens and other subjects concerning the Great War. . . . During the same period, each brigade or sub-district, as they were then called, had an Intelligence Officer. He was usually a 2nd Lieutenant, appointed locally and not 'graded'. These officers were frequently changed 'owing to the exigencies of the Service' and had little opportunity to become acquainted with their work or with the characteristics of the people. They were usually employed as orderly officers to the Brigade Major, Officer I/C Signals, or some other job not concerned with Intelligence.[62]

This tells us several things. First, as might be expected, the Great War was the primary concern and intelligence personnel were being moved around depending on wartime needs. Therefore, if Sapper Florence Donoghue was indeed Florrie O'Donoghue, it is almost certain that he must have spent some time serving abroad, even if only for a few months. The known intelligence operation in Cork was based in Queenstown and was run by Captain Wallace Dickie, who went searching for the Volunteers' arms in 1916 – he was even named as such in *Guy's Postal Directory* for Cork for 1916. It is unlikely that this is what the writer of the Record was referring to above. Intelligence officers employed by O/C Signals on the other hand, were members of the Royal Engineers. In other words, secret service in Cork operated under the cover of the Royal Engineers. 'Before the independent Corps of Signals was formed in 1920 a Royal Engineer Signal Service existed. This Signal Service included a large and complex Intercept organization, which provided Britain with a source of intelligence that

---

[62] A Record of the Rebellion in Ireland, 6th Division Report, TNA WO 141/93.

was quite exceptional'.[63] In the words of the regimental historians of the Royal Corps of Signals, the corps itself and their predecessors in the Signals Service of the RE constituted an 'Invisible Elite'.[64] It would make perfect sense that the intelligence branch operating under the aegis of the Signals Service of the Royal Engineers would pay its members through another Royal Engineer section such as the IW&D, in other words 'some other job not concerned with Intelligence'.[65] The most likely scenario is that, from the summer of 1916, O'Donoghue was paid through the Royal Engineers in Queenstown, though he is still likely to have had some involvement with MI5 right up to the end of the War of Independence.

Indeed, there are reasons to believe that Inland Waterways and Docks is likely to have been a cover for the recruitment of agents. In addition to Sapper Donoghue, Michael 'Mickeroo' Walsh was certainly a member of the IW&D, and 'Cruxy' O'Connor is likely to have been one too.[66] Thomas Downing, shot as a spy in late 1920 was a former Royal Engineer employed as a telegraphonist at the RE headquarters in Victoria Barracks.[67] One of the themes that run through the recollections of IRA men and indeed in documentation written at the time is how often the word 'transport' is used as a euphemism for spying activity. This is a theme that regularly crops up in the correspondence of Michael Collins and Richard Mulcahy. Early agents sent into Ireland in the summer of 1920 after a brief course of training in Hounslow were sent to Ireland to pose as Royal Engineers officers.[68]

---

[63] Cliff Lord and Graham Watson, *The Royal Corps of Signals, Unit Histories of the Corps and its Antecedents (1920-2001)* (2003).

[64] Ibid.

[65] It should be pointed out that the IW&D proper did not begin to recruit in Ireland until 1917, when it appears it ran a top-secret supply operation near Passage West, Co. Cork.

[66] David Grant of Cairogang.com has pretty conclusively shown that 'Cruxy' O'Connor was Patrick Joseph O'Connor who won a Croix de Guerre as a sergeant in the Lancaster Fusiliers. There is an IW&D Royal Engineer WWI medal card made out to one Patrick J. O'Connor, a 'sapper' with regimental numbers 105731 and WR289565.

[67] And a Thomas Downing 'sapper' has an IW&D RE regimental numbers 321061 and WR319618.

[68] Captain R.D. Jeune, in William Sheehan, *British Voices from the Irish War of Independence* (Cork, 2005), p.85.

The likelihood is that 'transport' is connected to various pseudo branches of the Royal Engineers.

Much of this is reflected in the British Army's intelligence report on its pursuit of the conflict in Ireland: 'Irish persons who were prepared to act as genuine secret service agents, i.e. as Sinn Feiners or as IRA were difficult to find. . . A few however were used with success.'[69] 'Where adequate precautions were taken, numerous agents were never suspected.'[70] Indeed, it even suggests that O'Donoghue may have been more likely a British officer than a mere agent by 1920/21. 'Some officers successfully passed themselves off as officers of the IRA and obtained information of great value. This, it need hardly be said, not only demanded at times courage of rare quality but always required exceptional local knowledge.'[71] Nobody had more 'exceptional local knowledge' than Florrie O'Donoghue.

As we have seen, 'the secret society known as the Irish Republican Brotherhood has been an organization concerning which it has been exceedingly difficult to obtain information, and informers, members of the IRB, have been almost impossible to obtain. The only member of the IRB who turned informer and whose information has been of the utmost value, was obtained through the agency of a Special Crimes Sergeant.'[72]

Methodologies are also detailed. Agents 'were provided with a secret ink which was considered, for all practical purposes, immune from discovery.' In the case of proper secret agents: 'The agent then corresponded with no Government official except the head of the London bureau, writing his information in the secret ink and sending his letters to a cover address. This went far to inspire a sense of security amongst those engaged in this difficult task.[73] While this refers to agents recruited in England and then sent to Ireland and may not apply directly

---

[69] A Record of the Rebellion in Ireland and the part the Army played in dealing with it. (Vol II, Intelligence), Hart. *British Intelligence in Ireland*, (Cork, 2002) p. 48.
[70] ibid, p.49.
[71] ibid, pp. 54-55.
[72] A Report of the Intelligence Branch of the Police, ibid, p.72.
[73] ibid, p.78.

202

to O'Donoghue after 1919 since he now simply had to give his information to Josephine – it does give an insight into the methods used. The army's report noted: 'There were many offices in London in which secrets of the highest importance were received and where there was no leakage.'[74] This is almost certainly a reference to MI5's veiled and fitful engagement with Ireland after 1919, as well as that of Thomson at Scotland House. 'Another branch of the secret service, based in London, is said to have cost about £15,000 a year. The information that came through this source was always 24 to 48 hours delayed and this militated against its usefulness.'[75]

The ambiguous position of someone like O'Donoghue may also have been noted: 'Had agents been planted five years ago throughout the country, they would, assuming the policy as actually carried out not to have been altered, in all probability have become ardent Sinn Feiners by 1920.'[76] Even someone very like Josephine gets a mention: 'Specially selected women, as usual, proved excellent intelligence clerks, but the difficulty of their accommodation limited their employment.'[77] The military did have some difficulties with Josephine's living on the Old Blackrock Road, to the extent of installing new locks for her additional security. They may have been watching out for her from the school across the road.[78] Disappearing neighbours like the Blemenes may also have been a 'difficulty'. They may even have taken the additional step to have their principal undercover officer, George Egan, aka Florence O'Donoghue, lodge with her. They may, or may not, have been introduced by Father Dominic. Love stories begin here.

Sometimes in his correspondence O'Donoghue gives the game away. Writing to Moirin Chavasse, Terence MacSwiney's biographer, in the 1950s, O'Donoghue writes about the rifles taken off the Volunteers in Cork in 1916. 'I could not get from Volunteer sources an accurate figure of arms surrendered, but I have the British figures . . . the British knew pretty accurately what arms the Volunteers had then and they knew that

---

[74] A Record of the Rebellion in Ireland and the part the Army played in dealing with it. (Vol II, Intelligence), op.cit, p.44.
[75] ibid, p.56.
[76] ibid, p.56.
[77] ibid, p.59.
[78] Josephine O'Donoghue, MSP34REF55794.

they did not get 50% of the serviceable ones.'[79] This tells us that the British had a very accurate picture of what arms the Cork Volunteers had at Easter 1916 – which they could only have got from an inside source – 'but I have the British figures. . .' According to himself, he was not in the Volunteers until 1917 and was not a serious intelligence officer until 1920, and Josephine was not bringing out anything until 1920 either. These kinds of British documents were not released to the British National Archives until the 1990s. So where could he have got the British figures in the 1950s unless he had them himself? (Access to such documentation of course made O'Donoghue one of the best historians of that period. Clearly, he had an unfair advantage.)

One of the few ways apparently of recognizing a trained secret service agent in a crowd is that he is likely to be the one observing what is going on above street level. Most people on a street have their gaze focused at the level of the people around them – understandably, I suppose, if you do not want to bump into your fellow pedestrians. Secret service agents with any training, on the other hand, will always be aware of what might be going on at roof level or what might come out of an upstairs window. They are trained to watch their surroundings. There is a photograph of Tomás MacCurtain's funeral where the chief mourners, led by Terence MacSwiney and Father Dominic, are walking after MacCurtain's coffin. All but one are suitably grave and staring forward in mourning. The exception is Florrie O'Donoghue. Though his face is forward, his eyes are looking up, staring straight at the person who is taking the photo from an upstairs window. This is a man who is watchful and who, even on the most solemn occasion, misses nothing, the one professional military man visible in the cortege.[80] And he does not appear particularly upset at the funeral either. In fact, he may even have a slight smirk on his face.

The writer and historian – and almost certainly secret service agent in the Foreign Office – Robert Conquest had what he referred to as 'the Second law of Robert Conquest': 'Every organization seems to be run

---

[79] O'Donoghue to Moirin Chavasse, 26 February 1952, O'Donoghue Papers, NLI, 31, 282(1).

[80] *Irish Independent*, 23 March 1920. See photo in the *Sunday Times* of 6 October 2019 of a much more recent MI5 agent at an IRA funeral who is also the only one in the crowd who has noticed the camera.

by secret agents of its oppressors.'[81] The one person who would not be surprised to find all this coming out a hundred years later was O'Donoghue himself. He was under no illusions that this stuff might see the light of day. He told Ernie O'Malley in the context of the RIC: 'In Cork they had lost the RIC as an Intelligence resource. Large areas were without police as their barracks had been burnt out and their contacts were gone, gone as far as we knew. *Yet in time the secret history may be that of 1798.*'[82] This is a reference to the betrayal of the men of the 1798 Rebellion in Wexford and Carlow by an insider, who went on, or at least so it is alleged, to write the history of the rebellion from the safe haven of a cushy job at the local hospital in Carlow. Alone of the survivors of the Cork IRA, O'Donoghue seemed to be acknowledging that the Cork Brigades were betrayed from within, and by a future scribe. Was he suggesting that history might be repeating itself? It certainly looks like that.

In a letter to Liam Lynch written in the summer of 1922 O'Donoghue explained his reasons for resigning from the IRA on the outbreak of civil war. The letter encapsulates neatly his rather odd combination of decency and deviousness. 'In no circumstances could I be party to a conflict which would bring about such deplorable results, and it is only in the event of the return of the English that I would take up arms again. Should that happen, as I think it will, I'll be somewhere in the ranks.'[83] He never made a truer statement. O'Donoghue was no stranger to self-knowledge.

---

[81] He also had a First Law: 'Generally speaking, everybody is reactionary on subjects he knows about.' Kingsley Amis, *Memoirs*, (New York, 1991), p.146.

[82] Florrie O'Donoghue, O'Malley, UCD, P17b/96.

[83] Florence O'Donoghue to Liam Lynch, 3 July 1922. O'Donoghue Papers, NLI, Ms 31,187.

21

What do you think spies are?

What the hell do you think spies are? Moral philosophers measuring everything they do against the word of God or Karl Marx? They're not! They're just a bunch of seedy, squalid bastards like me: little men, drunkards, queers, hen-pecked husbands, civil servants playing cowboys and Indians to brighten their rotten little lives.[84]

So what was O'Donoghue's motivation in all this? It would be easy to dismiss him as a scoundrel, a tout, a low life of the type so beloved of spy stories and republican mythologies. But clearly he did not give that impression to anyone while he was alive. One of the few negative comments made in connection with my book on the death of Michael Collins was that it was an 'impertinence' to even imply that O'Donoghue might have anything to do with it. This just goes to show how persuasive and successful O'Donoghue had been at putting out his own version of history. All it really meant, of course, was that he was just very good at what he was doing. He fought a long campaign of lies and the sowing of half-truths like weeds in order to disguise whole fields of historical realities. If he had not left his papers with their very occasional lapses, he might well have got away with it.

On the matter of spies, we saw in Chapter 9 how he wrote:

I was sceptical of popular ideas about spies . . . . Looking at the facts I could not see spies being successful against the tight organization we then had. By this time everybody of any consequence knew everybody in the Brigade, in the adjoining Brigades and at GHQ. We were not accepting anybody on his own valuation. The man who could horn in successfully would need to be a genius.

As noted previously, maybe O'Donoghue regarded himself as a genius – and perhaps he was, of a kind anyway. But he is also right in

---

[84] Alec Leamas in John le Carré's *The Spy Who Came in from the Cold.*

one respect. It would have been very difficult, well-nigh impossible, for a spy in the ordinary sense of the term to come in from outside and penetrate the IRA at a senior level in 1920 or 1921. He would have been outed and shot within days. But what if he had been there from the very beginning, from the days when the Volunteers were set up, effectively a sleeper? What if he had been in the IRB even before the Volunteers were created?

This is the situation where we find O'Donoghue. He was a professional secret service agent, in the pay of British military intelligence since 1911. He was most likely an officer by the time of the War of Independence. It is not difficult to elucidate his motivation at one level, at least in the early days. In 1911 Britain was in the middle of a spy scare. Thanks to the novels of William le Queux, and indeed Erskine Childers, there was a belief that Britain was overrun with German spies. This was entirely fanciful, of course, but it helped create the climate of general anti-German sentiment and paranoia about German intentions that led, *inter alia,* to Britain joining World War I when she would have been far better off staying out of it.

Be that as it may, the perception was that there were German spies everywhere. Young lads with a sense of patriotism and duty, especially if they were fans of spy thrillers such as those written by Sexton Blake, as O'Donoghue says he was, would have been very attracted to tradecraft. The initial brief – at least as outlined in the early internal histories of MI5 – was German subversion. This was to lead on the outbreak of war to the need to gather information on the passing of German submarines, as well as preventing information from British ports getting to the enemy. In the summer of 1914 it is safe to assume, Irish subversion was pretty much down the list of priorities of Kell and the other intelligence mandarins in London. There was one enemy and that was Germany.

From this we can conclude that, at least initially, O'Donoghue was most likely used as an agent against German spies, either real or alleged. At least two well-known German spies visited Cork and Killarney before they were apprehended, largely based on information gathered by MI5. On the outbreak of war, the surveillance extended to German submarines and coastal protection, something which, as we have seen, passed in Cork from the Royal Engineers to the Special Reserve in the course of the war. Only from 1915, when Seán O'Hegarty was arrested in Enniscorthy, is there evidence of O'Donoghue's involvement with the IRB and presumably as a British spy within the IRB. However, if the blurb of his biography of Tomás MacCurtain is correct, he was probably in the IRB by 1916 and in the Volunteers since 1913.

The fact that he joined the Special Reserve as a teenager in 1910 and moved into the full-time army in 1911 in order to be recruited into the secret services suggests that O'Donoghue saw himself essentially as a military man. This comes through in his very demeanour and all through his writings. He had the neat and clipped look, typical of the British military type in many of his photographs.

But surely there must be something in his make-up that leads a man to live the double life of a spy. This is not something that would attract everyone; the paranoia alone would drive most people crazy. (Interestingly, when I passed on samples of O'Donoghue's handwriting to handwriting expert Denis Sexton, he wondered if perhaps O'Donoghue might have suffered from some motor control health problems in later life, even though he knew nothing whatsoever about 'Florence'.[85] I wrote back suggesting that he was ever careful about his handwriting. What I actually believed, though, was that his small gnomic handwriting was from a lifetime's habit of writing tiny notes – often probably in invisible ink on tiny pieces of paper. The spy game does not allow for literary extravagance.) According to John le Carré's character Alex Leamas's definition of a spy, O'Donoghue does not easily fit the profile, except that he was small and possibly gay. His homosexuality, if indeed it was real, or even a factor in this, seems to have been superficial at best. (My belief on this is that he was simply a pretty boy who was placed in positions where pretty boys were useful. There was no need for him to have been actively homosexual. It was enough for him to be trusted – and loved.)

But most people do not want to become spies. If nothing else, the sheer fear of being found out would be enough to put most people off. It seems to me that the very act of spying, especially over such a long period, must surely require a certain degree of anger or resentment against the society being spied upon – in this case Irish separatism and nationalism and later republicanism – and perhaps even against Ireland itself. We only get hints of this in O'Donoghue's writings: his appalled

---

[85] Denis Sexton, email to author, 27 January 2017.

208

reaction at the 'lower class' nature of the boys he joined at the Volunteer Hall, his distaste for their thieving instincts and his displeasure at the attack on Clarke's at Farran to rob 'a Saxon foe' who wasn't 'probably even a Saxon'. But for the most part, he manages to keep his real opinions to himself – except for the occasional aside. To keep up such a veneer for such a long time requires considerable skill. 'A spy has to be an actor, but an actor that doesn't need a public or a stage, and doesn't require the approval of others. . . someone who is average-looking, does not attract attention and does not require external approval.'[86] O'Donoghue had no audience, except probably for Josephine and one or two others, including whoever was handling him. Still, it is hard not to feel that he must have had it in for somebody.

One of the odd things about O'Donoghue is that he never seemed to be quite clear about what age he was. In most published work about him he is described as having been born in 1895. This is what is generally accepted. Yet he was actually born a year earlier – in July 1894. Apart from the 1901 census, which has his correct age, in all other public documents, including the 1911 census (bar his Royal Munster Fusilier attestation form where he had to say he was a year older in order to join up) he is described as being a year younger than he actually was. So did something happen between 1901 and 1911 that made him subsequently claim that he was a year younger? I believe it did and here lies key to his career as a double agent.

Florence O'Donoghue entered First Class in Rathmore National School in September 1901. His final full academic year, Sixth Class at the school, ended in May 1908 – though he was back attending for three days the following September before being accepted into the school in Tralee from which he was to be recruited into the Special Reserve. In other words, he spent seven years getting through a six-year curriculum – and it looks like he would have spent another year in Sixth Class had he not been accepted elsewhere.[87]

The key detail that emerges is that he spent two academic years, 1905-06 and 1906-07, in Fifth Class. In other words, to quote the phrase that was common when I was a kid in the 1960s, he 'was kept back in

[86] Elena Vavilova and Andrey Bronnikov, Soviet sleeper spies in the United States in the 1980s, *A Woman Who Can Keep Secrets*, (In Russian, 2019).
[87] Rathmore National School Roll Books.

209

school'. People nowadays have no idea of the level of stigma that was attached to this. Being 'kept back in school' was a label that denoted stupidity and backwardness, that a person was 'a bit slow' and probably also meant – given the practice of National School teachers at the time of capital punishment – that he was regularly beaten for this inability to learn. Since we know that O'Donoghue was far from stupid, there is one most likely explanation: that he was dyslexic, a condition that was not understood at the time.

There is evidence right through his papers, especially in documents in his own handwriting, of mild dyslexia. We have seen how it is even evident in the *Sayanora* document written for British military intelligence and also in misspellings of names and common words. When he graduated from the school in Tralee, he stated in this attestation form that he received only a third class grade. So he was not the bright lad he would appear to be later. The stigma of apparent stupidity, allied to his diminutive stature, must surely have meant that he grew up with a chip on his shoulder. This was a boy with a lot to prove, if only to himself. He never after admitted his true age. He was always a year younger than he actually was.[88]

He claimed in his memoir that one of the reasons he did not go off to war in 1914 was that, as an only son he felt a sense of responsibility towards his sisters and parents. This may have been true, but it is also related to another factor. There is evidence in his records of an avaricious streak which may have come about because of the poverty of his background or perhaps out of that sense of responsibility. Eighteen acres of poor land outside Rathmore is not wealth. It is barely enough to eke out a living, especially with four sisters of various ages. It is clear from his memoir that he clearly felt the need to look after them. At many points in his written record he mentions how hard-up he was – although he was probably no more hard up than anyone else of his age once he reached Cork city.

There is an almost comic absurdity in some of the correspondence he had with the IRA Pensions Board between 1934 and 1938. In 1934 he was overpaid to the tune of £23 by the pensions board since his earnings 'from public monies', that is to say his salary as a rate collector,

---

[88] It has to be said that truthfulness about dates was not a strong point in his family. Both his mother and father gave different ages in the 1901 and 1911 censuses.

exceeded £450 p.a.. A blizzard of correspondence ensued, some of which is quite strident. O'Donoghue refused to return the £23 until by 1938 the State Solicitor threatened to bring him to court. He finally paid up at the end of that year.[89] It should be pointed out that he was by now living a comfortable middle-class life in Douglas, one of the more salubrious suburbs of Cork city, with a permanent, pensionable job and two stepsons – Reggie and Gerald Marchment – studying in University College Cork, which he did not have to pay for, since both received Kitchener Scholarships courtesy of the British government. He was not badly off.

Nor did he die a poor man. When he passed away in 1967, he left £14,487 in his will – and Josephine, who died the previous year, left a further £1,281.[90] This would have been enough to buy a substantial farm at the time, or several large suburban homes. This was a man who accumulated a substantial wad of cash during his lifetime. W.T. Cosgrave, who served his country to a much higher level than O'Donoghue and who died in the same year, left only £829.[91] And this is on a single salary as a rate collector. And he certainly did not make it out of his books – based on the size of the market for revolutionary books in Ireland. Or maybe he did make money from his books. Perhaps he was still being paid a stipend from British Intelligence for his literary endeavours to spread a smokescreen over the years of the Irish revolution. Somebody somewhere was certainly paying well. Espionage worked well to set up a nice middle-class life. By their fruits ye shall know them.

---

[89] Florence O'Donoghue MSP files, 34B37 and MSP34REF2091.
[90] Will and Probate Records, National Archives Dublin.
[91] *Cork Examiner*, 10 October 1966.

Epilogue

This is clearly not the last word on the career of Florrie O'Donoghue as a British agent. There are many questions still left unanswered. For a start, the fact that he was deeply embedded in the British intelligence system and was likely to be their greatest asset in the South of Ireland means that many of the events described in my book *The Year of Disappearances* need to be revisited. If the head of IRA intelligence and the adjutant of the Cork No.1 Brigade was a British agent, then this means that many of those shot by the IRA in Cork city were fingered in order to protect this prize asset. There was always something deeply suspicious about many of the killings that took place in Cork in late 1920 and the first months of 1921. Trying to imply that they were all spies, as some have done, when contemporary British records show that there was only one spy among the many killed, is disingenuous to say the least.

Also, what was the role of O'Donoghue's closest confidantes in all of this? What about his wife Josephine? Or Father Dominic O'Connor, the man who supposedly introduced them? And why did O'Donoghue cover the tracks of some agents while sending men half way around the globe to try to assassinate others?

And finally – and this is what will be of interest to most readers – what was his relationship with Michael Collins? Did Collins have suspicions about O'Donoghue? Did the fact that O'Donoghue was a British agent have a bearing on Collins's death at Bealnablath? Was O'Donoghue working for the British – or at least some part of the British military establishment – in luring Collins to Bealnablath? It is hardly news to say there have always been claims that there was British involvement in Collins's death.

As we saw in *The Great Cover-Up* there can be little doubt that O'Donoghue was heavily involved in getting Collins to Bealnablath in the first place and effected various levels of cover-up afterwards. Did he just 'happen' to meet with Collins that morning of Bealnablath? Was he trying push Collins into the path of the oncoming train that was the IRA ambush or was there more to it than that? These are difficult questions and easy answers may not be forthcoming. Nonetheless, it would be a dereliction of duty on my part not to make some attempt to answer them. These will be the subjects of the final volume in this series.

Literature Cited

Andrew, Christopher, *The Defence of the Realm: The Authorized History of MI5* (London, 2009).

Andrew, Christopher, *Secret Service: The Making of the British Intelligence Community* (London, 1985).

Andrew, Christopher and Dilks, David (eds), *The Missing Dimension: Governments and Intelligence Communities in the Twentieth Century* (London, 1984).

Borgonovo, John, *Florence and Josephine O'Donoghue's War of Independence: A Destiny Which Shapes Our Ends* (Dublin, 2006).

Borgonovo, John, *Spies, Informers and the 'Anti-Sinn Fein Society': The Intelligence War in Cork City 1920-1921* (Dublin, 2007).

Borgonovo, John, *The Dynamics of War and Revolution, Cork City, 1916-18* (Cork, 2013).

Cook, Andrew, *M: MI5's First Spymaster* (Stroud, 2004).

Cronin, Jim, *Making Connections: A Cork GAA Miscellany* (Cork, 2005).

Crowley, John, Sheehan, John and Murphy, Mike, *The Iveragh Peninsula: A Cultural Atlas of the Ring of Kerry* (Cork, 2009).

Deasy, Liam, *Brother against Brother*, (Cork, 1982).

Deasy, Liam, *Towards Ireland Free* (Dublin, 1973).

Documents Relative to the Sinn Fein Movement, (HMSO, London, 1921).

Dublin's Fighting Story (Cork, 1999).

Dudgeon, Jeffrey, *Roger Casement: The Black Diaries* (Belfast, 2002).

Dwyer, T. Ryle, *Tans, Terror and Trouble: Kerry's Real Fighting Story 1913-23* (Cork, 2001).

Girvin, Kevin, *The Life and Times of Sean O'Hegarty, O/C First Cork Brigade,* MPhil Thesis, (UCC, 2003).

Guy's Postal Directories for Cork.

Hart, Peter, *British Intelligence in Ireland: The Final Reports* (Cork, 2002).

Hart, Peter, *The IRA and its Enemies: Violence and Community in Cork, 1916-1923* (Oxford,1998).

Herlihy, Jim, *The Royal Irish Constabulary Officers, 1816-1922* (Dublin, 2005).

IRA Jailbreaks, Foreword by Florence O'Donoghue, (Tralee, 1971, reissued Cork, 2010).

James, Admiral Sir William, *The Eyes of the Navy* (London, 1955).

Jeffery, Keith, *MI6: The History of the Secret Intelligence Service, 1909-1949* (London, 2010).

Judd, Alan, *The Quest for C: Mansfield Cummings and the Founding of the Secret Service* (London, 2000),

Kerry's Fighting Story, (Tralee, 1949).

Kings Regulations 1912 (HMSO, London, 1912).

Lord, Cliff and Watson, Graham, *The Royal Corps of Signals: Unit Histories of the Corps and its Antecedents (1920-2001)* (London, 2003).

Macready, Nevil, *Annals of an Active Life Vol I* (London, 1925).

McEoin, Uinseann (ed.), *Survivors* (Dublin, 1980).

McMahon, Paul, *British Spies and Irish Rebels* (London, 2008).

Moynihan, Jamie, *Memoirs of an Old Warrior*, Donal O'hEalaithe (ed.), (Cork, 2014).

Muenger, Elizabeth A., *The British Military Dilemma in Ireland* (Kansas, 1991).

Murphy, Gerard, *The Year of Disappearances: Political Killings in Cork 1921-1922*, (Dublin 2011).

Murphy, Gerard, *The Great Cover-Up: The Truth about the Death of Michael Collins* (Cork, 2018).

Murphy, Seán A., *Kilmichael: A Battlefield Study*, (Cork, 2014).

Norway, Mary Louisa and Arthur Hamilton, *The Sinn Fein Rebellion as They Saw It*, Keith Jeffery (ed.) (Dublin, 1999).

Ó Corráin, Donnachadh (ed.), James Hogan, *Revolutionary, Historian, Political Scientist* (Dublin, 2001).

O'Donoghue, Florence, *No Other Law* (Dublin, 1986).

O'Donoghue, Florence, *Tomás MacCurtain, Soldier and Patriot.* (Tralee, 1955).

O'Neill, Tom, *The Battle of Clonmult: The IRA's Worst Defeat* (Cork, 2006).

Porter, Bernard, *Plots and Paranoia: The History of Political Espionage in Britain 1790-1988*, (London, 1989).

Rebel Cork's Fighting Story (Tralee, n.d.).

215

Sheehan, William, *British Voices from the Irish War of Independence* (Cork, 2005).

Sheehan, William, *A Hard Local War* (Stroud, 2011).

Spindler, Karl, *The Mystery of the Casement Ship*. (Tralee, 1965).

Tomaselli, Phil, *Tracing Your Secret Service Ancestors* (Barnsley, 2009).

Thom's Directory (Thom's Irish Almanac and Directory).

Thomson, George Malcolm, *Lord Castlerosse: His Life and Times* (London, 1973).

Twohig, Patrick J., *The Dark Secret of* Bealnablath (Cork 1991).

Vavilova, Elena and Bronnikov, Andrey, *A Woman Who Can Keep Secrets*, (In Russian, 2019).

White, Gerry and O'Shea, Brendan, *'Baptized in Blood': The Formation of the Cork Brigade of the Irish Volunteers 1913-1916* (Cork, 2005).

Winter, Denis, *Death's Men: Soldiers of the Great War*, (London, 1978).

Index

219

Printed in Poland
by Amazon Fulfillment
Poland Sp. z o.o., Wrocław

72922016R00139